S0-CPE-764

The Poetic Writings of Thomas Cradock, 1718–1770

A

FRIENDLY CHARACTER

OF THE LATE

Rev^d^. THOMAS CRADOCK,

Rector of St. THOMAS's *Baltimore* County,

MARYLAND.

Who departed this LIFE, *May* 7, 1770, in the Fifty Second Year of his Age.

HE was universally allowed to be a sincere Christian, a polished Scholar, an elegant and persuasive Preacher, a tender Parent, and an affectionate Husband; and though for many Years by the Will of Providence he was render'd incapable of performing the common Offices of Life, he seldom omitted his Duty as a Minister of the establish'd Church, and by his CHARITY, PIETY, BENEVOLENCE, and HOSPITALITY, he had the rare Felicity of rendering Himself acceptable to those of a different Communion with himself, and to every other Person who had the Pleasure of his Acquaintance; nor was he less fortunate in his domestic Happiness. Conscious to Himself of his own Integrity, he never suspected that of Others, and firmly persuaded of the great Importance of a virtuous Life, he met Death with that calm Resignation, that pleasing Tranquility so essentially necessary in the CHRISTIAN, the SCHOLAR, and the GENTLEMAN: If he had any Faults, they were trivial, when put in competition with his Virtues.

Printed by THOMAS WORRALL, No. 99, *Bishopsgate* without.

A broadside owned by the late Rev. Thomas Cradock Jensen of Garrison, Maryland, and reprinted with his permission.

The Poetic Writings of Thomas Cradock, 1718–1770

Edited with an Introduction by
David Curtis Skaggs

Newark: University of Delaware Press
London and Toronto: Associated University Presses

Associated University Presses, Inc.
4 Cornwall Drive
East Brunswick, N.J. 08816

Associated University Presses Ltd
27 Chancery Lane
London WC2A 1NF, England

Associated University Presses
2133 Royal Windsor Drive
Unit 1
Mississauga, Ontario
Canada L5J 1K5

Library of Congress Cataloging in Publication Data

Cradock, Thomas, 1718–1770.
The poetic writings of Thomas Cradock, 1718–1770.

Includes bibliographical references.
I. Skaggs, David Curtis. II. Title.
PS737.C42A17 1983 811'.1 81-72059
ISBN 0-87413-206-1

Printed in the United States of America

For my parents,
Eleanor Elizabeth Baer Skaggs
and
David Curtis Skaggs
of Pratt, Kansas

". . . teach your youth betimes the beauty and loveliness of virtue, lead them early into the mighty advantages that attend a Christian faith and practice; and then will your labours be crown'd indeed, and you'll secure for them as well as for yourselves a happy and glorious Immortality."

Thomas Cradock, "Sermon on Education. Acts 26:24–25"

Contents

List of Illustrations 10
Acknowledgments 11

Part I: Introduction: Thomas Cradock and the Golden Age of Chesapeake Culture

1 Prolegomenon: An Extraordinary Sermon 19
2 The Cradocks of Trentham 22
3 Defender of the Faith 31
4 The Christian Muse 46
Augustan Poetry 46
Devotional Poetry 52
Satiric Poetry 59
Drama 71
5 The Chesapeake Golden Age 84
6 The Manuscripts and Editorial Method 95
Bibliography 100

Part II: Cradock's Poetry

7 Devotional Poetry
To Thyrsis (1744) 115
A Poem Sacred to the Memory of Miss Margaret Lawson, Miss Elizabeth Lawson, Miss Dorothy Lawson, and Miss Elizabeth Read (1753) 118
Seven Hymns 121
Hymn for Christmas 121
Hymn for Whitsunday 122
Sacramental Hymn 123
Resignation 123
Hymn for Ascension 124
Funeral Hymn 125
On Viewing the Grave of Arthur Cradock 126
A Fragment 127

Crurulia, Part the Second 128
1—The Check 128
2—Afflictions mercies 130
3—The Resolve 131
4—The Relapse 133
5—The Recovery 134
6—The Prospect 136
8 Maryland Eclogues 138
1—Split-text 139
2—Daphne 150
3—Shoat 159
4—The Maryland Divine 166
5—Toss-Pot 170
6—Celsus 180
8—Jemima 185
9—Gachradidow 190
10—Worthy 198
9 The Death of Socrates 201
Act 1. 202
Scene 2 202
Scene 3 204
Scene 4 205
Scene 5 209
Scene 6 210
Act 2. 216
Scene 1 216
Scene 2 217
Scene 3 222
Scene 4 224
Scene 5 225
Scene 6 230
Scene 7 230
Act 3. 233
Scene 1 233
Scene 2 237
Scene 3—The Court of the Areopagus 239
Scene 4 249
Act 4. 250
Scene 1 250
Scene 2 253
Scene 3 253
Scene 4 255

Scene 5 256
Scene 6—The Prison 259
Act 5. 265
Scene 1 265
Scene 2 265
Scene 3 267
Scene 4 267
Scene 5—The Prison 271
Scene 6 272
Scene 7 275
10 Trifles, Part 2d 276
Marcus Valerius Martialis
To His Book 276
To Attalus 276
To Sextus 276
To Posthumus 277
On His Stay in the Country 277
George Buchanan
Mutual Love 278
Theocritus
On the Death of Adonis 278
Epigram 280
Moschus
Love at the Plough 280
Anacreon
Dove 280
Quintus Horatius Flaccus
Petition to Apollo 281
Boethius
A Poem 282
James Thomson
Celadon and Amelia 283
Lucian of Samosata
Mars; Muercury, a Dialogue 285
Phaedrus
The Dog and the Wolf 286
Cradock
On the Two Miss *****'* 287
Textual Notations 293
Index 309

Illustrations

A Friendly Character of the late Revd. Thomas Cradock	frontis
Genealogy of the Cradocks	24
Saint Thomas' Church	112

Acknowledgments

Thomas Cradock first came to my attention in early 1965 when I sought to find political information in the few Cradock sermons then held by the Maryland Diocesan Library in the Peabody Institute in Baltimore. It was then I first saw the famous General Assembly address of 1753 described in the first chapter of the introduction. Several years later, after I prepared that sermon for publication, my attention was brought to a cache of Cradock sermons at Trentham, the family home in Baltimore County. Thus began a decade of association with Cradock that climaxes with this publication of the poetic writings of this colonial Maryland cleric.

Financial assistance so essential to this project came in the form of travel grants from the American Philosophical Society and from the Faculty Research Committee of Bowling Green State University. The late Reverend Thomas Cradock Jensen, son of a rector of Saint Thomas' Parish and the inheritor of Trentham from the last of the Cradock family owners, provided much-appreciated hospitality and eventually donated the remaining Cradock sermons to the Maryland Diocesan Archives, which by that time had been moved to the Maryland Historical Society. Throughout this long project the historiographer of the Episcopal Diocese of Maryland, F. Garner Ranney, has been most helpful. Similar assistance has come from the staff of the Manuscripts Division of the Maryland Historical Society, where the Cradock Papers, MS. 196, are housed. In the initial phases of this project P. William Filby, then director of the society, provided considerable encouragement and made copying facilities available to me.

For years the Cradock work has brought me assistance, advice, and encouragement from two of this country's most distinguished students of early American literature—Richard Beale Davis, Alumni Distinguished Professor Emeritus of American Literature at the University of Tennessee, and J. A. Leo Lemay, H. F. du Pont Winterthur Professor of English of the University of Delaware. The former recently described Cradock as, next to Dr. Alexander Hamilton of Annapolis, "the most significant southern writer of the [late colonial] period still largely unpublished." Leo Lemay's long-term support obviously reached its acme when he encouraged the University of Delaware Press to publish this volume.

Searching for background evidence has brought me to many archives in both Maryland and England whose staffs have been most helpful. These include the William Salt Library and the Staffordshire Records Office in Stafford, the Lichfield Diocesan Archives in Lichfield, the Somerset Records Office in Taunton, the Bedford Office in London (particularly Mrs. M. P. G. Draper), the Hall of Records in Annapolis, and the John W. Garrett Library of Johns Hopkins University. Correspondence with the Reverend Prebendary F. S. L. Ramsden, rector of Trentham Parish, Staffordshire, the Lord Bishop of Lichfield, the Reverend Paul Hounsfield, rector of Donington Parish, Wolverhampton, and Mrs. P. H. Hardy, secretary to the archbishop of Dublin, provided numerous leads and answers relative to my subject and his family. Hospitality that will always be fondly remembered was extended to my wife and me by the Misses E. E. and V. M. Fen of Trentham, Staffordshire. Similar courtesies on visits to Maryland have been provided by our longtime friends Mr. and Mrs. Daniel Spintman of Bowie.

Over the years numerous graduate and undergraduate students at Bowling Green State University have assisted in the transcription and interpretation of Cradock's writings. They include Kevin Diels, Diane Van Skiver Gagel, James Gedes, Mara Ann Pinto Oess, Neil Weiser, Harold Zienta, and, most important, W. Jeffrey Welsh, whose master's thesis on Cradock's sermons provided many insights. Many colleagues at Bowling Green provided advice, including Lester Barber, Lawrence Daly, Richard Hebein, Virginia Platt, and Ronald Seavoy. Under the direction of Mrs. Phyllis Wulff the secretarial staff of the history department has typed and retyped various drafts of this manuscript until they have almost believed the spelling irregularities of both Thomas Cradock and David Skaggs. My hat goes off particularly to Judith Gilbert, Connie Montgomery, and Cindy Smith. The patient counsel of the Reverend James L. P. Trautwein of Saint John's Parish, Bowling Green, has been of considerable import.

The kind permission to reprint C. Day Lewis's translations of *The Eclogues and Georgics of Vergil* (1964) was granted by Literistic, Ltd. of New York. The illustrations are reprinted from Ethan Allen, *The Garrison Church: Sketches of the History of St. Thomas' Parish, Garrison Forest, Baltimore County, Maryland, 1742–1852* (1898). Numerous courtesies were extended by the present staff of the Garrison Church, particularly by Mrs. Marian H. Hurd, parish secretary.

Finally, there has been the tolerance of my family, who has spent days away from more desired vacations and has endured years of my concentration on this project. To Margo, Jason, and Philip—a hearty thanks.

In the end, the research, the writing, the conclusions, and the mistakes are mine.

The Poetic Writings of Thomas Cradock, 1718–1770

Part I
Introduction: Thomas Cradock and the Golden Age of Chesapeake Culture

For me while breath inspires this vital frame,
The glories of my God shall be my theme;
With joy sincere his praises I will sing,
And to his honour'd name attune the string.
While impious men by his resentment fall,
And direful woes their guilty hearts appall,
The great creator shall my soul inspire,
Shall fill my tongue, and animate my lyre.

Thomas Cradock, *A New Version of the Psalms of David* (1756), Psalm 104

1
Prolegomenon: An Extraordinary Sermon

The two Anglican ministers accosted numerous people all day Saturday. Before they finished, rumors circulated through the capital village of Annapolis that a "very uncommon Discourse" would be delivered the next morning.[1]

The older of the two was the hot-tempered, Catholic-baiting Thomas Chase, rector of Saint Paul's Parish, Baltimore Town. Now aged fifty, the irascible Parson Chase drank hard, scribbled verse, preached antipapist diatribes, and sued and countersued all those whose conduct affronted him and the dignity of his position.[2] His companion, some fifteen years younger, was Thomas Cradock, rector of Saint Thomas' Parish in western Baltimore County. A resident of the colony for only nine years, Parson Cradock had already achieved a reputation as a preacher, teacher, poet, and convivial companion among the Chesapeake gentry. The two men were boon companions who often drank together and exchanged verses.[3] For Cradock, the next day represented a rare opportunity to present his ideas to a much larger and more sophisticated audience than his frontier congregation. He intended to take advantage of it.

On Sunday, October 7, 1753, Saint Anne's Church was crowded as the Reverend Thomas Cradock preached one of the most important sermons in the history of Lord Baltimore's Province. He spoke before the governor, council, delegates, and Annapolitans of all classes in the sermon marking the opening of the annual session of the General Assembly. This year's address was not typical of what the assembled dignitaries usually heard on such occasions.

For nearly an hour the portly parson of Saint Thomas' Parish lectured recently arrived Governor Horatio Sharpe and the leading gentlemen of the colony on the unholy state of the Church of England in Maryland. He described how he and "the worthier part of the *sacred Order* have long suffr'd the Chagrin of *many joining* in the Ministry, who have fully shown by their horrid actions, how unfit they were for it, such as have turn'd out *Monsters in Wickedness.*" Cradock urged the establishment of a colonial bishopric for the closer supervision of the provincial clergy, many of whom were "of no Worth, no Learning, no Religion."[4]

This sermon created an immediate sensation. Jonas Green wrote in the next edition of the *Maryland Gazette* that the "excellent Sermon, on the Irregularities of some of the Clergy" was so well received that "we hear it will soon be printed."[5]

At a meeting of eight provincial clergy a few days later, Cradock repeated his discourse. All the assembled clerics recognized the potentially disturbing implications of the sermon. It attacked the core of the authority system of the eighteenth-century world. Here was a cleric of an established church preaching anticlericalism. In publicly discrediting some of his colleagues, Cradock opened the door to a wholesale attack on the religious and proprietary establishments as well as on the basic social theory of the day, which stressed the stratification of society and the necessary deference one should give to his social and intellectual superiors. On the other hand, even his conservative, proprietary-supporting colleague, the Reverend Thomas Bacon of Talbot County, recognized that the sermon laid the clergy "under a Necessity of doing something by way of Address to the Proprietor for establishing a legal Ecclesiastical Jurisdiction" for Maryland.[6]

In the end, nothing would change. Cradock's proposal failed to receive clerical, legislative, or proprietary approbation. He disturbed the advocates of proprietary privilege, he offended colonial Anglican laymen who wanted a voice in church governance that a bishop would deny, and he outraged dissenters who desired no episcopal jurisdictions in the New World. Besides, his sermon was an outspoken plea for the old order, for the transplantation of European institutions to America. For many this was anathema. Yet in recent times it has received the accolades of numerous scholars. Richard Beale Davis called it "perhaps the most courageous sermon of colonial America."[7]

Thus, what Parson Bacon called "a Sermon of a very extraordinary Nature, tending to prove . . . the absolute Necessity of an Ecclesiastical Jurisdiction over the Clergy"[8] had little immediate impact upon the religious establishment. But it has given Cradock a small niche in history. The recent deposit of Cradock's sermons and poetry in the Maryland Historical Society has provided us with an opportunity to view him in a broader way and thereby has enabled modern scholars to discern the values, ideas, and moral imperatives of a largely neglected segment of colonial American society—the Anglican communion and its clergy. But to understand the man fully we must comprehend the world that sent him to preach the gospel in a remote corner of the British empire.

NOTES

1. [Thomas Bacon], "Proceedings of the Parochial Clergy," *Maryland Historical Magazine* 3 (1908):366.
2. Rosamond R. Beirne, "The Reverend Thomas Chase: Pugnacious Parson," *Maryland Historical Magazine* 59 (1964):1–14.
3. David Curtis Skaggs, "Thomas Cradock and the Chesapeake Golden Age," *William and Mary Quarterly* 30 (1973):93–116.
4. David Curtis Skaggs, "Thomas Cradock's Sermon on the Governance of Maryland's Established Church," *William and Mary Quarterly* 27 (1970): 638, 641.
5. *Maryland Gazette* (Annapolis), October 11, 1753.
6. [Bacon], "Proceedings of the Parochial Clergy," p. 365.
7. Richard Beale Davis, "Intellectual Golden Age in the Colonial Chesapeake Bay Country," *Virginia Magazine of History and Biography* 78 (1970):136. See also Charles A. Barker, *The Background of the Revolution in Maryland* (New Haven, Conn.: Yale University Press, 1940), p. 276; Henry F. May, *The Enlightenment in America* (New York: Oxford University Press, 1976), pp. 66, 69.
8. [Bacon], "Proceedings of the Parochial Clergy," p. 365.

2
The Cradocks of Trentham

By the eighteenth century the outposts of the first British empire had become the refuge of cadet branches of various English families, where men attempted to recoup or expand their family's fortune or fame. A good example of the migration to the provinces can be seen in the Cradocks of Trentham, Staffordshire, who achieved positions of some prominence in the Anglican establishments in eighteenth-century Ireland and Maryland.

The Cradocks had once been a family of some importance in Staffordshire. They claimed descent from the most ancient of Welsh princes and, at least collaterally, from Sir Matthew Cradock (1468?–1531), royal official in southern Wales. Most important of the Staffordshire branch of the family was Matthew Cradock (1520–92), M.P. for the borough of Stafford, a wool merchant who prospered in the staple trade and in the purchase and rental of suppressed religious properties in the county. Two of his grandsons (also named Matthew) achieved some fame, one as merchant and M.P. of London and the first governor of the Massachusetts Bay Company and the other as M.P. and first mayor of Stafford. The elder branches of the family either migrated to London and sold their local estates or terminated in heiresses, through whom the Cradock properties passed into other families.

Presumably the William Cradock of Trentham who rented a cottage from Sir Richard Leveson in 1662 was a member of a younger branch. No direct link has been established between him and the John Cradock (d. 1687) of Trentham Parish who married Elizabeth (c. 1648–1728/29), daughter of Arthur Taylor (d. 1674/75) on August 20, 1673. From this marriage were born William (1674–1734), Richard (b. 1680/81), Elizabeth (d. 1684), and Arthur (ca. 1683–post-1749). No rental lists for the manor of Trentham are extant between 1662 and 1691, but apparently John Cradock rented property from the Leveson-Gowers, as his widow did in the latter years.

The Trentham Free School, established in 1674 by the will of Lady

Katherine Leveson, relict of Sir Richard, presumably was where the Cradocks' eldest son and possibly his brothers received their education. This William Cradock (sometimes Craddocke) was admitted sizar (a working scholarship student) at Jesus College, Cambridge, in 1694, receiving his B.A. in 1697/98 and M.A. in 1701. He served in a series of positions in the patronage of John Leveson-Gower (1674/75–1709), first Baron Gower. These included curate of Trentham (1702), chaplain to Lord Gower, rector of Swinnerton (1703/4), rector of Donington, Salop (1705–34), and prebend (beginning in 1720), sacrist, and principal officer (1723–34) of the Collegiate Church of Wolverhampton.

The Reverend William Cradock's connections with his patrons were close. Apparently Mrs. Cradock had been a nurse to Gertrude Leveson-Gower (1714/15–1794), and in her widowhood she was brought by Gertrude, after 1737 the wife of John Russell, fourth duke of Bedford, into the duchess's household at Woburn Abbey, Bedfordshire.

William and Anne Cradock's eldest son, John, attended the Trentham Free School and went on to Saint John's College, Cambridge, receiving his B.A. in 1728/29, M.A. in 1732, B.D. in 1740, and D.D. in 1749. He was a fellow of the College from 1732 to 1756, prebend and sacrist in Wolverhampton, and rector of several parishes before becoming chaplain to Bedford and rector of Saint Paul's, Covent Garden, from 1755 to 1758. When the duke became Lord Lieutenant of Ireland in 1757, John Cradock followed him there and was consecrated bishop of Kilmore that December. The high point of Dr. John Cradock's career was undoubtedly his translation to the archbishopric of Dublin in 1772. Thus in three generations the Cradocks of Trentham moved from minor tenants in the English midlands to the primacy of the Anglican church in Ireland.[1]

Considerably less distinguished were the other descendants of John and Elizabeth (Taylor) Cradock. Arthur Cradock, their youngest son, learned the trade of a tailor and lived with his mother until his mid-thirties, when he married Ann Marson in 1717. About the time of his marriage, Arthur Cradock began to assume a number of responsibilities in the Trentham community. In 1715 he served as warden of the parish, in 1717 he assumed the legal obligation for the payment of the annual rent for the grounds his mother leased from Lord Gower, and from 1716 to 1746 he served almost constantly as a juror on the manor court. In 1726 the court directed him and one of Lord Gower's largest leasors to "sufficiently scowere their several & respective ditches in the highway lane leading to Barlestone," showing that he

Genealogical Table

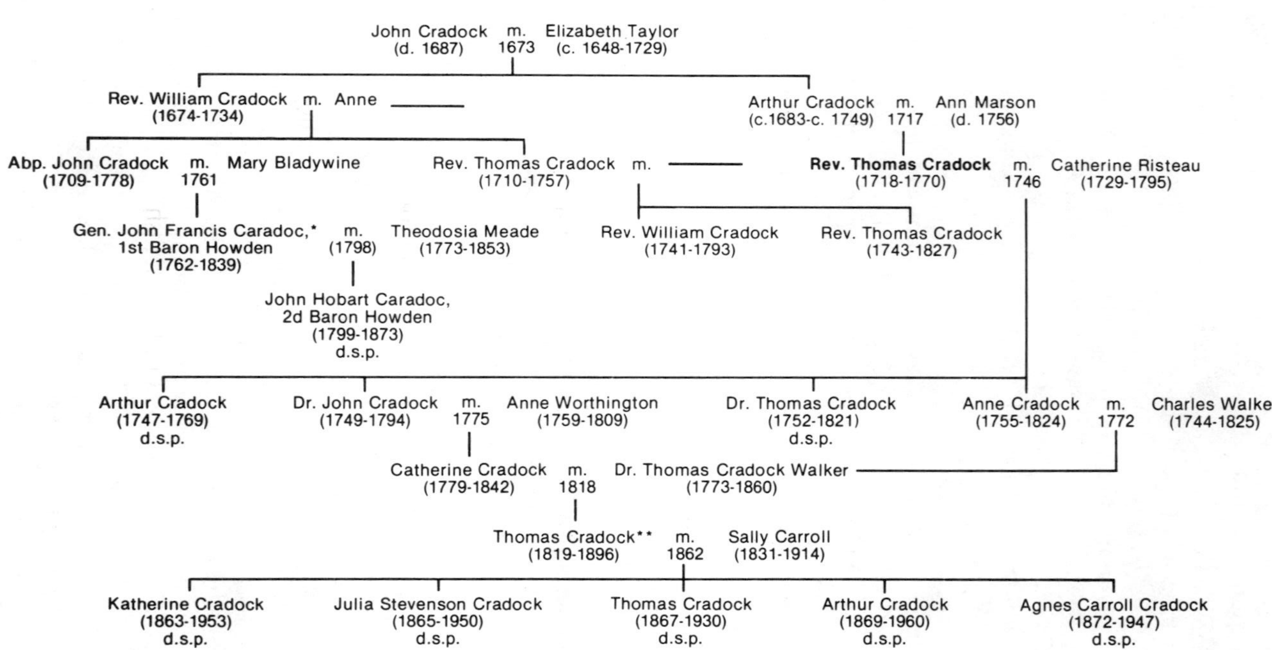

* Name changed because of supposed descent from ancient Welsh hero Caractacus or Caradoc

** Name changed by act of Maryland legislature to Thomas Cradock from Thomas Cradock Walker.

SOURCES: See notes 1-4 of chapter 2 and Dawn F. Thomas and Robert Barnes, *Green Spring Valley: Its History and Heritage*, 2 vols. (Baltimore: Maryland Historical Society, 1978), 2: 26-28, 107-110.

was expected to carry out other responsible duties within the community. The fact that he could sign his own name probably indicates he could read and write.

Arthur Cradock did not provide much of a living for his family. He was constantly in arrears in payment of his rents. Arthur and Ann Cradock enjoyed, however, a peculiar place among the Trentham tenants. His arrearages were not usually kept in the annual "Arrears Book," nor were they kept in the running totals of the "Collecting Rental" books. The absence of any vigorous prosecution of the Cradocks, except for the reducation in the size of the holdings of an aging tenant, seems to indicate that they enjoyed a special place in the eyes of the Leveson-Gowers.[2]

This place may have been due to Arthur's wife. She does not appear to have been a native of Trentham, since the family name is not in the parish register, but she is listed as a member of the parish at the time of her marriage. She neither was born nor died in the parish. Her American descendants believed her a personal servant to a British noble lady, possibly Lady Evelyn Pierrepoint (d. 1727), first wife of Earl Gower. (One must be exceptionally cautious about these family traditions, since they were not recorded until the mid-nineteenth century and confuse Thomas Cradock, son of Arthur and Ann [Marson] Cradock of Trentham with Thomas Cradock, son of William and Anne Cradock of Donington and Wolverhampton.) Arthur and Ann Cradock had six children, only two of whom, Thomas (1718–70) and James (1722–ante-1771), appear to have left descendants. She may have brought a love of learning into the household that infected at least her eldest son. Her halfbrother, John Worrall, was a London bookseller and publisher of enough note to receive an obituary notice in *Gentleman's Magazine.* Worrall deeded substantial sums to Ann Cradock's widowed daughters-in-law and to their children in England and America. Worrall seemed particularly proud of his nephew Thomas Cradock, because he published a glowing elegiac broadside praising the parson's "friendly character" when he learned of Cradock's death in 1770.[3]

This Thomas Cradock (1718–70) is the subject of this study. Following the family tradition, he studied at the Trentham Free School, where he received the classical training necessary for admission to the universities of the day. His master was the Reverend John Hargreaves (c. 1685–1760), who came to the Staffordshire School founded by Lady Katherine Leveson immediately upon receiving his B.A. from Jesus College, Cambridge, in 1707. Hargreaves served as Trentham's schoolmaster for nearly thirty-five years. He was paid not only the £20 fee from Lady Katherine's endowment but also £12 per year for instructing up to sixty scholars from some of the best-known gentry and clerical families of the county. Thomas Cradock praised Hargreaves in the dedication of his first translation of the psalms for "the pious Care that he took in my education." How many Trentham students went on to college is unknown, but five were admitted to Saint John's, Cambridge, in the years 1725–30. Probably John Cradock was his prize pupil, but the future archbishop's younger cousin was no mean scholar. Thomas Cradock matriculated at Magdalen Hall, Oxford, in 1737, but he never took the examinations necessary for the bachelor's degree.

Possibly he returned to Trentham to aid in the payment of his father's debts. During the early 1740s they were considerably reduced. During this period he decided to enter the clergy, and on September 20, 1741, the Right Reverend Richard Smalbroke, Lord Bishop of Lichfield and Coventry, ordained him to the diaconate. At the same time, Cradock became master of the Trentham Free School, succeeding Hargreaves. On September 25, 1743, Deacon Cradock journeyed to the Lord Bishop's residence at Eccleshall, where he received ordination into the priesthood. Bishop Smalbroke licensed him to serve as curate of Blurton (a chapel in Trentham parish) and "occasionally assistant at Kingsbury, Warwickshire." The latter post was so far distant from his home parish and schoolmaster responsibilities that it is doubtful that he ever served there. The benefits of this pluralism were small and he undoubtedly expected greater rewards from his patrons. Exactly what happened is unknown, but less than five months after his ordination, Cradock was in London securing license from Bishop Edmund Gibson to perform ministerial functions in the province of Maryland.[4] Thus another Cradock left Staffordshire to seek his future on frontiers of the British empire.

Cradock's decision to emigrate could have been prompted by economic, religious, political, or romantic reasons. Perhaps the greater economic opportunity of a Maryland parish over those in England induced the departure. He received, however, a new parish of modest income upon his arrival and never held a living equal to many parceled out to those in the Bedford and Leveson-Gower favor in the mother country. He may even have expected his British patrons to provide him some lucrative and prestigious position in Maryland—the first colonial Anglican episcopate, for instance? It is, however, doubtful that this was the case. The lords Baltimore were reluctant to allow the bishop of London even licensing authority in their domain;

it was hardly likely that they would allow a bishop on the shores of the Chesapeake to interfere with their powers.

Perhaps he came to the New World purely out of a devotion to the spread of Anglicanism in America. His was a time of an extraordinary flowering of the Church of England in the colonies and he may have been caught up in the missionary fervor that drove notable Britons like Dean George Berkeley across the Atlantic.

Or he might have been caught in a power play that squeezed him out of a place in the politics of religious preferment that characterized eighteenth-century England. The Levesons had been Royalists during the English Civil War and high Tories in the century following. Then suddenly in the mid-1740s, John Leveson-Gower (1694–1754), first earl Gower, joined his son-in-law, Bedford, in an alliance of Whiggish opportunism that left his Tory allies adrift. Since the Gowers dominated every parliamentary election in Staffordshire and the local boroughs throughout the eighteenth century, such a shift could have left a family retainer trained at the highly royalist stronghold of Oxford without a place in the new order. This could partially explain the Jacobite charges leveled against Cradock shortly after his arrival in Maryland.[5]

Finally there is the romantic reason. According to Cradock family legend, the young priest cast longing eyes toward a female member of the Leveson-Gower family. It may be that the object of his affection was Frances Leveson-Gower (1720–88), whose liaison with Lord John Sackville resulted in the birth of a child at Woburn Abbey (home of her sister, the duchess of Bedford) on December 30, 1743, and the marriage of the couple two days later.[6] Either pressure from his patrons or the personal decision of a disappointed lover could have resulted in his rapid removal to the New World.

Whatever rationale explains the young parson's departure for America, he arrived in Maryland by mid-1744, served as chaplain to the colony's commissioners negotiating with the Iroquois Confederacy that summer, and became first rector of the newly created Saint Thomas' Church in the Garrison Forest area of west Baltimore County early the next year. Thus began his twenty-five- year pastorate and an over two-hundred-year association of the Cradock family with the Garrison Church, as this parish is usually known. He apparently began his ministry with hopes of returning to England, but his ties to the New World became stronger with his marriage in March 1746 to Catherine, seventeen-year-old daughter of John Risteau, a prominent landholder of the Garrison Forest and Lord Baltimore's high sheriff for Baltimore County. Sheriff Risteau, a Huguenot refugee, deeded the couple a 170-acre farm on which they erected a house that Cradock, reflecting his Staffordshire heritage, named Trentham. Here they raised three sons—Arthur, John, and Thomas—and a daughter, Anne. By the time of his death in 1770, the parson had established a family with an estate of 800 acres of land and a heritage of Anglicanism and gentility that would continue at Trentham for over two centuries.[7]

The young parson brought more from the midlands than the names of his home and his children. He established at Trentham a school modeled after the one where he had studied and taught. He published two English translations of the psalms (one in London in 1754, the other in Annapolis in 1756). He preached before gatherings of provincial dignitaries in Philadelphia, Baltimore, and Annapolis. He left a collection of manuscript sermons that is one of the largest extant by a colonial Anglican priest. Included in his papers is a satiric commentary on provincial life entitled "Maryland Eclogues in Imitation of Virgil's." These nine pastorals constitute a burlesque on colonial society typical of those written by many Britishers who came to America. The poems provide us with a number of insights into the lives of the Britons, Negroes, and Indians who made up his Chesapeake world. His longest manuscript is a five-act play, *The Death of Socrates*.[8]

Individually considered, none of Cradock's works are great literature, but collectively they do show how the process of cultural transference from England to America occurred. Coupled with the Cradocks in Ireland, the career of Thomas Cradock in Maryland also demonstrates how one family utilized the patronage opportunities afforded by an expanding empire to elevate its social and economic position. Further studies of the emigration of English families throughout the empire will provide additional examples of this process of upward social mobility[9] and of the diffusion of British culture.

NOTES

1. The origins of the Cradocks of Trentham are obscure, so much so that even Archbishop Cradock's son, Lord Howden, made no serious attempt to find them: see *Burke's Peerage* (1837 ed.), s.v. "Howden, Baron." The data used here is mostly taken from the following: *Trentham Parish Register* (Staffordshire Parish Register Society, *Publications* 28 [Stafford, Eng., 1906]), 91, 93, 97, 98, 118, 121, 231; Rentals for the Manor of Trentham, (1662) D 593/G/s/1/27, folio 2, (1691) D 593/G/2/1/28, folio 1, Staffordshire Record Office, Stafford, England (hereafter cited as SRO); John Montgomery Traherne, *Historical Notices of Sir Matthew Cradock, Knt. of Swansea in the Reigns of*

Henry VII and VIII (Llandovery, Wales: W. Rees, 1840); J. S. Horne, "Matthew Cracock" (typescript, Guildhall Library, London, ca. 1937); Robert F. Scott, *Admissions to the College of St. John the Evangelist in the University of Cambridge*, 4 vols. (Cambridge, Eng.: At the University Press, 1882–1931), 2: 45, 158, 383, 699; 4: 211–13; John and J. A. Venn, comp. *Alumni Cantabrigienses . . . Part 1 . . . to 1751*, 4 vols. (Cambridge, Eng.: At the University Press, 1922–27), 1: 411; 4: 515; Thomas Baker, *History of the College of St. John the Evangelist*, ed. John E. B. Mayor, 2 vols. (Cambridge, Eng.: At The University Press, 1869), 2: 708–9; *Dictionary of National Biography*, s.v. "Cradock, John," "Caradoc, Sir John Francis," and "Caradoc, Sir John Hobart"; J. C. Dickinson, "The Priory of Trentham," and A. K. B. and R. H. Evans, "The College of St. Peter, Wolverhampton," in M. W. Greenslade, ed., *A History of the County of Stafford* [*Victoria History of the Counties of England*], vol. 3 (London: University of London Press, 1970), pp. 255–60, 321–31; Donington Register Book, No. 2, 1689–1796 (information on the Cradocks graciously supplied the author by the Reverand Paul Hounsfield, rector of Donington, Shropshire, in a letter of January 1, 1971); Josiah C. Wedgwood, "Staffordshire Parliamentary History" *Staffordshire Historical Collections*, 3d ser. (1919), pp. 345, 379, 409; (1920), pp. 6, 22; J. G. Cavenagh-Mainwaring, "The Mainwarings of Whitmore and Biddulph in the County of Stafford," *Staffordshire Historical Collections*, 3d ser. (1933), part 2: 62–63. This also corrects a number of errors in the family origins of Archbishop Cradock described in J. B. Leslie, Fasti of Christ Church Cathedral, Dublin (typescript in Library of Representative Church Body, Dublin) graciously supplied me by the office of the present archbishop in a letter of May 11, 1970. Archbishop Cradock's career may be seen in part in his letters to Bedford, July 22, 1756, August 29, 1758, September 16, 1765, Bedford Manuscript Letters, HMC #8, XXXII, folio 33, XXXVII, folio 116, LII, folio 142, Bedford Office, London. I wish to acknowledge with thanks the trustees of the Bedford Settled Estates, who have given permission to use these manuscripts.

2. Collecting Rentals for the Manor Trentham, (1716) D 593/G/2/1/32, (1718) D 593/G/2/1/35, (1729) D 593/G/2/2/6, (1731) D 593/G/2/2/11, (1741) D 593/G/2/3/2, (1749) D 593/G/2/3/22, (1750), D 593/G/2/3/24, Staffordshire Record Office; Survey of the Liberties of Trentham, (1716) D 593/H/14/1/3, (1729) D 593/H/14/3/36, Staffordshire Record Office; Court Rolls, Manor of Trentham, (1716–46) D 593/J/7/2/3–4, Staffordshire Record Office. The exact date of Arthur Cradock's birth and death are uncertain. No entries of births appear in the *Trentham Parish Register*, 1681–1700, and it is assumed that Arthur, probably named after his grandfather, Arthur Taylor, was born ca. 1683, two years after the birth of Richard Cradock, son of John and Elizabeth (Taylor) Cradock. It is presumed that he moved out of the parish about 1749 and died sometime before 1754, when Thomas Cradock's *A Poetical Translation of the Psalms of David from Buchanan's Latin into English Verse* (London: R. Ware, 1754) was published by "Ann Cradock, at Wells in Somersetshire."

3. *Trentham Parish Register*, pp. 147, 149, 152, 156, 158, 220, 225, 236, 244, 271. Ann (Marson) Cradock died in 1756. St. Cuthbert Parish, Wells, Baptisms and Burials, 1740 to 1787, D/P/W. St. C 2/1/4, Somerset Records Office, Taunton, England. In 1772 her half-brother willed part of his estate to the widows and children of her two sons, Thomas and James. John Worrall's will, Probate 11/971/392, Public Record Office, London; obituary notice, *Gentleman's Magazine* 41 (September 1771): 426. The family tradition on the Cradock origins is in Ethan Allen, *The Garrison Church: Sketches of the History of St. Thomas' Parish, Garrison Forest, Baltimore County, Maryland, 1742–1852*, ed. Hobart Smith (New York: James Pott and Co., 1898), pp. 7–12. The Maryland Cradocks supplied this information to the Reverand Dr. Allen in the mid-nineteenth century. They believed their ancestor to be the archbishop's brother rather than his cousin and that the family rented lands from Bedford rather than from Gower. Thomas Cradock undoubtedly had great affection for Bedford, however, since he named the home on a second farm after the duke's large London holdings; see William V. Elder III, "Bloomsbury, a Cradock House in the Worthington Valley," *Maryland Historical Magazine* 53 (1958): 371–75. See also the broadside "A Friendly Character of the Late Rev'd. Thomas Cradock . . ." (London: Thomas Worrall, 1770?).

4. Venn, comp., *Alumni Cantabrigienses,* s.v. "Hargreaves, John" (1707), 2: 307; on Trentham School see Scott, *Admissions to the College of St. John,* 2: 45, 57, 60, 62, 119, 383; s.v. "Cradock, Samuel" (1734–35) and "Cradock, Thomas" (1737), in Joseph Foster, comp. *Alumni Oxonienses: The Members of the University of Oxford, 1715–1886* (London: Parker and Co., 1888), 1: 312; Thomas Cradock, *A Poetical Translation of the Psalms,* p. iii; certificate of Thomas Cradock's ordination to the diaconate, September 20, 1741, Cradock's license as master of the Free School of Trentham, September 21, 1741, certificate of his ordination to the priesthood, September 25, 1743, his license to preach in Maryland, February 21, 1743/44: originals in the Maryland Diocesan Library, Maryland Historical Society, Baltimore.

5. On the Leveson-Gower political activities see D. A. Pennington, "County and Country: Staffordshire in Civil War Politics, 1640–1644," *North Staffordshire Journal of Field Studies* 6 (1966): 12–24; Wedgwood, *Staffordshire Parliamentary History* in *Stafffordshire Historical Collections,* 3d ser. (1920, 1922), esp. pp. 243–66; Ann J. Kettle, "The Struggle for the Lichfield Interest, 1747–68," ibid., 4th Ser., 6 (1970):115–35; S. M. Hardy and R. C. Baily, "The Downfall of the Gower Interest in the Staffordshire Boroughs, 1800–30," *ibid.,* 3d Ser., (1950–51), p. 267; Lewis Namier, *The Structure of Politics at the Accession of George III,* 2d ed. (London: Macmillan, 1957), pp. 104–5, 125, 339 n2. On Cradock's alleged Jacobitism see William Hand Browne, et al, eds., *Archives of Maryland,* 71 vols to date (Baltimore: Maryland Historical Society, 1883–1971), vol. 28 (1908), pp. 373, 374; Thomas Cradock, *Two Sermons with a Preface Shewing the Author's Reasons for Publishing Them* (Annapolis, Md.: Jonas Green, 1747), pp. i–vi.

6. The story of Cradock's alleged affection for a sister of the duchess of Bedford is related in Allen, *Garrison Church,* p. 9. For the story of the birth at Woburn Abbey, see Bedford to Duke of Dorset, January 1, 1744; Gower to Bedford, January 2, 1744; and certificates of marriage of Lord John Sackville with the Hon. Frances Leveson-Gower, Bedford Manuscript Letters, HMC #8, IX, folios 24, 26, 66, Bedford Office, London. A "Mrs. Cradock" witnessed the baptism; probably she was the widowed mother of the future archbishop.

7. On Cradock's Maryland life see Allen, *Garrison Church,* pp. 7–12, 22–27, 176–77, and David Curtis Skaggs, "Thomas Cradock's Sermon on the Governance of Maryland's Established Church, *William and Mary Quarterly* 27 (1970): 630–37. This introduction corrects the errors in Dr. Allen's account of Cradock's English background. On the Cradock landholdings see Debt Books, Baltimore County, 1770, folio 18, Hall of Records, Annapolis, Maryland.

8. Cradock, *Two Sermons;* Cradock, *A Poetical Translation of the Psalms;* Skaggs, "Cradock's Sermon," pp. 630–53; Thomas Cradock, *A New Version of the Psalms of David* (Annapolis, Md.: Jonas Green, 1756), constitute most of his published writings. For a description of his manuscripts housed in the Maryland Historical Society, Baltimore, see the bibliographical note by David C. Skaggs and F. Garner Ranney, "Thomas Cradock Sermons," *Maryland Historical Magazine* 67 (1972): 179–80.

9. See, for instance, Jacob M. Price, "One Family's Empire: The Russell-Lee-Clark Connection in Maryland, Britain, and India, 1707–1857," *Maryland Historical Magazine* 72 (1977): 165–225.

3
Defender of the Faith

The Anglican communion is an anomaly in western Christendom. Professor Crane Brinton succinctly described the place of that faith in his *Shaping of the Modern Mind:*

> The Church of England is no simple thing. . . . Basically a conservative Protestant Church, respectful of civil authority . . . , theologically and liturgically close to the Roman Catholic Church, lacking the Protestant zeal to clean up this world, the Church of England kept under its elastic control—the metaphor here is fairly exact, for the Anglican mind can stretch—a whole host of potential rebels. . . . At various times these potential rebels have become real rebels, but the Church has stayed on, a puzzle to the logically minded, an offense to the moral perfectionist, a delight to the admirer of the irrational English.[1]

Seeking to articulate the ethos of his church in the age of Elizabeth, Richard Hooker (1554?–1600) defined the three keynotes of Anglicanism. The church was biblical, apostolic, and rational. The Church of England was reformed in that it preferred biblical authority over church tradition, it was apostolic in its use of tradition where the Bible was silent or ambiguous, and it was unabashedly rational in its outlook whenever both Scripture and tradition were unclear.[2] Such a philosophy would never satisfy the convinced Roman Catholic or Calvinist, and for nearly a century after Hooker, England's turbulent history may in part be seen as an attempt to resolve the role of the established church in English society and politics.

The compromise emerging out of the Glorious Revolution left the Church of England intact but allowed dissenting Protestants a measure of religious toleration. The established church retained the support of public taxation, it coexisted and cooperated with the Crown and Parliament, and it kept the ecclesiastical orders of early Christendom—bishops, priests, and deacons. But the turbulence of the seventeenth century left the Church of England without an accepted doctrine and without accepted lines of authority. The Act of Uniformity of 1662 did not centralize Church discipline in the hierarchy, and the combination of Newtonion science, Arminianism, nonjurors, place hunting, latitudinarianism, deism, and evangelicalism made all forms of traditional authority suspect.[3]

It was during this age of uncertainty that both Archbishop John and Parson Thomas Cradock preached. The archbishop's career was primarily one of climbing the ladder of ecclesiastical preferment—with considerable help from the duke of Bedford—while the parson served as one of the clerical subalterns whose duty it was to preach the gospel in the thousands of rural parishes that covered Britain.

Despite all the ridicule of these country parsons and despite the penury of many clerical livings, there existed an extraordinary rapport between the rural clergy and their parishioners. The archetypal country rector was James Woodforde, vicar of Weston Longville, Norfolk, 1774–1803. Parson Woodforde's *Diary* depicts the tranquil life of an obscure village rector. He loved his country, sport, good food, and the established religious and political institutions. Warmhearted and generous, he expressed a candor in his discussion of the squires, servants, and publicans of Norfolk that is similar to the acid comments expressed in Thomas Cradock's "Maryland Eclogues." On the other hand, Woodforde's sermons reflect the concerned and pious vicar of East Anglia.[4]

This was the clerical tradition Cradock inherited from his native Staffordshire. The ideal clergyman was a true shepherd of his flock: he delivered sensible, scholarly, sound sermons, he remained companionable to all his parishioners, and he engaged in those community merriments befitting a man of the cloth and of the people. The Anglican worship of his boyhood was neither unworldly nor intense, but taken naturally and for granted. Religious and moral truths were presented to a receptive audience, one that wanted its religion taught with reason, politeness, and toleration. Neither the enthusiasm of the true believer nor the deism of the nonbeliever received a considerable following. The ordinary man with his ordinary ideas sympathized with the old orthodoxy rather than with enthusiasm or disbelief.

Most significant in eighteenth-century churchmanship was the growth of private benevolent activities: charity schools, tract societies, settlements for the British poor, and missionary activities. Charitable conduct became an increasingly important aspect of popular piety. Anglican clerics became more interested in benevolence than in theology. It was this tradition in England after the Glorious Revolution that contributed to some of the most conspicuous acts of Anglican charity.[5]

Spurred by Queen Mary II and Queen Anne, visionary clerics like Thomas Bray sought to expand Anglicanism outside the British Isles. The Society for the Promotion of Christian Knowledge (S.P.C.K.) established libraries of Christian and Anglican doctrine throughout the colonies. Bray's second enterprise, the Society for the Propagation of the Gospel in Foreign Parts (S.P.G.), sent missionaries throughout the world, but was particularly active in those colonies where there was no taxation in support of the Church of England. Bray and various governors secured the establishment of the church in the southern colonies: Maryland (1702), South Carolina (1706), North Carolina (1711), and Georgia (1750) joined Virginia as locations of established Anglican churches.

Undoubtedly, mixed motives prompted James Oglethorpe and others to found Georgia, but conspicuous among them was a philanthropic urge to provide a haven for the unfortunate. Missionary efforts brought such notable Anglican evangelicals as Charles and John Wesley and George Whitefield to that fledgling province. A similar fervor caused the most notable British philosopher of the eighteenth century, Dean (later Bishop) George Berkeley, to establish an abortive College of Saint Paul in Bermuda and to reside for several years in Rhode Island. From Newfoundland to Barbados, the S.P.G. and S.P.C.K. tried to satisfy the spiritual wants of the colonists. There can be little doubt that by mid-century Anglicanism was an expanding faith ministering to natives and settlers throughout His Majesty's dominions.[6]

But these efforts failed to replicate the Church of England in America. The most obvious difference was the lack of church hierarchy. Although the bishop of London held licensing authority over clergy sent to the colonies, his ecclesiastical authority and spiritual offices failed to cross the Atlantic. In effect, America had a nonepiscopal Episcopal Church. As two English historians wrote: "To say this was like acting the play of Hamlet with the character of the Prince of Denmark omitted, would be to understate the case."[7]

The only representatives of the hierarchy in America were the bishop's commissaries. The indeterminate status of their authority meant that they were incapable of administering the effective discipline over the clergy that their position supposedly allowed. Nowhere was this more apparent than in Maryland. What little symbolic authority these men possessed permanently disappeared when Lord Baltimore visited Maryland in the 1730s. The vested interests of the proprietor were stronger than those of the bishop of London, the Crown, the General Assembly, and the incumbent clergy. The proprietor's charter claims denied the Maryland church any semblance of governance similar to that which it enjoyed in England.[8]

The Church of England had become the established religion in Maryland in 1702 when the province was under direct crown control while the proprietary government was temporarily suspended. The restoration of proprietary powers in 1715 brought a nominally Anglican proprietor important powers relative to the religious establishment. The most significant of these was the right of presentation of clerical livings to persons in the proprietor's favor. By the time of the Declaration of Independence, forty-four parishes yielded a combined income of over £8,000, with the typical rector receiving approximately £200 per anum. No other province provided such lavish support for the Anglican clergy, and these livings were coveted by many whose piety was less important than their influence with Lord Baltimore. With no episcopal oversight and with no lay supervision of clerical conduct, the Maryland clergy was the proprietor's own. Consequently, there were many unworthy members of the priesthood whose misconduct contributed significantly to the disrepute of the church and state.[9]

This problem of unworthy clerics bothered Cradock considerably and remained a concern throughout his career. This in no way, however, caused him to reject his faith. Instead he concentrated on its defense in the face of adversity. In this assertion of Anglicanism, Thomas Cradock epitomized the cultural imperatives of the Chesapeake's established clergy when faced with the great controversies of the early modern world.

Peter Gay describes the eighteenth century as the beginning of the rise of modern paganism wherein secular solutions, religious skepticism, and experimental science contributed to the demise of medieval Christian unity. The volatile world of the seventeenth century with its "religious war, economic dislocation, political instability, and philosophical uncertainty"[10] led to a search for stability in the midst of seeming chaos. For some men, stability came from absolute political, economic, and religious truth; for others it involved a freedom of thought that abolished all the cultural inheritances for a new intellectual order. The English-speaking world sought a compromise between these two extremes, which was expressed in rational Christianity.

Torn apart by the Puritan values and ultraroyalism, the Anglican communion, somewhat reluctantly, accepted a philosophy of latitudinarianism. Forced conformity declined with the Toleration Act of 1690, and with it disappeared both the Puritan vision of a redeemed nation and the Anglican vision of a unified Erastian church. Nonconformity was confined to the walls of dissenting chapels and no longer played a central role in British political life.[11]

The English church was divided between its two wings. Toryism included a few nonjurors who refused to take the oath to William and Mary and the more numerous high churchmen. The latter accepted the political settlement resulting from the Glorious Revolution but distrusted the hypocrisy of "occasional conformists" whose rare communions allowed them to overcome the exclusion from civil and military office imposed upon nonconformists. The sacerdotalism of the Tories created considerable controversy between them and the Whigs over liturgy, prompting Bishop Benjamin Hoadley of Bangor to question the necessity of the visible church. The Whigs played down dogma and preached a religion of reasonable faith, piety, and morality. Creeds were less important to them than ethics; charity was more important than particular tenets. To the Tories, the Whigs' moderation was an excuse for apathy. The farcical nature of much of the argumentation prompted Jonathan Swift's High-Heel versus Low-Heel satire in *Gulliver's Travels*.[12]

"Our church," wrote Lord Halifax in 1684, "is a Trimmer between the phrenzy of Platonic visions and the lethargick Ignorance of Popish Dreams." To "trim" such a course when buffeted by the winds of rationalism required a most unusual sailing vessel—one that appeared to be sailing with the wind when actually it was tacking. Such was the problem confronting churchmen of the eighteenth century as rationalism replaced mysticism as the basis of Christianity. The great thinkers whose ideas served as the basis of the new philosophy—Isaac Newton, Robert Boyle, and John Locke—saw no conflict between their ideas and the essential ingredients of Christian faith. Reason vindicated revealed religion. God, said Locke, designed a harmonious universe not only in the physical but also in the moral world. While such works as Locke's *The Reasonableness of Christianity* (1695) would never satisfy the traditionalist, they were part of an effort to explain the faith through human reason. Yet "Liberal Anglicanism and the dawning deist Enlightenment were connected by a thousand threads: both saw the universe as rational and God as beneficent, both despised enthusiasm and mysticism, both were critical of the written tradition and long catalogs of dogma."[13] However distinct the rational Christians thought themselves from their deistic contemporaries, these threads bound them together.

It is, of course, virtually impossible to reconstruct all the ingredients of Cradock's intellectual background. We know that the diocese of Lichfield and Coventry in which he grew up was led by vigorous antideists. Conspicuous among such bishops was Edward Chandler (bishop 1717–30), whose *Defence of Christianity from Prophecies* (1725) was an attack upon those who rejected argument from prophecy. His successor, Richard Smalbroke (bishop 1731–49), studied at Magdalen College, Oxford, and wrote against both deists and Methodists. It may well have been Smalbroke who influenced Cradock to attend Oxford rather than Cambridge, where Cradock's uncle, his cousin, and his schoolmaster had been educated. It is clear that Cradock's youthful intellectual environment was one in which both deism and itinerant preaching were frowned upon.[14] This heritage did not mean that Cradock rejected either a rational Christianity or an evangelical approach to religion. In fact, there are several reasons to believe that he was devoted to both a rational and an evangelical church.

In contrast to the Methodists, who tended to be concerned with lay leadership and itinerant preaching, the Anglican evangelicals were resident clergy who emphasized church liturgy and private philanthropy to mitigate the evils of poverty and illiteracy in the world. Evangelicals feared Wesley's drift away from the church and sought to exercise their concerns for morality within its teachings. Such men sought to go beyond the rationalism of Tillotson and Clarke. Many of the influential evangelicals like James Hervey, Samuel Walker, Thomas Adam, and William Romaine attended Oxford colleges in the same period as Cradock.[15]

We have few direct references by Cradock to the evangelicals, but Bishop Beveridge is cited in his General Assembly sermon of 1753.[16] On the other hand, enough evidence of Cradock's preaching exists to indicate his popularity. He frequently spoke outside his home parish—to groups in Baltimore in 1745 and 1746, to the Maryland General Assembly in 1753 and possibly in 1757, to Anglican, Lutheran, and Moravian congregations in York and Cumberland counties of Pennsylvania in 1758, and to a Philadelphia assembly sometime after 1749.[17] Moreover, his own congregation grew so much that a gallery had to be constructed to accommodate increased communicants, and he and his son Arthur journeyed to locations throughout the large parish to preach, to administer the sacraments, and to minister to his flock. By the time of his death, only small Quaker and Baptist congregations whose existence antedated Cradock's arrival in 1745 served the few dissenting Christians in his parish.[18]

Like other evangelicals, he preached outside his parish only when invited to do so. That differing denominations wanted to hear him indicates that he preached an ecumenical Christianity that was typical of the age. He remained loyal to the Church of England's discipline and theology but constantly sought expressions of faith through a lifetime of devotion, piety, and benevolence rather than through enthusiastic outbursts of conversion.

Cradock asked of his parishioners a simple, lifelong faith that required them to have a "firm belief of things at present not seen" and a "Conviction upon the mind of the Truth of the Promises and Threatenings of God" that confirms "the certain Reality of the Rewards and Punishments of the Life to come."[19] Cradock joined traditional creeds with piety and benevolence in a manner typical for his times.

Orthodoxy of this type did not reject the rationalism of the Age of Reason, however. The rector of the Garrison Church combined evangelicalism with rationalism to achieve a faith that effectively integrated tradition with reason. Thus he sought to bridge the dilemma between the mysticism of faith and the deism of the age by accepting the Enlightenment belief in an ordered universe and by using its principles to prove the existence of God. He fought the spread of deism and disbelief by imitating the Christian apologists of the Mother Country, such as Bishops Beveridge, Chandler, and Smalbroke, as well as theologians Jeremiah Seed and Samuel Clarke.

It was the care of the Anglican faith that prompted Cradock to make his famous appeal to the General Assembly in 1753. He feared that the continued licentiousness of too many of its clergy contributed significantly to the low estate of public morality in the province. "To see the Ignorance and Immorality, that prevails among the *meaner,* and the Indifference to religious duties that too frequently distinguishes the *higher,* Classes of People," struck him "with melancholy Reflections." Too many went unchurched, while others fell prey to the erroneous doctrines of "Dissenters or Papists"; even more ominous was the increase of "that other set of men . . . who are of no Religion at all, and make jest of the Christian Scheme and Ordinances, those very wise men, who laugh at *the Bible* 'as fit only for the Amusement of old Women and Children, and have Souls too large and gen'rous forsooth' to be terrified by at the severest Denunciations of God's Wrath."[20]

Too many persons did not bring up their children in the fear of God. His opposition to the growing secularism of the day reflected iself in a sermon on education preached in Philadelphia. Cradock probably intended to attack Benjamin Franklin's *Proposal Relating to the Education of Youth in Pensilvania* (1749). He objected to Franklin's nondenominational approach to education on the grounds that it would result in nonreligious, if not antireligious, instruction. The rector of Saint Thomas' made education and religion inseparable; to neglect the one would harm the other. Learning without religious principles could lead to moral anarchy, while religion without scholarship was antagonistic to the precepts of Protestant Christianity. This was not to say that all learning must be of a religious nature, for the study of the arts and sciences would also be beneficial in forming students' minds to piety and virtue. But one should never separate religious training from the general education of pupils. Cradock urged a humanist approach to pedagogy: "teach your youth betimes the beauty and loveliness of virtue, lead them early into the mighty advantages that attend a Christian's faith and practice; and then will your labours be crown'd indeed, and you'll secure for them as well as yourselves a happy and glorious Immortality.[21] Citing examples from biblical Israel, ancient Greece and Rome, and modern Europe, Cradock demonstrated that when morality departed the educational process, society plunged into moral and political decline.

To avoid such a demise of greatness in the British empire, the rector of Saint Thomas' preached a love of king and country that transcended the petty political quarrels of the day. When the darkness of military defeat combined with the factionalism of provincial politics to lead to despair, Cradock was called outside "the narrow circle of his own Parish" to preach to other audiences. Based upon the famous "house divided" text (Luke 11:17), this sermon is the only one in the Cradock Papers of which there are two versions. It seems reasonably clear that it was this "war sermon" that proprietary interests in Pennsylvania had him deliver on a tour of York and Cumberland counties in 1758. He may have delivered the one version to the Maryland General Assembly in the fall of 1756 or possibly the spring of 1757. The most probable time is April 1757, when the assembly met in Baltimore because a smallpox epidemic prevented meeting in Annapolis.[22]

Cradock's call for "concord and unanimity" in the councils of government was an obviously political sermon, and he apologized for it, hoping that he would not be received "with contempt or disgust nor . . . scorn or resentment" because "he meddled with subjects that did not concern him, and ought rather to confine his discourses to the more private virtues of a Christian life."[23] Still, he proceeded.

Tracing English history from the fourteenth to the seventeenth century and combining this with examples from the ancient and medieval worlds, Cradock proclaimed that political survival required "all to join hands and hearts together to promote peace and unity, and to discountenance both by our words and actions all grumblings and uneasiness that may rise among us."[24] His words obviously pleased the proprietary factions in Maryland and Pennsylvania, who found themselves confronted with intransigent opposition that was willing to risk the security of frontiersmen to wring political advantage from the proprietors. Cradock tried to avoid being involved in partisan rancor: "my Christian brethren, I blow not the trumpet of contention; tis peace, tis unity, tis unanimity that I with so much earnestness plead for."[25] Cradock understood that "the nature of our constitution" made Britons "more slow in our resolves and consequently more dilatory in the execution of them" than the "cruel and perfidious" French and Indians that opposed them, but all colonists must join together "to preserve ourselves, to preserve our wives and little ones, our flocks and herds, our lands and possessions."[26] The long-term effect of Cradock's charge was minimal; for a brief moment in 1757 and 1758 cooperation ensued, but his words had little lasting impact upon the contentious politics of the proprietary colonies.

Throughout his career, Cradock took the opportunity to affirm his patriotism and his zeal for the Church of England: "We are Britons; . . . we are the Sons of those who valued Life less than Liberty, and readily gave their Blood to leave that Liberty to their Posterity. . . . Let us chiefly remember, that we can chuse our Religion . . . and not tamely, basely submit to the slavish Yoak of a *Roman Pontiff*."[27] The Protestant nationalism embodied in this statement typifies Cradock's attitude toward the Church of Rome. Had Bonnie Prince Charlie successfully led the 1745 Jacobite Rebellion, Cradock predicted not only that "the mild gentle sway, which his present gracious Majesty exercises over his Subjects" would be lost, but also that Britons would be subject "to all the Fopperies and Absurdities of the *Roman* Church."[28]

Although Cradock acknowledged that the modern Catholic church was purged of many of her errors of immorality, she still clung to "Errors" of doctrine that were so obviously false that he wondered "that any man of common Sense can be so blinded as to follow and support a Religion, that gives the Lie to every sensible Faculty about him."[29] The Catholics, he argued, are "our Enemies . . . who wou'd make us slaves and half-Christians like themselves, and like the grand Enemy of Mankind . . . bring us into their own deplorable condition."[30]

Cradock's Protestantism differed greatly in practice from that of seventeenth century Puritans or that of his Methodist contemporaries. The rector of the Garrison Church felt no compunction at joining his parishioners in a few drafts after services. In fact, he seems to have made it a regular practice to ride to "Mr. Metcalfe's" tavern after the sermon and to treat those gathered to a glass of wine. Moreover, he would often drive his wife home, only to rejoin his drinking companions in the afternoon.[31] Such conviviality was typical of the English country parson of his day and undoubtedly endeared the rector to many who would otherwise have avoided contact with him.

If Cradock despised the Catholics for false scriptural doctrine, so also he despised the Puritans for false morality. His discussion of the miracle of turning water into wine at the wedding feast at Cana provided an opportunity to show "how little ground there is, for that stiff and precise Temper which condemns all outward Expressions of Mirth." In what Professor Richard Beale Davis calls "The Merry Sermon" preached on Saint George's Day in Baltimore Town, 1745, Cradock condemned those who "dress'd up Religion in such a gloomy, frightening manner, that they have taken away the Beauty and Comeliness of it." Men are mistaken if they place "Religion in Gloominess" and call "a sorrowful Countenance, and a sullen Behaviour, true Piety and Godliness."[32] Provided the enjoyment of God's bounty is done in moderation, we are not brought into sin by its enjoyment. The "blame is not due to the things, but to the Abuse of them." "Mirth . . . as long as it is attended with Prudence and Innocence, is so far from being criminal, that it is Praise worthy." We should, he concluded, "all be prudently merry; and reflect on . . . the wholesome Advice in an old English Proverb; *Let us take Care to be merry and wise.*"[33]

Cradock left England while evangelicalism was in its infancy. Because of this, he never observed the more rigid sobriety and discipline characteristic of later evangelicals. Yet, like them, he worried about the public and private morality of his congregation. Too many were accenting the proverbial wish to be "merry" without heading its caution to be "wise." In a "fast sermon," probably preached in memory of the victims of the disastrous Lisbon earthquake of November 1755, Cradock warned his listeners of their "manifold and continued transgressions that have drawn down the vengeance of a just God upon you." In this Jeremiah-like discourse, he exhorted them. "The day of the Lord seems indeed to be at hand. Within this year what terrible signs and forerunners have we not had of it? . . . Earthquakes alone have not been the only forerunners of this terrible day, Wars, Famines, Storms, Burnings, such as have scarcely ever been heard of before, join their united force, and seem to declare to us the near arrival of" the day of judgment.[34]

Cradock then lambasted the sinners in his own parish: "Vice had . . . grown up with us and become the beloved of our souls." His ire fell upon the deists, the nominal Christians "who almost never name the name of God but in a blasphemous oath or curse," the "silken sons of pleasure" whose lives were spent "in drunkenness and debauchery," "the worldly wise . . . who place all their happiness in riches," "the proud, the spiteful, the malicious," the envious, the malignant, the unmerciful and unforgiving spirits "whose inhumane hearts are quite strangers to the gentle and those gospel graces of meekness and mercy," and, finally, the intolerance of Christian denominations other than their own whose professed piety "is a mere mockery, a profanation, nay, an affront to the divine mercy and justice."[35] Few New England Calvinists expressed greater outrage at the worldliness of their congregation and predicted more dire consequences of continued wayward behavior than did this Anglican vicar of Maryland's Garrison forest.

Like other evangelicals, Cradock felt that more than preaching was required to foster a rebirth of piety. For this purpose he organized a "Society" that met one Saturday noon per month for lunch and prayer at the homes of various parishioners. Parson Cradock served as director of the group and supervised all admission thereto and dismissals therefrom. Besides regular attendence at the Society's meetings, "all the Members, considering the sad Consequences of Vanity and Amusements over the Nation, . . . look upon themselves as oblig'd to use particular Caution, with respect to many of the usual amusements, however innocent they may be, or be thought to be in themselves; least by joining therein they shou'd be a Hindrance to themselves, or to their Neighbours." Obviously this marks a departure from the hedonistic attitudes expressed in the Saint George's Day discourse. Yet there is not a total prohibition from such activities. At the opening session Cradock discussed the Society's objectives: "1. To glorify God. 2. To be quickened and confirmed . . . [in Christian faith and living]. 3 To render us more useful to our Neighbors."[36]

In "The Office of Devotion us'd at the Meeting of the Society," Cradock brought together prayers and devotions from a variety of services in the *Book of Common Prayer*. In the middle of these devotions, Cradock composed his own prayer for the society and its members, which runs to five manuscript pages. Near the end of these devotions, a three-page "Exhortation to Humility" was to be read that sought to eliminate the sin of pride, "because the proud Person quits his Reliance on God to rest in himself: which is to exchange a Rock for a Reed."[37] Clearly modeled after the various extemporaneous prayer groups utilized by the Methodists and evangelicals of England, this society had been adopted by Cradock to meet the peculiar needs of his frontier congregation.

But Cradock did not seek merely the salvation of the select few in his society. Like the English evangelicals, he ministered to those of all social ranks, to the planters and tenants, to the servants and slaves, to the wives and maidens who constituted his congregation. No other phenomenon so differentiated the evangelists from more traditional Anglicans than this desire to preach the word of God to all men and to escape the supposed bounds of hierarchy and squirearchy.

But this urge to address the entire community did not involve the disruption of conventional values. Although Cradock often spoke "to a numerous Audience of all Ranks,"[38] he endorsed the natural order in the cosmology of the Great Chain of Being. This intellectual construct held that there were gradations of life from the lowest forms to the divine Creator himself. The hierarchial nature of the chain did not make all humans part of a single link. Rather, the system of human existence requires gradations in talent and virtue among men. This variation in ability was part of the necessary cosmic division of labor that allowed each human being to use his peculiar talents so that they contributed to the well-being of all. This traditional paradigm, which was reinforced by the writings of Richard Hooker and Alexander Pope, reached the acme of its acceptance in the eighteenth century.[39]

The social order sought by the advocates of the Chain of Being received emphasis from Cradock when he told his congregation that the faithful Christian "shews deference to superiours, is open clear and friendly with equals, [and is] easy of access to Inferiours."[40] It was the obligation of the patron not to reduce the client to servility but to treat him so that the interdependence of both was acknowledged and the self-respect of both maintained. These mutually interlocking obligations resulted from God's having "endow'd different men with different abilities, sufficient to make them excell in their different studies: And has taken care that no Employment shall want Labourers."[41] The economic well-being of the whole community benefited from these interdependencies. The worker must not "live an idle and unprofitable life" and he must avoid being "*faithless, lazy* and *dishonest*" because "god wou'd resent this usage as done to himself, and shou'd he delay to punish you here, he wou'd not fail to do it *hereafter*."[42]

Thus the vicar of the Garrison Forest sought to preserve in America the concepts of an organic community and hierarchical society that he found prevalent in the Staffordshire manor of his youth. This philosophy of a stable social order was undercut by a new economic theory. Economic liberalism undermined traditional deferential concepts by arguing that growth lay with the unleashing of the economic interests of the populace.[43] Cradock sought to subordinate competition and social mobility in the better interests of community harmony. That Cradock continued successfully to preach the old values indicates their persistence in the New World environment.

Any summary of Cradock's defense of the Anglican faith would reflect the sensitiveness of the vicar of the Garrison Church to the social and theological controversies of his day. Thomas Cradock was a man of simple religious belief and genuine pastoral zeal for the welfare of all his people. While he drank with his parishioners and, as we shall see, wrote bawdy verse for the eyes of other Chesapeake gentlemen, the rector of Saint Thomas' Parish represented the dominant churchmanship of his age—Protestant, evangelical, latitudinarian, and nationalist. He spoke to his congregation in a simple, homespun style with sermons lacking sophisticated systematic theology. Yet he presented a tradition of sincerity and pastoral piety that endeared him to his audiences and provides us with extraordinary insight in the ethical and personal value systems of the colonial Anglican clergy. Cradock sought to lead his flock down the path of traditional piety and respect for authority. He personified the normative and the orthodox, and he typified the Church of England tradition and the continuity of British society and intellectual life on the Maryland frontier.[44]

NOTES

1. Crane Brinton, *The Shaping of the Modern Mind* (Englewood, N.J.: Prentice-Hall, 1953), p. 69.
2. John S. Marshall, *Hooker and the Anglican Tradition* (London: Adam and C. Black, 1963).
3. Norman Sykes, *Church and State in England in the XVIIIth Century* (Cambridge, Eng.: At the University Press, 1934) provides the best discussion of churchmanship in the Hanoverian era. For a study of regional Anglicanism see Arthur Warne, *Church and State in Eighteenth-Century Devon* (New York: Augustus M. Kelley, 1969).
4. John Beresford, ed., *The Diary of a Country Parson: The Reverend James Woodforde, 1758–1781*, 5 vols. (Oxford, Eng.: At the University Press, 1926–31); Norman Sykes, "The Sermons of a Country Parson: James Woodforde in His Pulpit," *Theology: A*

Monthly Review 38 (1939): 97–106, 341–52. For another eighteenth-century rural cleric's preaching, see Byron Petrakis, "Jester in the Pulpit: Sterne and Pulpit Eloquence," *Philological Quarterly* 51 (1972):430–47; Barbara Lounsberry, "Sermons and Satire: Anti-Catholicism in Sterne," ibid. 55 (1976):403–17.

5. R. S. Crane, "Suggestions toward a Genealogy of the 'Man of Feeling,'" *Journal of English Literary History* 1 (1934):205–30.

6. John H. Overton and Frederick Relton, *The English Church from the Accession of George I to the End of the Eighteenth Century (1714–1800)* (London: Macmillan and Co., 1906), pp. 306–45; Sykes, *Church and State,* pp. 147–88; Frank J. Klingberg, "The Expansion of the Anglican Church in the Eighteenth Century," *Historical Magazine of the Protestant Episcopal Church* 16 (1947):292–301; Frederick V. Mills, "Anglican Expansion in Colonial America, 1761–1775," ibid. 39 (1970):315–24.

7. Overton and Relton, *The English Church,* p. 307.

8. Alison Gilbert Olson, "The Commissaries of the Bishop of London in Colonial Politics," in Olson and Richard Maxwell Brown, eds., *Anglo-American Political Relations, 1675–1775* (New Brunswick, N.J.: Rutgers University Press, 1970), pp. 109–112; Nelson W. Rightmyer, *Maryland's Established Church* (Baltimore: Diocese of Maryland 1956), pp. 64–95; Daniel J. Boorstin, *The Americans: The Colonial Experience* (New York: Knopf, 1958), pp. 123–31; Carol Lee van Voorst, "The Anglican Clergy in Maryland, 1692–1776," Ph.D. diss., Princeton University, 1978, pp. 8–97.

9. Rightmyer, *Maryland's Established Church,* pp. 37–112; Nelson W. Rightmyer, "The Character of the Anglican Clergy of Colonial Maryland," *Maryland Historical Magazine* 44 (1949): 229–50; David C. Skaggs and Gerald E. Hartdagen, "Sinners and Saints: Anglican Clerical Conduct in Colonial Maryland," *Historical Magazine of the Protestant Episcopal Church* 47 (1978):177–95.

10. Peter Gay, *The Enlightenment: An Interpretation—The Rise of Modern Paganism* (New York: Knopf, 1966), pp. 280 et passim.

11. Russell E. Richey, "Effects of Toleration on Eighteenth-Century Dissent," *Journal of Religion* 8 (1975):350–63.

12. J. R. H. Moorman, *A History of the Church in England,* 3d ed. (London: Adam and Charles Black, 1976), pp. 269–89; A. R. Humphreys, *The Augustan World: Life and Letters in Eighteenth-Century England* (London: Methuen, 1964), pp. 142–49.

13. Gay, *Enlightenment,* p. 327. See also H. Daniel-Rops, *The Church in the Eighteenth Century,* trans. John Warrington (New York: E. P. Dutton, 1964), p. 55; Humphreys, *Augustan World,* pp. 149–63; Gerald R. Cragg, *Reason and Authority in the Eighteenth Century* (Cambridge: At the University Press, 1964), pp. 1–61.

14. Overton and Relton, *The English Church,* pp. 49–50; L. W. Cowie, "The Church of England since the Reformation," in M. W. Greenslade, ed., *A History of the County of Stafford* [*Victoria History of the Counties of England*] (London: Oxford University Press, 1970), 3:62, 65.

15. Lewis P. Curtis, *Anglican Moods of the Eighteenth Century* (New Haven, Conn.: Archon Books, 1966), pp. 7, 71–72; L. E. Eliott-Blinns, *The Early Evangelicals: A Religious and Social History* (Greenwich, Conn.: Seabury Press, 1953), pp. 95, 129–48, 168–69, 208.

16. David Curtis Skaggs, "Thomas Cradock's Sermon on the Governance of Maryland's Established Church," *William and Mary Quarterly* 27 (1970):646–47.

17. Thomas Cradock, *Two Sermons, with a Preface Shewing the Author's Reasons for publishing Them* (Annapolis, Md.: Jonas Green, 1747); Thomas Cradock, "On Education, Acts 26:24–25" (see note 19 below); Roland Baumann, *George Stevenson (1718–1783): Conservative as Revolutionary,"* Cumberland County Historical Society Publications 10 (1978):18; David Curtis Skaggs, "Thomas Cradock and the Chesapeake Golden Age," *William and Mary Quarterly* 30 (1973):101–4.

18. Ethan Allen, *The Garrison Church: Sketches of the History of St. Thomas' Parish, Garrison Forest, Baltimore County, Maryland, 1742–1852,* ed. Hobart Smith (New York: James Pott and Co., 1898), pp. 18, 26–27.

19. Thomas Cradock, "On Faith and Patience, Hebrews 6:12," ff. 1, 3. Unless otherwise noted, all manuscript sermons are located in the Maryland Diocesan Archives, Maryland Historical Society, Baltimore.
20. Skaggs, "Cradock's Sermon," pp. 648–50.
21. Cradock, "On Education," f. 23. This sermon was probably preached shortly after the Academy opened in 1751.
22. Thomas Cradock, "On Patriotism, Luke 11:17." The main body of the two versions is virtually the same, only the beginning and the final sections have substantial alterations. The original of the second version is personal property of the author in Bowling Green, Ohio, and the other version is in the Maryland Diocesan Archives, Maryland Historical Society, Baltimore. The quotation above is from f. 2 of the first version, all others are from the second version.
23. Ibid., f. 3.
24. Ibid., f. 15.
25. Ibid., f. 17.
26. Ibid., ff. 17, 20, 21.
27. Cradock, *Two Sermons,* p. 5.
28. Ibid., pp. 9–10.
29. Skaggs, "Cradock's Sermon," p. 646; Cradock, *Two Sermons,* p. 10.
30. Thomas Cradock, "Four Sermons on the Errors of Popery, Luke 16:29," 2: f. 6.
31. Cradock, *Two Sermons,* pp. ii–iii n.
32. Thomas Cradock, "On Miracles, John 2:11," f. 10; Cradock, *Two Sermons,* pp. 2–3; Richard B. Davis, *Intellectual Life in the Colonial South, 1585–1763* (Knoxville, Tenn.: University of Tennessee Press, 1978), 2:749–50. The sermon is reprinted in Richard B. Davis, C. Hugh Holman, and Louis D. Rubin, Jr. *Southern Writing, 1585–1920* (New York: Odyssey Press, 1970), pp. 136–40.
33. Cradock, "On Miracles," f. 11; Cradock, *Two Sermons,* pp. 4–6.
34. Thomas Cradock, "Fast Sermon, JOel 1:14–15," Manuscript Collection, St. Thomas Church, Owings Mills, Md., ff. 1, 3–4.
35. Ibid., ff. 5, 7–11, 13.
36. "Rules for the Society in St. Thomas's Parish in Baltimore County," Manuscript Collection, St. Thomas Church, Owings Mills, Md., ff. 4, 21.
37. Ibid., f. 18.
38. Skaggs, "Cradock's Sermon," p. 637.
39. Arthur O. Lovejoy, *The Great Chain of Being: A Study in the History of Ideas* (Cambridge, Mass.: Harvard University Press, 1936). The theme as it pertains to Cradock is more thoroughly explored in David Curtis Skaggs, "The Chain of Being in Eighteenth-Century Maryland: The Paradox of Thomas Cradock," *Historical Magazine of the Protestant Episcopal Church* 45 (1976):155–64.
40. Cradock, "On Faith and Patience," f. 4.
41. Thomas Cradock, "On Children and Parents, Prov. 17–6," f. 5. See also J. G. A. Pocock, "The Classical Theory of Deference," *American Historical Review* 81 (1976):516–23.
42. Thomas Cradock, "Execution Sermon, Isa. 58:7" [1752], p. 24. A typescript copy of this sermon made in the 1930s is in the Cradock Papers, MS 196, Md. Hist. Soc.
43. Joyce Appleby, "Ideology and Theory: Tensions between Political and Economic Liberalism in Seventeenth-Century England," *American Historical Review* 81 (1976):499–515; Appleby, "The Social Origins of American Revolutionary Ideology," *Journal of American History* 64 (1977–78):935–58.
44. For more detailed analyses of Cradock's preaching see: William Jeffrey Welsh, "The Rhetoric of Thomas Cradock, 1744–1770: A Study in the History of Ideas," (MA thesis, Bowling Green State University, 1977). Other observations may be found in Van Voorst, "Anglican Clergy in Maryland," pp. 276–85.

4
The Christian Muse

The time Thomas Cradock spent at his writing desk was not entirely devoted to homiletics. Like many clergy of his day, he devoted many hours to the production of poetic exercises. These metrical compositions represent the continuity of British literary traditions to the Chesapeake region. Therefore, to comprehend fully Cradock's belletristic style we must begin with an exploration of British ideas and forms.

AUGUSTAN POETRY

Many students of late-seventeenth- and early-eighteenth-century English literature describe this period as the "Augustan Age." Although some would confine the meaning to the age of Joseph Addison (1672–1719) and his urbane circle of poetic and prose writers, the term generally conveys a broader meaning that encompasses the neoclassic impulse of 1660–1760.[1]

Several Augustan modes found expression in Cradock's poetry. Such features included using satire and copying Latin models that used the past to parody the present. This combination of satiric commentary with the classics allowed the Augustans to criticize their world in contrast to the "golden age" of Caesar Augustus, whose supposed social harmony contradicted the social fragmentation of their own age. The use of the pagan authors was particularly important in the literary expressions of Anglican clerics. These articulate and civilized men saw no need to abandon the ancients because they antedated Christ. Led by Richard Bentley (1662–1742) of Trinity College, Cambridge, classical linguists translated and commented upon the works of Cicero, Horace, Terence, Thucydides, and numerous other Latin and Greek authors.[2]

No ancient writer exerted greater influence upon eighteenth-century English poetry than Vergil. Augustan poets admired his pastoral *Eclogues* for their framework, phraseology, and polished style. In particular, his regularized forms provided models that they could follow. In the eyes of the Augustan, imitation of this form added value to the worth of one's works. Alexander Pope thought the *Eclogues* the "sweetest poems in the world," and he sought to imitate that sweetness in his own *Pastorals*. Such a poetic mode sought to evoke "the action of a shepherd," wrote Pope. "The complete character of this poem consists in simplicity, brevity, and delicacy; the first two of which render an eclogue natural and the last delightful."[3]

Pope and his followers sought to emulate Vergil by imitating the framework of his *Eclogues*, by echoing his phraseology, and by polishing their work with the same care as the Roman poet. James Thomson (1700–1748) combined Vergil's powers of description and love of nature in his own *Seasons*, which enjoyed extraordinary popularity among English-speaking peoples. Thomson possessed the imagination to cast the familiar images of a natural scene into a mold, which gave them originality, distinctiveness, and truth. Although Thomson's great work is superficially pastoral, it evokes the mood of Vergil rather than merely duplicates his style.

Other adaptations of Vergil's style occurred in the works of minor Augustan poets. John Gay and Lady Mary Wortley Montagu cleverly adapted the bucolic landscape to the satiric urban environment and satirized the beaux and belles of the Hanoverian court. Their first three "Town Eclogues" appeared in 1716 under Pope's name, although his contribution was minimal. For thirty years, three other eclogues that Lady Mary wrote circulated as manuscripts among trusted friends because some of them bordered on slander of the royal family. Finally in 1747 *Six Town Eclogues* appeared in print after much of their personal satire had lost its sting, but they were excellent *vers de societé*.[4]

Some of their impact may be deduced from the second poem, entitled "The Drawing-Room," in which "Coquetilla"—the duchess of Shrewbury—is reputed to constitute an evil influence over Caroline, princess of Wales, for whom she is lady of the bedchamber.

> That Coquetilla, whose deluding airs
> Corrupt our virgins, still our youth ensnares;
> So sunk her character, so lost her fame,
> Scarce visited before your highness came:
> Yet for the bed-chamber 'tis her you choose
> When zeal and fame and virtue you refuse.[5]

Although dozens of other pastoral poems appeared in the eighteenth century, few combined satire and an American setting location before Cradock composed the "Maryland Eclogues." He chose a wilderness American environment rather than the placid rural scene of Staffordshire to ponder in satire Vergil's bucolic verse.

Satire is the literary trademark of eighteenth-century England. For clerics, satire provided a mode for assessing the conduct of the community that must be redeemed or reformed and for comparing it with an ideal world. Especially among the divines of the established church, satire constituted a means of displaying a target and proposing a means for its reformation. Satire became a vehicle for exposing the thin veneer of gentility that covered the corruption, disease, violence, filth, and death that underlay surface civility. It also provided a device for social criticism, a vehicle for continuing the ministerial jeremiad tradition while supporting the status quo. Moreover, the genre had an extraordinary impact. Who could deny that Jonathan Swift's *The Tale of a Tub* (1704), *Gulliver's Travels* (1726), and *A Modest Proposal* (1729) made a greater impression upon their readers than all the sermons preached by the dean of Saint Patrick's, Dublin? At the same time, satire was a dangerous literary vehicle. Its potential for sedition and its impact upon patrons in an age when patronage was critical to the economic survival of a social critic were among its chief dangers. For instance, a staunch churchman like Swift lost Queen Anne's favor because of his *Tale of a Tub* and thereby forfeited his chances for greater preferment in the English religious establishment.[6]

If satire enabled one to criticize without giving offense and to avoid disturbing the social fabric while skirting controversy, it still affronted those who thought it was scandalous when it came from the pen of a clergyman. One literary mode appropriate to men of the cloth and laymen was that of devotional poetry and hymns. Joseph Addison, Isaac Watts, and Charles Wesley predominated in this style of writing, but many clergy, regardless of denomination, contributed to the growing corpus of religious lyrics.

Addison, whose name frequently appears in Cradock's writings, wrote an "Ode" in *The Spectator* (August 23, 1712) that presaged Cradock's justification of God based upon the harmony in nature, particularly in the grandeur of the sun, moon, and stars.

What though, in solemn silence, all
Move round the dark terrestrial Ball?
What tho' nor real Voice nor Sound
Amid their radiant Orbs be found?
In Reason's ear they all rejoice

And utter forth a glorious Voice,
For ever singing as they shine,
"The Hand that made us is divine."

(Ll. 17–24)

The father of English hymnody was Isaac Watts (1674–1748), a dissenting clergyman famous for his *Hymns and Spiritual Songs* (1707) and *The Psalms of David, Imitated in the Language of the New Testament* (1719). Seldom does any Augustan divine achieve an intensity of image and emotion greater than did Watts in his famous "When I Survey the Wondrous Cross," one of the classic hymns of Protestant Christianity.[7]

This was an age when the clergy were at the forefront of literary developments. Not only is there the conventional devotional poetry and religious disputation, but also clergymen like Swift mastered the forms of satiric literature, and Laurence Sterne (1713–68) founded modern psychological fiction with his *Tristram Shandy* (1759–67). Addison, son of the dean of Lichfield Cathedral in the diocese in which Cradock grew up, wrote a weekly lay sermon for *The Spectator* that was widely read. Sermons poured from the presses *ad nauseam*. Religious polemics flourished as deist and orthodox, High Churchmen and Low, dissenters and Methodists, participated not only in trivial argumentation but also in important theological and reverential discourse. One cannot examine the literature of the age without recognizing the importance of Christian thought in all aspects of literature.[8]

One field in which few clergy participated was that of drama. Considered by many to be frivolous, if not actually licentious, the theater attracted few clerics—Maryland's James Sterling is one exception, and even he did not write plays after ordination. Some dramas involved themes of traditional morality, none more so than Addison's *Cato* (1713). First performed at the Theatre Royal, Drury Lane, London, in 1713, this story of a Roman general fighting against the tyranny of Julius Caesar became the most popular play of the century. Part of this appeal was due to its political overtones. To the Whigs, Cato seemed the resolute defender of liberty against French tyranny; to the Tories, Caesar was a Roman duke of Marlborough whose military successes threatened English liberties.

But there is more to attract one to *Cato* than its political implications. The neoclassic revival made Plutarch's hero particularly inviting to Augustan audiences. Moreover, the appeal to patriotism above personal welfare found a willing reception in an age of intense British nationalism. Additionally, the Christian Stoicism of Cato provided the perfect exemplar of the virtuous citizen. In fact, Cato's tragic self-sacrifice of life and love in the cause of liberty constituted a notable contrast to the normal public and private conduct during the eighteenth century. Finally, there was a tragic romance.[9]

Addison's tragedy is set in 46 B.C. in Utica, where Marcus Porcius Cato (95–46 B.C.) refused to collaborate with Caesar. Betrayed by a senator and a Numidian general, he was stoutly defended by a Numidian prince, who was also in love with Cato's daughter Marcia. Another romantic subplot involved the love of Cato's two sons for Lucia, the daughter of a loyal senator. When resistance to Caesar's army became hopeless, Cato provided for his followers' escape before taking his own life. Cato's lament for Rome as he pondered the corpse of one of his sons slain in the defense of liberty provided Addison with the opportunity to express those conceptions of virtue and piety that he felt should endure forever:

> . . . Let not a private loss
> Afflict your hearts. 'Tis Rome requires our tears,
> The mistress of the world, the seat of empire,
> The nurse of heroes, the delight of Gods,
> That humbled proud tyrants of the earth,
> And set the nations free; Rome is no more.

Cato advised those who mourned with him to retire from politics and return to "thy paternal seat" where, like their "frugal ancestors," they might toil in the soil and live in "humble virtue, and a rural life."

> There live retired, pray for the peace of Rome;
> Content thyself to be obscurely good.
> When vice prevails, the impious men bear sway,
> The post of honour is a private station.[10]

Such appeals excited an enthusiastic response among colonial American theater patrons. In the South, *Cato* was widely performed and well received. In 1735–36 it was produced in Charleston and in Williamsburg. The Walter Murray–Thomas Kean players performed it in New York, Philadelphia, and various Chesapeake Bay towns from 1749 to 1752 and the famed Hallam company brought *Cato* as one of twenty-four pieces in their repertoire of 1752–53.[11] On October 21, 1752, the Murray–Kean troupe presented *Cato* in Annapolis as part of a Maryland season that extended from June through October.[12]

This positive reception of Addison's play indicates the growing importance of British cultural values in mid-eighteenth-century colonial

America. Thomas Cradock brought not only the love of theater across the Atlantic but also the love of classics and poetry. The Chesapeake intellectual environment in which he settled was most receptive to Augustan literary developments. Throughout the eighteenth century, Maryland received a continuous influx of British ideas from migrants like Ebenezer Cook, Daniel Dulany the elder, Richard Lewis, James Sterling, Thomas Bacon, and Dr. Alexander Hamilton. Their anglophilic values combined with those of many native Marylanders who journeyed to the Old World for education and returned with the metropolitan culture as part of the "intellectual baggage" they carried with them. Stephen Bordley, William Brogden, Henry Addison, Charles Carroll of Carrollton, and Daniel Dulany the younger were among the best known of these American-born scholars. It seems clear from most recent studies that, however divergent British America's economic, social, and political life may have been from that of the mother country, cultural life in the colonies became more English as the eighteenth century progressed.[13]

However derivative this tradition was, we should not condemn it for that reason. The colonials sought to bring the metropolitan culture to the provinces and to create an environment where it would flourish. Nowhere, writes Richard Beale Davis, did this mimetic impulse express itself more completely than in the fine arts—architecture, formal gardens, painting, music, literature, and the theater.[14] All this demonstrates the British dominance of colonial aesthetic tastes and intellectual development. Normally the American man of letters adopted English models, although he might convert them to American themes.

We should not downgrade the quality of the Americans' literary efforts merely because they were written by provincials. While the center of British culture was undoubtedly London, there were other significant intellectual centers in Edinburgh, Dublin, and Philadelphia that made important additions to Augustan thought. As John Clive and Bernard Bailyn have noted; "provincialism sometimes served to inhibit creative effort. But . . . there existed important factors which more than balanced the deleterious effects. The complexity of the provincial's image of the world and of himself . . . tended to shake the mind from the roots of habit and tradition. It led men to the interstices of common thought where were found new views and new approaches to the old." The innovative ideas of a David Hume, George Berkeley, Jonathan Swift, or Benjamin Franklin originated in the provinces of Britain and America.[15] While Jack P. Greene sees a sense of provincial inferiority pervading the colonial

American society, J. A. Leo Lemay and Richard Beale Davis demonstrate that Chesapeake literature became increasingly sophisticated and is worthy of study in its own right.[16]

One of the centers of provincial culture lay around the shores of the Chesapeake Bay, where nearly one-third of His Majesty's American colonists lived. Cradock migrated to a Chesapeake world in which his English upbringing constituted a significant intellectual asset. Educated at a grammar school that sent several scholars on for Oxbridge training, well grounded in ancient languages, history, and contemporary letters, Cradock understood the satiric commentaries of Jonathan Swift, enjoyed the classical imitations popular in the coffeehouses and salons, and delighted in the psalms and hymns of Isaac Watts. All of these he sought to bring to the Garrison Forest and its environs. At Trentham, his small home just off Reisterstown Road, surrounded by his growing family and his students, the rector found time not only to write scholarly sermons but also to indulge in his delight in verse. Moreover, the study of this obscure man of modest talent provides a fuller measure of both the extent and nature of Chesapeake culture than if one relies exclusively on the occasional literary genius like William Byrd. Until we know more about men like this frontier parson, we shall have an incomplete picture of the thought and society of colonial America, and we shall more likely reach erroneous conclusions about its ethical paradigms and intellectual accomplishments.

Cradock's verse may be grouped into three categories: devotional, satiric, and dramatic. As one would expect, the greatest bulk is designed to reinforce religious values. His inspiration was that of Christian muse.

DEVOTIONAL POETRY

Cradock probably began his writing of religious poetry early in his Maryland career. He mingled with a group of "Baltimore Bards" about whom we know little except from the derisive comments about them made by Dr. Alexander Hamilton, leader of the rival "Tuesday Club" of Annapolis. We are certain of the identity of only two members of the Baltimore Bards, Cradock and the Reverend Thomas Chase of Saint Paul's, Baltimore Town. A 1746 petition signed by thirty "Members of a Club kept" in Baltimore Town may well constitute such a list. If so, it contains some of the first families of the region—Buchanan, Fell, Gough, Hammond, Harrison, Lux, Ridgely, Tolley, and Walker.[17]

The earliest known Cradock poem is "To Thyrsis," written in Baltimore County in 1744 and printed in the *American Magazine* of 1757–58.[18] He begins with a line from Pope's "Epistle on Taste" that describes vice as being triumphant in England and then implores the muse Thyrsis to guide his poetic hand:

> While *Vice* triumphant lords it o'er the plain,
> And holds o'er abject man her tyrant-reign;
> * * * *
> Dear *Thyrsis,* scorn the listless, impious, throng,
> And harken to the precepts of my song.
> Observe the muse that tempts the moral lay,
> And boldly follow, where she leads the way.[19]

He then beseeches the deity to guide his thoughts, tongue, and actions so that he might follow "the blest path" that God had revealed to man:

> And firm regard to *Heav'n* devoutly paid;
> *His* pow'r acknowledg'd, and implor'd *his* aid;
> The *Parent's, Sov'reign's, Reason's* laws observ'd;
> The *Naked* cloath'd, the *Fainting* soul preserv'd;
> The duties of each station well perform'd,
> And in her strongest holds *vice* bravely storm'd;
> *Goodness,* by pattern more than precept, taught.
> (Ll. 83–89)

Such conduct, of course, "will give thee bliss, which ne'er shall end" (l. 93).

"To Thyrsis" typified Cradock's devotional poetry. It lists those temptations of this world that can lead to damnation in the afterlife. It may involve some important personal references. There is a reference to a "killing scandal" (l. 54) and to such "foul *Deeds*" as "The maid deflour'd, the easy friend deceived" (ll. 70–71). Could this refer to the scandal of Lady Frances Leveson-Gower that may have contributed to his trans-Atlantic migration?

In Cradock's poetry, one finds an echo of the appeal in his sermons to both revelation and rationalism as the basis of belief:

> To *Reason's* strength call *Revelation's* aid,
> Nor be by too presuming *Self* betray'd;

By *Both* assisted, soon thou'lt gain the field,
Without the aid of *Both* as soon wilt yield.
("To Thyrsis," ll. 39–42)

One also notes the neoclassic tendency to seek the assistance of the Greek goddesses in the composition, but it is conventional Christianity that predominates.

Another style of devotional verse appeared in his "A Poem Sacred to the Memory of Miss Margaret Lawson, Miss Elizabeth Lawson, Miss Dorothy Lawson, and Miss Elizabeth Read." This blank verse elegy uses a dream vision to present orthodox Protestant religious concepts. The poem was occasioned by the death of the four young ladies in a skating accident when the ice broke and they drowned. Three of the girls were daughters of a member of the same Baltimore men's club as Cradock and may have been his parishioners. In the panegyric, the youthful departed are idealized:

. . . beauteous *Margaretta,* peerless Maid!
The two *Elizas,* faultless both as fair,
And gentle *Dorothea,* heav'nly Child!
So sudden left us, left us, to bewail
Beauties and Graces, that with Rapture long
We'ad view'd sweet perfection op'ning . . .[20]
(Ll. 14–19)

The grieving poet is confronted by the specter of Margaret, who consoles him with visions of heavenly bliss: "Death's a mere Bug-bear, which, because untried, Vain Man thinks all that's horrible and dire" (ll. 69–71).

Here also the author repeats the theme of reason and mysticism in religious belief:

. . . Like the Sage,
Who, when exploring great Creation's Laws,
Finds Difficulties not to be explain'd,
And owns his Reason's dim short sighted Pow'rs.
(Ll. 21–24)

During his lifetime, Cradock composed a considerable amount of pietistic poetry. Much of it disappeared over the years, but in the mid-nineteenth century the Reverend Dr. Ethan Allen found "still in the possession of his descendants a fragment of a manuscript containing some of his poetical translation of Martial; an Elegy on a young lady, in about eighty lines; the Distitch on Notra Dames, paraphrased; the

Culprit, Smectymnus, or the Centinel, (a Satire;) Hymns, for Christmas, Good Friday, Easter day, Ascension day, Whitsunday; a Sacramental Hymn; a funeral Hymn; and one on Resignation, besides others."[21] Most of these poetic efforts have disappeared since Allen, a historiographer of the Episcopal diocese of Maryland, recorded their existence. Allen published three Cradock hymns and one poem entitled "Resignation" that indicate Anglican orthodox interpretations of Christmas, Whitsunday, Holy Eucharist, and the acceptance of death.[22]

Of those which survive, one of the more touching is "A Fragment," which is not in Cradock's hand nor in the hand of either of his daughters or of his friend Dr. Randle Hulse who lived at Trentham. Remembering that it could have been dictated to an amanuensis in his last years and that it makes reference to a "rook" or English crow and to land cultivated by the same family for generations, this thirty-six-line piece may honor Cradock's father, Arthur. On the other hand, it may have been written by the rector's son Arthur (1747–69). "A Fragment" opens with a reference to men of humble wealth who cultivate the soil, much in the vein of Cato's praise of rural living cited above. In it the poet describes a bucolic country scene in which he rests from the toil of farmwork beneath the trees that shaded his ancestors and these hears

> . . . The Rooks, whose Sires before
> Lull'd his Forefathers with their cawing Lore,
> On him like Tribute gratefully bestow.
> Tis all they have to give, tis all the Rent they owe.
>
> (Ll. 9–12)

Such a pastoral scene did not exclude reference to Christian obligations.

> On Sundays seated in his wicker Chair,
> His Wife, his Children, Friends and Neighbours near,
> He from the sacred Text a Chapter reads,
> Comments, explains each verse as he proceeds:
> Not to corrupt, but to apply the Word,
> Not make his Hearers Casuists, but good.
>
> (Ll. 17–22)

Similar sentiments are found in the longest piece of devotional verse in the Cradock Papers. "Crurulia, Part the 2d" is written in a fine hand, obviously not that of Parson Cradock. It contains a number of corrections that do, however, appear to be in his very shaky penmanship. If Cradock wrote "Crurulia," he dictated it in the last years of his life when illness prevented writing it himself. "Crurulia" is written in heroic stanzas of four lines rhyming *abab* and consists of six sections with from nine to eleven stanzas each. Probably its title comes from the Latin word *crura,* referring to the foundations or underpinnings of a bridge, presumably in this case the bridge to true faith.

The first section, called "The Check," recounts the bountiful blessings conferred upon the author by the deity—"a tender wife," dutiful children, "the genuine friendship of the few," a great country, a reasonable faith, and "the glorious hope" of eternal life. The nine stanzas of the section entitled "Aflictions" describe his trials with an illness in "pain's hard school," where he learned "the wholesome lesson" of mortality. The third section—"The Resolve"—asserts his resolution always to praise the Lord for his mercy.

> Yes, O my God, thy praise I'll ever sing,
> Thou heard'st men in the direful hour of pain,
> Didst kind relief in all my sad anguish bring,
> And gav'st me to behold the sun again.
>
> (3. 17–20)

The fourth section, "The Relapse," relates his failure to keep his constant devotion to the Lord:

> Base dastard as I am, I quit the field,
> To boist'rous passions leave my soul the prey;
> E'en at the first assault supinely yield,
> A rebel, where I bound my heart t'obey.
>
> (4. 5–8)

"The Recovery," the next section, describes how "wild passions now no more distort my frame" and with his "soul now glowing with devotion's flame" (5. 5, 7), his "heart again has peace" (5. 2). This contentment allows him in "The Prospect" to view the heavens.

> What rapture, O my soul! The minstrelsy
> Of *Seraph* & of *Cherub* strikes my ears;
> Amid the tuneful choir I seem to be,
> And listen to the musick of the spheres.
>
> (6. 25–28)

"Crurulia" is Cradock's great apologia, a confession of his own weaknesses as well as of a faith in a beneficent Creator who sacrificed his own Son for the salvation of all who believed in him. Because of its allusions to Generals Wolfe and Jeffrey Amherst (l. 28) and because of its handwriting, this was probably written after an illness in 1765 that left him paralyzed for the rest of his life. Nevertheless, he remained intellectually vigorous until the end, five years later.

Despite this handicap and his great weight of over 250 pounds, the parson normally conducted Sabbath services at the parish church. He was carried to the sanctuary and placed in a chair. He could not stand while officiating, and apparently his son Arthur did most of the clerical duties except consecrating the elements. Near his death he became so helpless that he could not control his limbs. If his head would sway to his shoulder, the sexton would return it to an upright position.[23] In such a pathetic condition, Thomas Cradock continued to dictate sermons and poetry.

Long before these unhappy events, Cradock composed what his contemporaries considered probably his greatest contribution to colonial culture—his two versions of the Psalms. The first, published in London in 1754, represented a translation into English of the Latin psalter of the famous Scottish classicist George Buchanan (1506–82). After one delay for quality paper and another awaiting a new font of type, an American version was published in Annapolis in 1756—four years after it was originally advertised as ready for the press.[24]

The first version was "Printed for Mrs. Ann Cradock, at *Wells* in *Somersetshire;* and sold by R. Ware on *Ludgate-Hill*" in London. Cradock dedicated this volume to "the Reverend Mr. John Hargreaves, Some Time Master of *Trentham* School, in the County of *Stafford* . . . In Acknowledgement of The pious Care that he took in my Education . . . By His dutiful and affectionate Old Scholar, Thomas Cradock." The second version is dedicated to Governors Horatio Sharpe of Maryland and James Hamilton of Pennsylvania and contains a list of subscribers that reads like a *Who's Who* of the two colonies plus others from Antigua, Virginia, and Delaware. Seventeen Anglican clergymen in four provinces subscribed, as did several members of the councils of these provinces. Even the great Roman Catholic layman Charles Carroll of Doughoregan purchased a copy, and another was found in the library of the famous Virginian Robert Carter of Nomini Hall, although he did not subscribe. Benjamin Franklin purchased twelve copies, presumably for resale. A survery of estate inventories revealed that Cradock's work was the second most common Maryland imprint in the colony's libraries, exceeded only by Thomas Bacon's *Laws of Maryland.*[25]

Translations of the psalms were common exercises of eighteenth-century schoolmasters, and Cradock's, like most other published versions, was merely competent. Its iambic-pentameter-couplet meter is satisfactory, but his rigid attention to literal translation of Buchanan's psalter prevents the flow of imagery present in versions by contemporaries like Watts and the Wesleys.[26] Yet his psalter indicates that emigration to the colonial frontier did not diminish the appetite for scholarly endeavor that he had acquired at Trentham School and at Oxford. Moreover, his learning impressed enough of his contemporaries to merit the publication of his psalms on both sides of the Atlantic.

A sample from the Annapolis edition's Twenty-third Psalm provides a reasonable view of his ability:

> The bounteous Lord my pastures shall prepare,
> And feed his servant with a shepherd's care:
> In a gay verdant plain, with flow'rs o'erspread,
> Where nature furnishes her softest bed;
> Where the clear stream in smooth meanders flows,
> He bids me take a sweet, serene repose,
> When in erroneous paths I simply stray,
> His gracious goodness leads me in the way;
> Recals my wand'ring steps, and points the road,
> The even path his David shou'd have trod
> Yea; tho' the gloomy vale of death I tread,
> Where dreary horrors compass round my head,
> E'en there no fatal ills my soul betide,
> Thy rod, thy staff, my comfort and my guide.
> Vainly my foes with hell-born envy burn;
> The choicest cates my loaded board adorn,
> My chearful bowls are fill'd with purest wine,
> And round my brows thy richest ointments shine.
> And, while my breath inspires this vital clay,
> On thee secure I'll rest, for every gay;
> Thy truth, thy mercy, shall protect me still,
> And constant I'll attend thy holy hill.[27]

This rendition of Buchanan's Renaissance Latin represents the continuation of the classical and religious modes of southern thought that would persist long after Cradock's death.[28] In fact, Cradock looked upon translations of classical poets as an intellectual exercise typical of a learned gentleman.

"Trifles, Part 2d By the Author of the First" (part one has not been located) is a booklet in the Cradock Papers containing translations of verse by Martial, Horace, Lucian, Anacreon, Theocritus, and George Buchanan. These are clearly drills designed to maintain one's skill in poetic translation from Latin and Greek. There is nothing exceptional in their quality. One does note, however, that Cradock never lost his sense of humor. One of the verses is Buchanan's poem entitled "Mutual love, on the friendship between Mary Queen of Scotland and Elizabeth Queen of England." Below the title Cradock wrote: "N.B. This is translated to shew that Poets are not always prophets." Although such translations are not devotional poetry, they constitute practical exercises leading toward Cradock's greater effort at the psalms.

Collectively Cradock's religious verse is of reasonable quality and he represents an important colonial manifestation of this genre; certainly he is not of the standing of the Presbyterian divine Samuel Davies, but he does not rank far below him.[29]

SATIRIC POETRY

The eighteenth century was the Golden Age of English satire. Some of the most imaginative satiric compositions in literature were composed between Samuel Butler's *Hudibras* of the seventeenth century and Lord Byron's *Don Juan* of the nineteenth. Satire is usually classified into three types—invective, burlesque, and irony. By these rhetorical devices it aims to instill a particular set of emotion or biases. David Worcester distinguishes the three forms:

> The writer of effective satiric invective keeps the abuse he is attacking always before the reader's eyes. The light is clear, the object plain. . . . The writer of burlesque gives flickering glimpses of his object; he distorts it, magnifies it, reduces it, pushes it forward and snatches it back. The reader sees the goal, but a pretty chase the author leads him before he reaches it. The ironist gravely argues in favor of the abuse and forces the reader to work furiously at inverting a long chain of reasoning.[30]

While invective and irony appear in colonial American satiric compositions, most are burlesques. The Maryland bards usually indulged in this type. Burlesque sought to make a series of comparisons between the ideal and the real through an extended simile. The full impact of the work depended upon the reader's knowing the object or style being parodied. This presents difficulties for the modern reader because it requires either an understanding of the model being used or copious notations by an editor. Burlesque is mimetic, and its mimicry is comic. Thus *Gulliver's Travels* becomes a funny story about big and little people unless the reader comprehends the political objects Swift's satiric mirror reflects.

One of the most common forms of eighteenth-century satire was the poem "designed to express the author's disapprobation of political, social, or personal actions, conditions, or qualities, written in heroic couplet, in real or fancied imitation of one or more of the Roman satirists."[31] This mode crossed the Atlantic with men like Thomas Cradock and Dr. Alexander Hamilton and became a popular literary device.

An excellent example of the use of satire came during the February 20, 1753, meeting of the Tuesday Club in Annapolis. Two Baltimore men, William Lux and Thomas Cradock, both honorary members, joined in composing a poem lamenting the illness of the club's president. Entitled "Carmen Dolorosum" (Song of Sorrows), it imitated Horace's "Carmen Saeculare" written in 17 B.C. to commemorate the annual games honoring the founding of Rome.[32] Obviously there is considerable burlesque involved in a poem imitating a celebration of the birth of the Eternal City set in the mud-filled streets of Annapolis. When he recorded this often bawdy piece, Dr. Hamilton noted those portions written by the honorary members that evening. Cradock added two six-line stanzas closely copying Horace. The first described the tears shed by one of the classic world's most pitiful figures, Niobe.

As Niobe, (what heart could bear the pain)
Her blooming race, by wrathful Phoebus slain,
(Thus tuneful Bards have sung in doleful Lay,)
In floods of tears dissolv'd herself away,
'Til every pulse and vital motion gone,
She stood a lifeless monument of stone.

(Ll. 7–12)

The usual version is that Leto, the daughter of Phoebe, had Apollo and Artemis slay the several children of Niobe, who then became a stock symbol for bereavement. According to Homer (*Iliad,* 24:602–17), Niobe wearied of tear-shedding and was turned into stone. A comparison between the classic tragedy and the temporary illness of Charles Cole, president of the Tuesday Club, constituted a great burlesque.

The second stanza attributed to Cradock notes the depth of grief the club members felt.

'Stead of the Joys that drill'd along the hour,
Incessant Griefs each aking heart devour,
They Loll, they heave, they yawn, they wail, they sigh,
And direful discords dash their Harmony,

Such their sad plight, alack and wail a day,
To cruel gout to keep our Cole away.[33]

(Ll. 29–34)

Although this poem becomes rather risqué in parts, the lines attributed to Cradock reflect the sense of exaggerated grief that the satirist tried to convey. Moreover, the first stanza demonstrates the use of classical myth to travesty the ancients. The whole contrasts the lofty theme of Horace with the prosaic and crude activities of the Tuesday Club.

Although Cradock attended the club six times between 1750 and 1754, he apparently never composed any other poems for the group.[34] He last attended on November 5, 1754, and "made several learned speeches in Club." In mock-heroic reply, Hamilton issued a "Proclamation:"

> Whereas it has been observed at sundry times that the honorary members, at their casual appearance in club, have taken upon themselves a behavior unbecoming their station as honorary members, and passed several Insults and open affronts on the president or the Club, this is therefore in name and by the authority of our honorable president to make to publicly known to all herein concerned, that if any honorary member for the future, shall misbehave himself or be Impertinent In Club, by speaking Irreverently or disrespectfully to the Chair, raising any disputes or disturbances in the Club, taking more the discourse than comes to his share, making speeches of any sort to the Chair without leave first asked and granted, or pretending to vote in Club in any manner whatsoever, contrary to an express law of the Club in that case made and provided such honorary member so offending shall be expelled the Club, and ipso facto forfeit his seal therein, never again to be admitted upon application, unless it be the Gracious will and pleasure of his honor the president.

When Cradock took umbrage at the proclamation and assured the gathering he always acted "to fit with that station and quality" to which he had been called and "could not base himself with any misbehaviour," President Charles Cole assured the minister that no personal affront was intended. With this, "Mr. Craddoc made a very low bow, sat down, and resumed his pipe." After a discourse by William Lux, Cradock rose to speak without asking leave and Lux cried out "The Proclamation!" Whereupon Cole "quashed this clamor" by "graciously" declaring "that an honorary member of the clergy might at anytime speak what he pleased without asking leave." Thus was added a corollary to the proclamation.[35]

This was not the first time Cradock was the butt of Hamilton's wit and pen. A decade earlier, Cradock wrote an eight-line poem on the beauty of a young lady sitting in a pew in front of him during a sermon by George Whitefield. This piece prompted the opening of a literary war between the "Baltimore Bards" and Hamilton's circle of "Annapolis Wits." Soon the Annapolis group ridiculed the original poem, and Cradock coauthored with the Reverend Thomas Chase a rejoinder entitled "The Baltimore Belles." In "An Infallible Receipt to cure the Epidemical and Affecting distempers of Love and Poetical Itch," an anonymous "Philalethes" (certainly a member of the Hamilton circle and probably the doctor himself) described the symptoms of the disease as having raised in its victims "the feverish Rage of poetical Fury" so as to cause them to lose "their Sight, as to be quite blind to all the astonishing Charms of the Fair Sex, especially their backward Beauties." After taking "half a Grain of the South-East and by East Side of the Pith of common Discretion, two Grains of moderate vulgar Sense and Solidity, . . . half a Dram of the inside of solid Thought and Reflection," etc., patients would be "effectually cured their Blindness, and restored . . . to their right Senses." With such a cure one would "neither heedlessly fall in Love at improper Seasons, or in improper Places; for Example, when hearing a Sermon, or while in Church, or vainly imagine himself a Poet."[36]

All of this satirical commentary is probably aimed at young Parson Cradock, then contemplating marriage to the daughter of Sheriff John Risteau. A few weeks after the publication of Dr. Philalethes' nostrum "for the *Furor Poeticus* and *Febris Amatoria,*" in February 1746, Dr. "Theophilus Polypharmacus" (a Hamilton pseudonym) wrote the press to announce that the earlier prescription had failed. Still the victim blurted out such poetic nonsense as:

> *See lovely* R——, *happy, hapless* Maid—
> Happy the Man whom this fair Maiden loves;
> O happiest he, whom this fair Maid approves!

Presumably this is a direct quotation from one of Cradock's love poems, and for the distemper of such poetry Dr. Polypharmacus devised a new receipt "of my own Invention and Composition:" "Take four Lines of any of Pope's poetical Works, six Lines of Milton's Paradise Lost, eight Lines of Garth's Dispensary, guarded with four Lines of Butler's Hudibrass" that the doctor is to "read very loud to the Patient, every Time he bursts forth into his Exclamation."[37] It all failed. A few weeks later Cradock and Miss Catherine Risteau were married, and the parson continued to suffer from the "Poetical Itch" but no longer wrote about his romance.

Whatever the satire involved in his contributions to "Carmen Dolorosum" and whatever the humor involved in the exchange between the Baltimore and Annapolis versifiers, the most important piece of satiric writing in the Cradock Papers is entitled "Maryland Eclogues in Imitation of Virgil's." The title page of one of the booklets containing them says they were written by "Jonathan Spritly, Esqr., Formerly a Worthy Member of the Assembly, Revis'd and Corrected by his Friend Sly Boots." Several explanations for the authorship are possible. "Slyboots Pleasant" was the Tuesday Club pseudonym of Walter Dulany, who also served in the General Assembly, "Jonathan Grog" designated Jonas Green, and "Smooth Sly" was the Reverend John Gordon, another honorary member. Several members of the club were assemblymen, including its most notable poet—Dr. Hamilton. The eclogues could have been collectively composed by members of the Tuesday Club and forwarded to Cradock. There are allusions to geographic features and to families in the Potomac–Patuxent valleys of southern Maryland. Colonel William Fitzhugh of Rousby Hall in Calvert County could have been the author. He was a former Virginia burgess and Maryland assemblyman and councillor, having associations with the Tuesday Club and other Chesapeake literati. Thus Fitzhugh might have been Jonathan Spritly.

Most indicators, however, point toward Cradock's authorship. The writing seems to be in his hand, he was addicted to imitations of classical poetry, and he was noted for his hypercriticism of his fellow priests. Because of the religious context of many of the eclogues, they almost had to be written by a clergyman or someone exceptionally well acquainted with Augustan criticisms of traditional Christianity. The rector of Saint Thomas' Parish was certainly such a man. The ninth eclogue's reference to the negotiations with the Iroquois at Lancaster in 1744 displays a knowledge possessed by few Marylanders aside from Cradock, who served as chaplain to the colony's commissioners. Notes in the entire series indicate the eclogues were being prepared for possible publication before a non-Maryland audience. Since Cradock printed an edition of psalms in England, a British printing could have been his design for the eclogues. There are additional copies of two of the pastorals in the Cradock Papers. An early version of the fourth eclogue is in the middle of the "Trifles" booklet, and another copy of the second eclogue is in a separate booklet. Finally, the Cradock family preserved the eclogues at Trentham for nearly two hundred years, along with his other writings. His descendants apparently considered them an important part of the family heritage. Thus we may assume Cradock wrote the "Maryland Eclogues."

Vergil's *Eclogues* are the earliest Latin pastoral poetry, copying the master of the genre, Theocritus, a Sicilian who wrote in Greek. Vergil composed ten poems, and Cradock imitated all but the seventh. The "Maryland Eclogues" are in two manuscript booklets: the first contains eclogues 1, 2, 9, 6, 5, in that order; the second includes numbers 3, 4, 8, and 10.

In the first booklet, Cradock attempts to follow Vergil and often inserts a few lines of the Latin original beside the "Maryland Eclogues." In eclogues 1, 2, 5, and 9 Cradock writes his version on the right page of the manuscript, and on the left page he copies the Latin version. For instance, in the first eclogue Vergil wrote:

> Non equidem invideo: miror magis, undique totis
> usque adeo turbatur agris. en, ipse capellas
> protinus aeger ago: hanc etiam vix, Tityre, duco.[38]
>
> (1. 11–13)

Cradock rather loosely paraphrased this as:

> I envy not your Bliss, but wonder much
> Their Hate for Pray'rs & Parsons here is such!
> Poor I am forc'd on this lank jade to ride.[39]
>
> (1. 15–17)

Finally, Cradock confesses at the opening of the sixth eclogue (the fourth in order of presentation) "The Imitation [of Vergil is] so small, that I shan't think it worth my while to mark out the few places where I have followed the Poet." Only in eclogue 5 of the remaining poems do the Latin verses reappear.

Instead Cradock found that the Latin pastoral provided a medium for social comment while the writer maintained a detached pose. Just as his sermons sought to copy the correct homiletic form of Archbishop John Tillotson, his literary model was the correct poetic form of Vergil. The pastoral scene provided a primitive paradise in contrast to the urban corruption of eighteenth-century London. To many this primitive past with its abundant fertility, eternal greeness, and tranquillity represented a golden age of simplicity. Vergil had no idealized vision of the countryside such as is often described by romantic city-dwellers. He sympathized with the country without idealizing it. He knew the harshness of rural life, but the pastoral convention required tales of love, nymphs and swains, flattery and song.[40]

Cradock exploded the pastoral myth in his eclogues. Instead, Maryland became the wilderness scene of greed, immorality, and conflict. Cradock used the Latin poetic form to show that rural society was not the scene of tranquillity and innocence that many English lyricists described. Like Vergil, Cradock dealt with lost illusion, profanity, irreligion, robbery, and denial of freedom. The "Maryland Eclogues" became a vehicle for social criticism while providing entertainment for his readers.

Cradock provided a few bucolic descriptions: "By this purling Rill,/These shady Locusts, and that pleasant Hill" (1. 60–61). Often the harsh realities contrast with the idyll: "Winter's most piercing Cold I might endure" (10. 79) and "in the Woods fell Wolves shall chuse to rove" (5. 87). Instead of Vergil's shepherds watching their flocks on Arcadian slopes, the colonial poet has indentured servants herding cattle in the Maryland forests. He satirizes the colonists' moral bankruptcy—their promiscuity, their contempt for religion, their abuse of Indians, servants, slaves, and women, their breech of promise, and their excessive drinking. The few lines of idyllic nature poetry jar against the satire. The "Maryland Eclogues" constitute a burlesque of the pastoral myth.

In the first eclogue, entitled "Split-Text," a Virginia clergyman, named "Crape," who has been expelled from his living in Virginia, visits Parson "Split-Text" in Maryland. The object is to describe the corruption of the Anglican church in Lord Baltimore's colony, where the immorality of "Crape" would not have cost him a parish since all livings were in the patronage of the proprietor and moral rectitude was not a prerequisite for continued clerical appointment. Such a theme reminds one of the 1753 sermon before the General Assembly in which Cradock called for ecclesiastical supervision of the clergy. In two notes to the poem, the author describes the differences in church polity in the two provinces: "The Vestries in Virginia have it in their Pow'r, if the minister behaves ill, to get rid of him; which the Maryland Vestries have not." Lord B[altimore,] Proprietary of Maryland, . . . has all the [clerical] Livings in his own Gift" (1. n. 9 and 19). Splittext came to Maryland from England as a poverty-stricken schoolmaster; seeing the low quality of rectors and their ample income, he returned to the mother country to receive ordination and the proprietor's blessing. Upon return to Chesapeake, he gladly prayed for Lord Baltimore's family along with the royal household and collected his forty pounds of tobacco from each parishioner. Thus even though

Maryland parsons were "such Clods of Clay" who resembled "those at Home no more,/Than Saints of Modern days do Saints of yore" (1. 29, 33–34), Split-text lived a blissful life. One senses that Cradock saw the approaching doom of the church establishment, although Crape issues no warning that his friend's idyll might end.

"Daphne," the second eclogue, concerns the pining of the Negro "Pompey" for a fellow slave. He finds his love rejected by Daphne, who would rather spend her evenings in the arms of their master. The poem is an attack on miscegenation as practiced by many colonials. Not only is "the coal-black Maid" (2. 3) the consort of the slaveowner, but Pompey notes, "My Mistress oft invites me to her Bed" (2. 23). The consequence of such liaisons is "proud Mulatto *Bess*" (2.17). Cradock's scorn of such sexual promiscuity is coupled with some of the best social comments of the entire series. Pompey describes social mobility of whites like their master, whose economic status was once as low as that of slaves. The daily life of slaves, in which their gardens and poultry supply extra food and Pompey plays the banjo and sings "as well as ever a Negro sung" (2. 32), seems more than a little idealized. This parody on Vergil closely follows the original in which the love of a shepherd is scorned by the city-bred object of his affection.

Cradock apologized for the poetry of the third eclogue, titled "Shoat," because he sought to have three convict servants speak in dialect. The dialogue consists mainly of exchanges between cowherds named "Scape-Rope" and "Cutpurse." Here again the sexual immorality of the day elicits comments in one of the best of the internal stories in any of the eclogues:

> Dogs I have none; My Mistress well you know
> To Dogs e'er since her Loss has been a Foe;
> By them her hapless Lover was betray'd,
> And thro' her Husband's Rage an Eunuch made;
> And now she hates them with the utmost spite,
> And the least Howl still puts her in a Fright.
>
> (3.29–34)

To which Cradock added a note that this was a "true story, and just as it is related here." These servants cavort with the slave women and the wives of their overseer and their master. They also continue to risk additional punishment for theft, a habit they cannot eliminate even though it might send them to the gallows if caught. Aesthetically this is the least satisfying of the eclogues, possibly because the Maryland poet tries to imitate Vergil too closely. On the other hand, "Shoat" evokes a continuing tradition of southern humor in which the ordinary citizens survive in a hostile environment.

In the fourth eclogue, "The Maryland-Divine," Cradock continues his attack upon the proprietor and the clergy. He calls upon local river deities, rather than upon the slaves and convicts of the previous poems to assist him on a higher note: "Ye *Severn* Nymphs, attempt a nobler song" (4. 1). Vergil used the fourth eclogue to foretell the birth of a great leader (some Christian writers saw it as a prophecy of Christ's incarnation), but Cradock used an entirely different theme. He castigated "Baldus," presumably Charles Calvert, Lord Baltimore, for sending to the province clergy of low quality and unorthodox ideas. He was particularly upset by their adherence to the deistic ideas of Matthew Tindal, Anthony Collins, Thomas Woolston, and the third earl of Shaftesbury. The consequence of such teaching became obvious:

> No more the beardless Boy Damnation fears,
> But at such *Old Wive's Fables* nobly sneers
> The tim'rous Girl that wont to fear an Oath,
> And trembled at the Thought of Breach of Truth,
> Now smiles at Perjuries—the Reason's plain
> By Gospel-Laws who wou'd themselves restrain?
>
> (4. 49–54)

None of the eclogues better reflect Cradock's opinions than this. Here are echoed themes from the sermons in a burlesque that illustrates the vicar of the Garrison Forest at his best.

The fourth eclogue also makes reference to Richard Lewis, an Annapolis schoolmaster and poet, who is now acknowledged to be among the finest versifiers in colonial America. Cradock sought to improve his poetic abilities so that not

> . . . e'en *L*[*ewis*]*s* poor, unhappy Bard,
> Be read with more Delight or more Regard.
> *Le*[*wi*]*s*, on whom the Muse her Favours Shed
> And yet to Want her Favourite betray'd.
>
> (4. 65–68

To this Cradock added an identifying note describing Lewis as a "Gentleman who had a pretty Vein in Poetry, and like other sons of Parnassus, was very poor; he was also a fine Gentleman, and laught at Religion with the rest." It is clear that Lewis's reputation lived in the province after his death in 1734, so that when Cradock arrived a decade later, the minister was told of the poet.

Entitled "Toss-Pot," the fifth eclogue is the most humorous of the nine pastorals. Vergil's version commemorated the loss of an ideal leader, but Cradock's has planters "Ever-Drunk" and "Love-Rum" singing hymns in honor the most notable of the local drunkards—"Toss-Pot." Cradock's 102 lines represent, it seems clear, a lampoon of the Latin poet, since the two planters elevate their "ideal" former companion to an alcoholic's heaven: "A Saint we've made him & his constant Task's/ To hover o'er the Punch-Bowls & the Flasks" (5. 79–80). Seldom is there a greater contrast between Vergil's Roman values and the low condition of Maryland morality exhibited than in "Toss-Pot."

The sixth eclogue, entitled "Celsus," the name of a schoolmaster who teaches blasphemy to his pupils, is an embittered attack on deists and nonbelievers. It may be that Celsus is Richard Lewis of the fourth eclogue; certainly Lewis of the earlier poem and Celsus of this both "laught at Religion" (4. n. 8). Celsus's impious lessons deride Christianity:

> And the whole *Bible*'s a notorious Cheat,
> A Maintenance for lazy Priests to get.
> * * *
> In short, Religion was the Child of Pow'r,
> To keep poor ign'rant Man from knowing more,
> Than what their *wise* Forefathers knew before.
> Hence then, this Inference he plainly drew,
> Our Passions shou'd be all submitted to;
> Pray why were they bestow'd if not employed,
> And what are Blessings, that are not enjoy'd?
> (6. 63–64, 81–87)

In the opening lines of this poem he pokes fun at those who seek a nobler subject than a schoolmaster and write of assemblymen, councilors, or charwomen. This may be an attack on Lewis's effusive praise of Lord Baltimore's visit to the colony upon its centennial in 1732.[42]

In a note at the end of the tenth eclogue, Cradock noted the omission of an imitation of Vergil's seventh poem: "What can be the Reason, I'm at a Loss." It may well have been that "To Thyrsis" was a partial imitation. In Vergil's poem, Corydon sings of pastoral idealism while Thyrsis is cynical, contrasting the harsh realities of rural life with his companion's idyllic vision. One easily sees why Cradock's critical "To Thyrsis" was so inscribed.

Jemima, the title character in the eighth pastoral, laments the loss of her lover, Dr. Crocus, a Scotsman who wed a wealthy Maryland girl, Dorinda. This poem may constitute a veiled attack on Dr. Alexander Hamilton. Heiress Margaret Dulany wed Hamilton in 1747. If Hamilton is the object of Cradock's derision, the poet took the opportunity to revenge any earlier slight from the pen of the Annapolis physician when he noted how difficult it was for the bridegroom to discard his Caledonian upbringing and urged the bride

> Dorinda go; the nuptial Candle light
> Perhaps one Candle he'll allow to Night;
> Too great th' Expence for him t' indulge again.
>
> (8. 37–39)

Cradock then added a note: "From this and sev'ral other Hints, 'tis plain this Eclogue has it's Foundations on Truth." Moreover, in an earlier note, Cradock described Crocus as a mere "ship surgeon, of which this Country is full, where they administer their Poysons under the pompus name of Doctors" (8. n. 3).

In Vergil's eighth eclogue, Damon laments the loss of Nysa and Alphesiboeus seeks through witchcraft to bring home a love, apparently succeeding. No such success comes to Jemima, whose mission to the local midwife and witch ends only in defeat: "Ah! poor Jemima! all thy Hopes are o'er,/ Die an old Maid, nor think of Lover more!" (8. 117–18). As in the fifth of Cradock's pastorals, this eclogue provides comic relief from the often serious social criticism appearing elsewhere.

Nowhere is that social commentary more apparent than in the ninth Maryland pastoral—"Gachradidow." The three characters in it are "Shuncallamie," "Tachanootia," and "Gachradidow," who correspond to Shikellamy, Tachanutie, and Gachraddodow, Iroquois sachems whom Cradock met at Lancaster in 1744. The first two Indians bemoan the fate of themselves and their nation at the hands of the avaricious and land-hungry colonists. After praising the prowess of the departed Gachradidow, they invoke the must of liberty:

> Here then, O Goddess, midst our Tribes remain;
> With Us, thy faithful Race, for ever reign;
> Poor as we are, our wide-extended Waste,
> Our Christal Streams, which yield a cool Repast,
> Our lofty Forests all shall witness be,
> How much we love, how greatly honour thee.
> Let vile Injustice & base Slav'ry sway
> The Christian Plains—we neither will obey—
> What Wonder that these Wretches seek our Shore,
> Since Wealth, not Thee, O Freedom, they explore?
>
> (9. 53–62)

The perfidy of Christians towards the Indians galled Cradock as unbecoming their faith. In this Cradock echoed other Anglican churchmen in seeking more humane treatment of the native Americans.[43]

Like Vergil's tenth pastoral, Cradock's last eclogue, entitled "Worthy," features a disappointed lover who is incapable of recovering from·unrequited love. Worthy, a planter, bemoans the loss of Flavia, who, after promising to marry the young man, "prudently" accepts a richer match and leaves Worthy to his fruitless complaints. Squire Worthy is obviously a gentlemen who cannot temporarily satisfy his loss with a woman of a lower social caste.

> O that an Overseer — I'ad only been
> This cruel Creature I shou'd ne'er have seen;
> Some Convict-Girl full well had serv'd my Turn,
> Black *Bess* at least with equal flame wou'd burn;
> And what tho' black she is—The Crabs brave food,
> Tho' it's Form's hideous, yet the meat is good.
>
> (10. 43–48)

Instead he proposes to flee to the backcountry and try to forget Flavia in company with the Scotch-Irish and Indian rovers of the woods. One might suspect that Worthy is Cradock himself, jilted by the Lady Frances Leveson-Gower, who seeks his solace in a mission to the New World.

The eclogues conclude with a quatrain apology to his readers:

> Enough has *Worthy* mourn'd—enough I've sung,
> Due Thanks, ye Planters, to my Lays belong:
> No more my Pipe with spritely Strains shall swell;
> Go mind your Hogs & Crops,—& so farewel.
>
> (10. 81–84)

With this conclusion, Cradock accomplishes his purpose. Like his sermons, the eclogues aim to reform morals and to reinforce the agreed standards of the age by pointing out deviant behavior—blasphemy, pretension, cruelty, infidelity, greed, and drunkenness. The objects of his wrath are clear, if not in the poems themselves, then in the author's explanatory footnotes. The reader is never misled. Acceptable behavior is obvious either by being the opposite of what is described or through the ironic voice employed from time to time.

Cradock's eclogues were definitely inferior to Ebenezer Cook's *Sotweed Factor* (1708). Cook's satire possesses a double focus, the colonials and those English readers gullible enough to believe the speaker's nonsense about America.[44] There is no such depth in the "Maryland Eclogues." Thus Cradock's work is a pale reflection of greatness in an age of great satire. But the ecologues are important as sources of social and historical commentary, portraying as they do the cultural and intellectual environment of provincial Maryland.

The eclogues constitute an important broadening of the scope of early American literature. Cradock romanticizes the noble savage and exhibits a combined admiration and disdain for the Scotch-Irish frontiersmen; he depicts Negroes as docile, happy, and singing, although the poet remains aware of their social disadvantages. In a tradition of American folk humor from Ebenezer Cook to Uncle Remus, his country bumpkins and slaves cleverly survive in a hostile environment. All these become stock characterizations of our literature. None of his natural descriptions evoke the quality of Richard Lewis's "A Journey from Patapsco to Annapolis, April 4, 1730," which is the best neoclassical poem of colonial America. Still, we do find attempts at natural depiction often missing in other colonial poets.[45]

DRAMA

The least known of Cradock's poetic endeavors is his blank-verse tragedy on the trial and execution of Socrates. Althoug there is no evidence that it was ever performed, this drama represents aesthetic continuity of the Old World on the shores of America.

Theatrical performances were an old Chesapeake tradition, dating at least to 1665 when "The Bare and the Cubb" was performed on the eastern shore of Virginia by members of the colony's working class. As in British schools, students of the grammar school attached to the College of William and Mary spoke pastoral colloquies in English and Latin, and the professors apparently wrote some declamatory pieces that were performed in 1702. Schoolboys and collegians continued to present plays both for the instruction they provided in Latin and in elocution as well as for simple entertainment. It appears that group readings of plays was a favorite indoor pastime of such planters as William Byrd II of Westover, and by the end of the colonial period they constituted a form of amusement common in manor houses throughout the region.

There are several instances of locally written drama in the colonial period. "The Bare and the Cubb" was probably a Virginia-composed farce, while at least one scholar credits Byrd with the coauthorship of "The Careless Husband," usually attributed to Colley Cibber. Byrd apparently directed the play at a performance held at the Harrison manor house of Berkeley, just a short trip upstream from Westover. In the late 1750s, the Reverend Adam Menzies wrote a satirical farce read at a tavern in Richmond County, Virginia. The play ridiculed Presbyterian evangelism from the viewpoint of an Anglican rector. In Mecklenburg County, Virginia, the Munford family both wrote and acted in locally produced dramas in the last third of the eighteenth century. Maryland attracted the Reverend James Sterling, who authored two plays in Ireland before crossing the Atlantic. It is clear that private as well as public performances and plays authored by colonials were a continuing feature of Chesapeake life.[46]

Thomas Cradock's literary interests easily fit into this milieu. That Cradock would both enjoy the theater and be interested in writing a play is to be expected. This was certainly the case of many gentlemen of his day in both England and America. Thus it is not surprising that a manuscript drama exists in the Cradock Papers of the Maryland Historical Society. What survives is an 84-page booklet beginning on page 7 and ending on page 90. Presumably the first six and last six pages of the manuscript are missing. It beings in the middle of act 1, scene 2, and stops in act 5, scene 7. The author numbered the lines consecutively in the first act, so we know that it has 136 lines missing. Because the front page is missing, the title is unknown, but for the purposes of this discussion it will be entitled "The Death of Socrates."

This five-act, blank-verse tragedy is probably the first serious drama written in Maryland. No record exists of its production, and it was most likely intended for performance by schoolboys or for a reading by adults gathered in the drawing room of a Chesapeake manor house. It appears to be written in the hand of Thomas Cradock; it reflects opinions known to be his; it is done in the style of Addison's *Cato,* so popular in the eighteenth century; and it was long treasured by the Cradock family. Thus, it would appear that, as in the case of the "Maryland Eclogues," Cradock authored this dramatic piece.[47] If so, it was undoubtedly written before his incapacitation in 1765 prevented writing such a manuscript.

As Cato became the embodiment of eighteenth-century patriotism and public virtue, so Socrates in the Augustan age was always exemplary of intellectual honesty and the search for truth. He became one of the most admired historical figures of the era. This image was best illustrated in James Thomsom's "Winter" from the 1746 version of *The Seasons,* in which the poet puts aside his Plutarch;

. . . and, deeply-musing, hail
The sacred Shades, that slowly-rising pass
Before my wondering Eyes. First Socrates
Who firmly good in a corrupted State,
Against the rage of Tyrants *single* stood,
Invincible! calm Reason's holy Law,
That voice of God within th' attentive Mind
Obeying, fearless, or in Life, or Death:
Great Moral Teacher! *Wisest of Mankind.*

(Ll. 437–45)

More elaborate sentiments of this sort appeared in John Gilbert Cooper, Jr.'s biography of Socrates published in 1749. By arguing that Socrates embodied the best of God's revelation to the non-Jewish world, Cooper attacked those who belittled the Athenian scholar because of his paganism. The "Athenian *Sage . . . constantly and invariably taught and believed the Immortality of the Soul, and a future Retribution of Rewards and Punishments.*" Moreover, Socrates taught that God "was One, eternal, uncreated, immutable, immaterial, incomprehensible Being; that he was omnipotent, omniscient, infinitely good and wise; that he created and continued to govern by his unerring Wisdom all Things in universal Harmony; that he regarded Mankind with a paticular Affection, and endowed them with Reason, that Ray of divine Light, to guide their Steps in this probationary State to temporal, and afterwards eternal Happiness, thro' the Paths of Virtue."[48]

While no direct connection can be made between Cooper's biography and Cradock's play, the similarities in emphasis are striking. It is probable that Cradock studied the ancient Socratica, particularly the writings of Plato, Xenophon, and Aristotle, and did not merely utilize the secondary writings of Cooper. Although the eighteenth century marks the dawn of the new history of David Hume and Edward Gibbon, the most popular historian of the age was Charles Rollin, the French chronicler whose moralistic interpretation of the ancient world circulated widely in British America. Cradock's library contained Rollin's ten-volume *Historie Ancienne des Egyptiens, des Carthaginois . . .* (Amsterdam, 1733–36), which he apparently translated for his own use and loaned to others. Just as Rollin saw history as a device for criticizing the immorality of the contemporary world, so also did Cradock see Socrates as a means for calling Britons and Americans away from their decadence and a vehicle for preaching the virtue of intellectual honesty in an age of hypocrisy. History had a purpose: to discover and promulgate the great moral laws of the past so that the next generation would know and obey these laws.[49]

For those who, like Rollin and Cradock, thought historical lives taught philosophical truths, the career of Socrates was an ideal case study. Rollin wrote that the pagan world never produced "any thing so great and perfect" as Socrates:

> When we observe to what height he carries the sublimity of his sentiments, not only in respect to the moral virtues, temperence, sobriety, patience in adversity, the love of poverty, and the forgiveness of wrongs; but, what is far more considerable, in regard to the Divinity, his unity, omnipotence, creation of the world, and providence in the government of it; the immortality of the soul, its ultimate end and eternal destiny; the rewards of the good and the punishment of the wicked: when we consider this train of sublime knowledge, we . . . are scarcely persuaded that from so dark and obscure a stock as paganism, should shine forth such brilliant and glorious rays of light.[50]

Following the criticisms of Saint Augustine, Rollin found a serious flaw in Socrates' character. In practicing the conventional rites of Athenian religion when he disbelieved them, Socrates clearly lacked the courage of conviction that distinguished the martyrs of the early Christian church. *The Death of Socrates* lacks this moral outrage, although we may be missing a prologue or epilogue that made such a distinction. Instead Cradock paralleled closely the appraisal of Cooper's biography, which is descriptive and laudatory, without the critical commentary that Rollin includes in the *Ancient History*. [51] We know that the Thomson-Cooper-Cradock vision of the ancient philosopher dominated the eighteenth century. In 1753 Cradock declared that both Socrates and Plato would have been not only Christians but also Anglicans, if they had been given the opportunity. Eighteen years after Cradock's death, the famous Maryland Roman Catholic Charles Carroll of Carrollton saw Socrates as a paragon of virtue in a corrupt world: "the godlike Socrates, ye ornament not of Athens only, but of human nature: him [the Athenians] doomed to die, because his precepts & practice were a constant reproach to their doctrines & vices."[52]

To understand Cradock's plot one needs an introduction to Athenian politics. In the fourth century B.C., conflicting factions of oligarchs and democrats contested for control of the city while the city was at the same time at war with Sparta and Persia. Each faction exacted retribution with executions or exile when it assumed control. A number of Socrates' former pupils were linked to the oligarchical faction, but Socrates remained above politics, exercising his sarcastic criticism upon both groups. Politicians resented his sarcasm more than his ethics. When the democrats seized control after a defeat by Sparta, two of them—Anitus and Lycon—conspired with Melitus to accuse Socrates of impeity and the corruption of the youth. The first charge concerned less his disbelief in some of the Olympian deities than his development of a novel religious doctrine of a single God and a human soul. This accusation probably had little to do with the verdict. More critical was the charge of corrupting the youth. This was a political indictment concerned with Socrates' instruction of the two arch-traitors of Athenian democracy, Critias and Alcibiades. Direct reference to these two was forbidden by the Great Amnesty of 404/3 B.C.—hence the vague accusation of corrupting his pupils.

Undoubtedly the accusers expected Socrates to flee into self-imposed exile. When he stood trial in early 399 B.C., they were as surprised as his followers. After conviction and sentencing, Socrates was again offered exile by the intentionally long delay before execution and by readily available opportunities for escape. Again Socrates refused, and he accepted his sentence despite the efforts of his wife, Xantippe, and his disciples Plato, Phedon, and Crito to dissuade him.

In this basic foundation to the plot, Cradock closely copied the ancient and modern Socratic writings. Like Addison in *Cato,* Cradock was not above inventing characters or expanding historical personalities in order to achieve dramatic affect. The most important of these innovations was Apame, sister of Melitus and sweetheart of Phedon. Caught between her familial obligations to Socrates' principal accuser and her love of one of the philosopher's most devoted pupils, Apame's tragic fate creates considerable audience sympathy. Additional sympathy arises for Xantippe, who is made into a far more important figure than in the classical writings. She is a minor character in Plato's works and a shrew in the eyes of Xenophon. In Cradock's version, Socrates' wife plays an important role.

Among the other historical modifications are the playright's elimination of characters to achieve dramatic simplicity. Cebes and Simmias, two pupils in Plato's description of the last hours of Socrates, do not appear in the Maryland play. This allows Cradock to place Plato at the execution, although he did not actually witness this event. Another change concerns the supposed mental anguish and subsequent Athenian lynching of Melitus. Even in Cradock's day these ancient rumors were considered fables, although they do allow a tragic element to enter the action.

Modern feminists will find in Apame an intriguing character. Admittedly physically weak and a member "of that thoughtless sex who seeks no further role" than to follow "the dull road their Mothers trod before them" (1. 4. 32–34), she aspires to higher intellectual ambitions. At one time she sought to be Socrates' student. Apame recalls that as a young girl

> I grew fond to hear
> The lessons that he taught; to learn from him
> Truths, hid before in sophistry's dark guise,
> And close to follow, where he led the way.
> The more I knew, more was my joy athirst
> For higher knowledge; and he still encreas'd,
> Still as he led me on, my love of wisdom.
> (1. 4. 37–43)

Also imitative were Cradock's theatrical format and literary style. Like Addison, he organized his play into five acts. And since the English playwright used French scenes for the first act of *Cato,* Cradock used them throughout his play. (This convention requires the designation of a new scene every time a character enters or exits the stage, even though the action is continuous. Thus throughout the play, rather than write "Exit Socrates" or "Enter Xantippe," the author merely began a new scene with or without the respective character.)

Also like Addison, Cradock increasingly used stage directions to specify action. Since he probably wrote the play for reading rather than for performance, one wonders about the reason for stage directions. Were they mere convention? Whatever the reason, they are unmistakably there. Some are hidden within the dialogue, while others are clearly stated and separated from the dialogue. Within the script one finds descriptions of movement and facial expression. Apame indicates that her brother has seen her and fled the stage: "Thou fly'st me; ah! infatuated brother!" (1. 3. 1). Phedon indicates Apame's reaction to a speech with "Listen to me,/ Nor with that frown indignant kill your *Phedon*" (1. 4. 59–60). Later, we get in essence the stage direction "Enter Phedon" when Plato states, "Tis now the hour- /that *Phedon* said he'd meet us." To which Crito responds, "He appears" (1. 6. 1–2).

Normally the directions merely occur as the scenes change, and the cast of characters is either decreased or enlarged. A major exception occurs in the sixth scene of Act 4. Cradock first provides the locale, "The Prison." He then uses a major theatrical convention, the discovery scene. The direction reads "Socrates discovered asleep." The author clearly envisioned a curtain that would open, revealing the philosopher on his couch. To this scene, Cradock adds "to him enter . . ." This climactic scene utilizes directions throughout, causing one to wonder if it were not at least locally produced. It is clear that its author was familiar with theatrical productions, and it is probable that he had witnessed them both before his departure from England and after his arrival in America.

Cradock's *Death of Socrates* is a historical drama allowing long orations on Socratic philosophy revolving around the trial and death of the famous Athenian. The dramatic effect is heightened by the wifely fears of Xantippe and the fate of the star-crossed affection of Apame and Phedo. Whether Cradock resolved the dilemma of these last two is lost with the missing manuscript pages, but it is doubtful whether Melitus's pending doom would have released Apame from the familial obligation that kept the two apart.

One is struck by the Christian parallels in the play. Cradock envisioned Socrates as a pagan John the Baptist sent to bear witness to the doctrine of the soul's immortality and to pave the way for the Savior's coming:

. . . God is good,
Is gracious ever—In some future time,
When man's prepar'd to hear the happy tidings,
Some blessed sage will rise t' instruct him, wither
He goes from hence, to teach the certain road
He must pursue to reach his destin'd goal.
(5. 6. 43–48)

Socrates describes an afterlife.

. . . death to thee but opens
A brighter prospect, rich with endless life,
With rich happiness! Not to be told,
Not to be thought, while thou art confin'd below!
(2. 1. 37–40)

While Xantippe called Socrates' single, sovereign god "this unknown Deity" (4. 1. 53), Plato understood that the teaching concerning "that Omniscient Power" (4. 1. 38) was the key to understanding Socratic philosophy. Other Judeo–Christian similarities include the apostle-like attitudes of the pupils and the Judas-like career of Melitus. A former student turned accuser, Melitus repents his actions towards the end of the play, although he is not sufficiently repentant to save Socrates' life. His end seems as foreordained as the suicide of Judas Iscariot.

Melitus finds himself emasculated by the dire doom his sister foretells after he persists in the attack on Socrates: "Gods! how she hath unman'd me!" (2. 6. 1). Anitus called him back to his senses with conventional attitudes toward the role of women:

> Sure the noble *Melitus*
> Will laugh at a weak woman's idle reasonings.
> The sex will oft assume a fancied power,
> And rate it shrewdly; but they're tinsel arguers;
> The man, whose soul is constant to herself,
> Carries with ease the pretty things they say.
>
> (2. 7. 5–10)

And Xantippe scorns her husband with the ultimate insult when she tells him his logic is "worse than womanish reasoning" (4. 1. 60). By all odds, Apame does not embody thoroughly those virtues that the eighteenth century expected in its women: "constant good humor and good sense, strong social love, and quiet unassuming wit."[53] She becomes angry with her brother, impatient with her lover, critical of her mentor, and, finally, intellectually equal to her male companions.

The Death of Socrates represents an important discovery in colonial American intellectual history. No previously known play exhibits the sophistication of characterization and dramatic unity that this one possesses. While blank verse was known in the colonies—Cradock used it in his 1753 elegy—nowhere else before the 1765 publication of Thomas Godfrey's *The Prince of Parthia,* another historic tragedy, is there a long attempt at poetic drama in early America.[54] *Socrates* is not great theater, but it clearly indicates the degree to which the neoclassic drama of Augustan London penetrated Chesapeake culture. However modest the literary merit of this play (the evaluation of its quality is left to others), this manuscript demonstrates that there was little stylistic cultural lag between England and the Chesapeake.

* * *

Throughout Cradock's poetic efforts, he sought to court a Christian muse, one whose ideas were consistent with the ideas announced in his sermons. For instance, the failure of reason to satisfy all one's needs was effectively argued by Xantippe:

> But we, that vaunt ourselves superior beings,
> That proudly talk of reason and her powers,
> What bliss have we? incessant fears alarm us;
> Incessant ills o'ertake us; and our joys

So thinly scatter'd, that they fleet unfelt,
Like empty bubles on a watry mirror.

(4. 1. 9–14)

In the fourth eclogue, Cradock extolled those who, despite the temptations to deism, kept their beliefs—those who

Will own a Savior, & will think him *God.*
Of honest Faith will Still endure the Load:
Will think the Sacraments art awful Things,
And great the Transports true Religion brings.
In short, in Spite of all these Sons of Reason,
Will still be *Godly,* tho' tis out of Season.

(4. 41–46)

Socrates' description of death as "this bug-bear to mankind" (2. 2. 123) is but an echo of Cradock's sentiment in his elegy to the four girls lost in the skating accident. The object of Cradock's poetry, like the object of his homiletics, was the promulgation of Christian piety and theology. Thus in sacred hymn and verse, in satiric lampoon, and in drama he sought the continuation of the values of orthodox Anglicanism.

NOTES

1. James W. Johnson, "The Meaning of 'Augustan,'" *Journal of the History of Ideas* 19 (1958):507–22; Irvin Ehrenpreis, *Literary Meanings and Augustan Values* (Charlottesville, Va.: University Press of Virginia, 1974), p. 3; Ehrenpreis, "Meaning: Implicit and Explicit," in Phillip Hart, ed., *New Approaches to Eighteenth-Century Literature: Selected Papers from the English Institute* (New York: Columbia University Press, 1974), pp. 118–20; Ralph Cohen, "The Augustan Mode in English Poetry," *Eighteenth-Century Studies* 1 (1967–68):3; Donald Greene, "Augustianism and Empiricism: A Note on Eighteenth-Century Intellectual History," ibid., pp. 33–38; Peter Gay, *The Enlightenment: An Interpretation* (New York: Knopf, 1966), 1:10; A. R. Humphreys, *The Augustan World: Life and Letters in Eighteenth-Century England* (London: Methuen, 1964), Hugh Ormsby-Lennon, "Poetic Standards on the Early Augustan Background," *Studies in Eighteenth-Century Culture* 5 (1976):253–80.

2. Cohen, "Augustan Mode," pp. 31–32; Gay, *Enlightenment,* 1:216–17; James D. Duff, "Scholars and Antiquaries," in A. W. Ward and A. R. Waller, eds., *From Steele and Addison to Pope and Swift,* Cambridge History of English Literature, Vol. 9 (Cambridge: At the University Press, 1913), pp. 368–81.

3. Alexander Pope, "A Discourse on Pastoral Poetry," in *The Poems of Alexander Pope,* ed. John Butt, (New Haven, Conn.: Yale University Press, 1963), pp. 119–20. For Pope's Pastorals, see ibid., pp. 123–38; Elizabeth Nitchie, *Vergil and the English Poets* (New York: AMS Press, 1966), pp. vii, 10, 163–72; Geoffrey Tillotson, *Augustan Studies* (London: Athlone Press, 1961), pp. 33–38. For an introduction to the pervasiveness of pastoral poetry, see John Barrell and John Bull, eds., *A Book of English Pastoral Verse* (New York: Oxford University Press, 1975).

4. Robert Halsband, *The Life of Lady Mary Wortley Montagu* (London: Oxford University Press, 1956), pp. 49–54, 243.

5. Mary Wortley Montagu, *The Letters and Works of Lady Mary Wortley Montagu,* ed. Lord Wharncliffe, 2 vols. (London: Swan and Sonnenschein, 1893), 2:434.

6. Herbert J. Davis, *The Satire of Jonathan Swift* (New York: Macmillan, 1947); J. M. Bullitt, *Jonathan Swift and the Anatomy of Satire* (Cambridge, Mass.: Harvard University Press, 1953); Sacvan Bercovitch, *The American Jeremiad* (Madison: University of Wisconsin Press, 1978); C. R. Kropf, "Libel and Satire in the Eighteenth Century," *Eighteenth-Century Studies* 8 (1974–75):153–68.

7. Bonamy Dobree, *English Literature in the Early Eighteenth Century, 1700–1740* (Oxford: Clarendon Press, 1959), pp. 153–58.

8. A. R. Humphreys, "Literature and Religion in Eighteenth Century England," *Journal of Ecclesiastical History* 3 (1952):159–90.

9. Dombree, *English Literature,* pp. 244, 248–49; Frederick S. Boas, *An Introduction to Eighteenth Century Drama, 1700–1780* (Oxford: Clarendon Press, 1953), pp. 117–23.

10. John Hampden, *Eighteenth-Century Plays* (New York: E. P. Dutton, 1961), pp. 44–45.

11. Frederick M. Litto, "Addison's *Cato* in the Colonies," *William and Mary Quarterly* 23 (1966):431–49; Hugh F. Rankin, *The Theater in Colonial America* (Chapel Hill: University of North Carolina Press, 1960), pp. 19, 24, 28, 31, 38, 41, 72, 93, 106, 115, 140, 169, 185, 193, 194.

12. Kathryn Painter Ward, "The First Professional Theater in Maryland and Its Colonial Setting," *Maryland Historical Magazine* 70 (1975):41; Richard B. Davis, *Intellectual Life in the Colonial South, 1585–1763* (Knoxville: University of Tennessee Press, 1978), 3:1284–1302.

13. Henry F. May, *The Enlightenment in America* (New York: Oxford University Press, 1976), pp. 26–27; Louis B. Wright, *The Cultural Life of the American Colonies, 1607–1763* (New York: Harper and Row, 1957), pp. 126–53; Michael Kraus, *The Atlantic Civilization: Eighteenth-Century Origins* (Ithaca, N.Y.: Cornell University Press, 1949); Davis, *Intellectual Life,* passim.

14. Davis, *Intellecutal Life,* 3:1110.

15. John Clive and Bernard Bailyn, "England's Cultural Provinces: Scotland and America," *William and Mary Quarterly* 11 (1954):213.

16. Jack P. Greene, "Search for Identity," *Journal of Social History* 3 (1969–70):205–18; J. A. Leo Lemay, *Men of Letters in Colonial Maryland* (Knoxville: University of Tennessee Press, 1972), pp. 73–342; Davis, *Intellectual Life,* 3:1354–1506.

17. *Archives of Maryland* 28 (1908):375.

18. This unsigned poem is ascribed to Cradock in J. A. Leo Lemay, *A Calendar of American Poetry in the Colonial Newspapers and Magazines and in the Major English Magazines through 1765* (Worcester, Mass.: American Antiquarian Society, 1972), p. 206.

19. *American Magazine or Monthly Chronicle for the British Colonies* 1 (1957–1958):605–7, ll. 1–2, 11–14. See *Gentleman's Magazine* 2 (1732):555, for reference to Pope's use of the phrase.

20. *Maryland Gazette,* March 15, 1753. On their death see ibid., December 28, 1752. The poem is reprinted in R. B. Davis et al., eds., *Southern Writing, 1585–1920* (New York: Odyssey Press, 1970), pp. 203–5.

21. Ethan Allen, "Sketches of the Colonial Clergy of Maryland: No. I Rev. Thomas Cradock," *American Church Review* 7 (1854):307.

22. Ibid., pp. 308–9, 311. On the place of the hymn in eighteenth-century literature see M. Pauline Parker, "The Hymn as a Literary Form," *Eighteenth-Century Studies* 8 (1974–75): 392–419; Richard Crawford, "Watts for Singing: Metrical Poetry in American Sacred Tunebooks, 1761–1785," *Early American Literature* 11 (1976): 139–46; Crawford, "An Historian's Introduction to Early American Music," *Proceedings of the American Antiquarian Society* 89 (1979): 261–98.

23. Allen, *Garrison Church*, pp. 25–26.

24. Thomas Cradock, *A Poetical Translation of the Psalms of David. From Buchanan's Latin into English Verse* (London: R. Ware, 1754); Cradock, *A New Version of the Psalms of David* (Annapolis, Md.: Jonas Green, 1756), p. iv; *Maryland Gazette*, July 23, 1752, August 23, 1753.

25. Cradock, *A New Version of the Psalms of David*, (Annapolis, Md.: Jonas Green, 1756) pp. v–viii; John Rogers Williams, comp., "A Catalogue of the Books in the Library of 'Councillor' Robert Carter, at Nomini Hall, Westmoreland County, Va.," *William and Mary Quarterly*, 1st Series, 10 (1901–2): 238; Joseph Towne Wheeler, "Books Owned by Marylanders, 1700–1776," *Maryland Historical Magazine* 35 (1940): 352.

26. Maxine Turner, "Three Eighteenth-Century Revisions of the *Bay Psalm Book*," *New England Quarterly* 45 (1972): 270–77, examines English psalters used in New England, plus those of Cotton Mather, John Bernard, and Thomas Prince.

27. Cradock, *New Version*, p. 22; Cradock, *Poetical Translation*, p. 25. In the London edition, line 2 reads "My God shall feed me with a shepherd's care," line 3 substitutes "fair" for "gay," line 6 replaces "a soft" for "serene," and line 10 has "David" replaced by "servant." In line 14 what may have been a typographical error of "my staff" in the London version becomes "thy staff" in the Maryland one. More substantive modifications occur in lines 15, 16 and 20. The first two read "Vainly my foes thro pining envy mourn,/Thy choicest cates my plenteous board adorn." The latter line originally was written "I'll rest secure, for ever blithsome gay." It is clear Cradock felt little need for substantive modifications in the two versions, but that he was constantly looking for those minor changes that provided better versification. Cradock's version of this psalm compares favorably with that of the most famous New England devotional poet. See Thomas M. Davis and Virginia L. Davis, "Edward Taylor's Metrical Paraphrases of the Psalms," *American Literature* 48 (1976–77): 470.

28. See, for instance, Clarence Gohdes, ed. "Old Virginia Georgics," *Southern Literary Journal* 9 (1978–79): 44–53.

29. Davis, *Intellectual Life*, pp. 1406, 1470, 1472.

30. David Worcester, *The Art of Satire* (Cambridge, Mass.: Harvard University Press, 1940), pp. 31–32.

31. Ibid., p. 161.

32. Charles Michael Carroll, "A Classical Setting for a Classical Poem: Philidor's *Carmen Saeculare*," *Studies in Eighteenth-Century Culture* 6 (1977): 97–99.

33. Alexander Hamilton, "Record Book of the Tuesday Club," John Work Garrett Library, Johns Hopkins University, Baltimore, Maryland, ff. 470–72; Hamilton, "History of the Ancient and Honourable Tuesday Club," Maryland Historical Society, Baltimore, 3: 160–66. I am indebted to Professors J. A. Leo Lemay and Elaine G. Breslaw for assistance in the location and analysis of "Carmen Dolorosum."

34. Cradock attended sessions of August 28, 1750, October 26, 1752, February 20, June 26, November 6, 1753, and November 5, 1754. Hamilton, Record Book. For descriptions of the Tuesday Club see Lemay, *Men of Letters*, pp. 188–89, 202, 208, 245–55, 323–24; Elaine G. Breslaw, "Wit, Whimsy, and Politics: The Use of Satire by the Tuesday Club of Annapolis, 1744 to 1756," *William and Mary Quarterly* 32 (1975): 295–306; Breslaw, "The Chronicle as Satire: Dr. Hamilton's History of the Tuesday Club," *Maryland Historical Magazine* 70 (1975): 129–48.

35. Hamilton, Record Book, pp. 585–86, 592.

36. *Maryland Gazette*, December 17, 1745.

37. *Maryland Gazette*, February 4, 1746. See also Lemay, *Men of Letters*, pp. 229–30.

38. Here and elsewhere for Vergil's Latin I rely on C. Day Lewis, *The Eclogues and Georgics of Virgil* (Garden City, N.Y.: Doubleday, 1964).

39. [Thomas Cradock], "Maryland Eclogues," Cradock Papers, Maryland Historical Society, Baltimore.

40. Nitchie, *Vergil and the English Poets,* pp. 162–63; Tillotson, *Augustan Studies,* pp. 56, 226; Winsor Leach, *Vergil's* Eclogues: *Landscapes of Experience* (Ithaca, N.Y.: Cornell University Press, 1974), pp. 23–24, 31–32, 42–44; Michael C. J. Putnam, *Virgil's Pastoral Art: Studies In the Eclogues* (Princeton, N. J.: Princeton University Press, 1970), p. 4.

41. For more on Lewis see Lemay, *Men of Letters,* pp. 126–84; Davis, *Intellectual Life,* 3: 1361–62, 1462–66.

42. Lemay, *Men of Letters,* pp. 166–72.

43. *Dictionary of American Biography,* s.v. "Shikellamy"; "Witham Marshe's Journal," Massachusetts Historical Society, *Collections,* 1st series, 7 (1801): 179–80, 195–96, 200; *Archives of Maryland,* vol. 28 (1908), pp. 335–36; vol. 44 (1925), pp. 121–22; Daniel Dulany to Charles, Lord Baltimore, July 16, 1744, *The Calvert Papers, No. 2,* Maryland Historical Society, Fund Publication No. 34 (Baltimore: The Society, 1894), p. 108; Charles P. Keith, *Chronicles of Pennsylvania from the English Revolution to the Peace of Aix-La-Chapelle, 1688–1748,*2 vols. (Philadelphia: Privately printed, 1917), 2: 867–70; Joseph S. Walton, *Conrad Weiser and the Indian Policy of Colonial Pennsylvania* (Philadelphia: George W. Jacobs, 1900), pp. 93–121; Paul A. W. Wallace, *Conrad Weiser, 1696–1760, Friend of Colonist and Mohawk* (Philadelphia: University of Pennsylvania Press, 1945).

44. Lemay, *Men of Letters,* pp. 86–87.

45. Davis, *Intellectual Life,* 3: 1393–95; Lemay, *Men of Letters,* pp. 138–50; Robert D. Arner, "Ebenezer Cooke's *The Sot Weed Factor:* The Structure of Satire," *Southern Literary Journal* 4 (1971–72): 33–47; Arner, "Clio's *Rhimes:* History and Satire in Ebenezer Cooke's 'History of Bacon's Rebellion,'" ibid. 6 (1973–74): 91–106.

46. Davis, *Intellectual Life,* 3: 1280–1306, is the best summary of southern dramatic life. Most other work, like Hugh F. Rankin, *The Theater in Colonial America* (Chapel Hill: University of North Carolina Press, 1960) and Mary Childs Black, "The Theatre in Colonial Annapolis," M. A. thesis, George Washington University, 1952, deals with performances by professional theatrical companies. The two best known colonial-written plays are by Robert Mumford: Jay B. Hubbell and Douglass Adair, eds., "Robert Munford's *The Candidates,*" *William and Mary Quarterly* 5 (1948): 217–57; Courtlandt Canby, ed., "Robert Munford's *The Patriots,*" *ibid.* 6 (1949): 437–503. On Byrd see Carl R. Dolmetsch, "William Byrd II: Comic Dramatist?" *Early American Literature* 6 (1971): 18–30.

47. [Thomas Cradock, "The Death of Socrates,"] Cradock Papers, Maryland Historical Society, Baltimore. Further citation will be by act, scene, and line number.

48. John Gilbert Cooper, *The Life of Socrates . . .* ,3d ed. (London: R. Dodsley, 1750), pp. vi–viii.

49. William Gribbin, "Rollin's Histories and American Republicanism," *William and Mary Quarterly* 29 (1972): 611–22; Henry Steele Commager, "The American Enlightenment and the Ancient World: A Study in Paradox," *Proceedings of the Massachusetts Historical Society* 83 (1972): 3–7. I examined the remnants of Cradock's library at Trentham in March 1971 and found inscribed in the flyleaf of the first volume of Rollin: "Borrowed August 1765 of the Revd. Mr. Cradock."

50. Charles Rollin, *The Ancient History of the Egyptians, Carthaginians, Assyrians, Babylonians, Medes, and Persians, Grecians, and Macedonians,* 2 vols. (Cincinnati, Ohio: Applegate and Co., 1856), 1: 395.

51. See Cooper, *Socrates,* pp. 167–74, and compare with Rollin, *Ancient History,* 1: 394–96.

52. David Curtis Skaggs, "Thomas Cradock's Sermon on the Governance of Maryland's Established Church," *William and Mary Quarterly,* 27 (1970): 642; Edward C. Papenfuse, ed., "An Undelivered Defense of a Winning Cause: Charles Carroll of Carrollton's 'Remarks on the Proposed Federal Constitution,'" *Maryland Historical Magazine* 71 (1976): 249.

53. Felicity A. Nussbaum, "Pope's 'To a Lady' and the Eighteenth-Century Woman," *Philological Quarterly* 54 (1975): 445. See also Marlene Le Gates, "The Cult of True Womanhood in Eighteenth-Century Thought," *Eighteenth-Century Studies* 10 (1976–77): 21–39.

54. Kenneth Silverman, *A Cultural History of the American Revolution* (New York: Thomas Y. Crowell, 1976), pp. 105–7.

5
The Chesapeake Golden Age

When British colonists crossed the Atlantic, they did not leave behind their cultural heritage in order to build a new intellectual community. Rather they sought to preserve that heritage in the face of considerable adversity. Nowhere were efforts more strenuously made to retain Britain's culture than in the Chesapeake colonies. To the docks of Virginia and Maryland plantations sailed vessels out of London, Bristol, and Glasgow loaded with books, pamphlets, fashionable clothing, and passengers who brought the latest ideas to the manors' dining and drawing rooms. They sailed away not only with their holds filled with hogsheads of tobacco and with grain, but also with planters' sons, who sought education in British schools and colleges. This lively exchange of people and ideas kept the Chesapeake in the mainstream of European developments.

Such an image is not the one scholars customarily have painted when describing the tobacco coast. More typical evaluations of the quality and ethical precepts of the region have been critical of intellectual activity. Most historians have agreed with Carl Bridenbaugh, who thought the region produced "men of intellect, not intellectuals," or with Daniel Boorstin, who wrote that "among Virginians there was no place for a literary class, a Grub Street, or a polite salon." The few obvious intellectuals like William Byrd and Thomas Jefferson are dubbed "sports" in an otherwise barren cultural environment.[1] One only has to peruse the table of contents of the *William and Mary Quarterly,* the leading scholarly periodical dealing with early American history and culture, to note the concentration of scholarly effort toward the intellectual life of the Puritan colonies. Normally, anthologies of American literature devote most of their space to the Northern Colonies, with a selection from Benjamin Franklin (a New Englander by birth) representing the Middle Colonies, and some bawdy quotes from William Byrd typifying the South. Few, if any, Southern poems, letters, essays, sermons, histories, or scientific observations have been included.

Southerners are to blame for much of this. Because the region sought so much to copy British modes, it did not feel the need to found the institutional supports of colleges and printing presses that Puritans felt were necessary. Commonly the Southern gentry relied on British institutions for their education and edification. Why, for instance, publish the sermons of a local minister when those of Archbishop John Tillotson could be so easily procured? Moreover, Southern parsons lacked the compulsion to publish their writings that dominated many New England divines. Many of the belletristic contributions of Chesapeake gentlemen circulated in manuscript among the planters and parsons, and such distribution was considered sufficient for men of quality and breeding. Thus it has not been until recently that discovery and publication of hitherto unknown or little-known manuscripts, combined with a revival of scholarly interest in the colonial South, has led to a reappraisal of the cultural life along the tobacco coast.

The beginnings of this renaissance may be traced to the books and edited works of Louis B. Wright. In his *The First Gentlemen of Virginia* (1940) and in his editing of the diaries and prose writings of William Byrd II of Westover, Wright laid a solid foundation for the Southern intellectual history that would follow.[2] In fact a whole school of Byrd scholarships arose, culminating in Pierre Marambaud's biography of the squire of Westover, published in 1971.[3] Meanwhile scholarship relating to the eighteenth-century South increased rapidly with the publication of a host of source documents[4] plus the production of a variety of scholarly commentaries dealing not only with literature,[5] but also with science, architecture, and painting.[6]

By the 1970s three decades of scholarship relating to the tobacco coast culminated in the publication of new syntheses of Chesapeake intellectual life. Maryland attracted J. A. Leo Lemay, who revised and expanded his doctoral dissertation into a book entitled *Men of Letters in Colonial Maryland* (1972). In a series of biographic sketches, he surveyed the literary life of early Maryland. Lemay found that His Lordship's province contained some of the finest belletristic writers of British North America. He elevated Richard Lewis (1700–1734) from obscurity to first place among eighteenth-century verse writers: "it is practically impossible to imagine a cultivated, well-educated man of the time caring for any other contemporary American poet."[7] The center of intellectual intercourse in the colony was the circle of Annapolis wits led by Dr. Alexander Hamilton, who founded and kept alive the Tuesday Club of that city. A convivial gathering of gentlemen who ate, drank, talked, wrote satiric verse, and composed and played music, this cultivated group included publisher Jonas Green, parsons Alexander Malcolm, James Gordon, and Thomas Bacon, plus a variety of merchants and planters interested in poetry and music.

Since the completion of Lemay's research, the scholarly inquiry on the Tuesday Club has expanded further with the writings of Elaine Breslaw and others.[8] Beyond the Tuesday Club circle, other studies describe a large number of parsons, planters, and merchants who collectively added to our comprehension of this "golden age" of colonial Chesapeake culture.[9] There were many men like Parson Malcolm, whose obituary notice described him as a "Gentleman who has obliged the World with several learned Performances on the Mathematics, Music, and Grammar."[10]

The principal study of Chesapeake culture, however, was not Lemay's study of Maryland, but rather a series of writings by Richard Beale Davis that culminated in his three-volume *Intellectual Life in the Colonial South, 1585–1763* (1978), winner of the National Book Award. Davis charted the direction of this work in a 1970 address to the Virginia Historical Society entitled "The Intellectual Golden Age in the Chesapeake Bay Country."

Davis's paper marks a major attack on the theories of a Southern intellectual vacuum espoused by Bridenbaugh, Boorstin, and their followers. Davis argues that such historians have written Marylanders and Virginians off "as non-intellectuals perhaps because they did not demonstrate their cerebral powers by struggling with the knotty problems of Calvinist theology."[12] Instead of this measurement, Davis wants other yardsticks of cultural activity to be used to gauge the profundity and diversity of intellectual life of the tobacco provinces. He suggests that the "beautiful architecture and gardens, verse in many forms and traditions, prose satire, annotated editions of the laws, pervasive and eloquent sermons" of the tobacco coast constitute "artistic and intellectual creativity" as worthy of study as that which occurred elsewhere on this continent.[13] Using such criteria, Davis concludes that in the Chesapeake region "from about 1720 to 1789 there was a strong expression of discriminating taste in the arts, as high a proportion of well-educated men as existed anywhere in the colonies, frequent discourses on religious doctrine and application, a creativity in belles-lettres, and a dynamic and reasoned expression springing from scores of thoughtful and sophisticated minds."[14]

In his *Intellectual Life in the Colonial South,* Davis seeks to document the arguments presented in his 1970 Virginia Historical Society lecture. Given the diversity of interests in such a mandate, it is remarkable that he can accomplish his objectives in three volumes that total over 1,800 pages. He finds the colonial Southern mind to have several characteristics. First of all, the Southerner was *religious,* although clearly in a different way from the Puritans. Much "that was happening in Great Britain and on the European continent had effects on the southern seacoast settlement which prevented the kind of unified, albeit changing, religious and theological unity that New England possessed."[15] Second, the Southerner was *hedonistic.* "From the colonial beginning the love of play, of recreation has gone hand in hand with the piety of rank and file society and with the more reasoned religious philosophies of the better educated."[16] The white Southern settler also had an *agrarian* viewpoint fully developed by the mid-eighteenth century. He "came not to build a city upon a hill" but rather "to cultivate a fertile valley until he won for himself the good life, the American dream as reality."[17] Moreover, the Southern mind was devoted to *classicism,* not only in its reading habits but also in such manifestations as architecture—an emanation of intellectual development most characteristic of the region's cultural achievements. Finally the colonial Southerner remained *British* in his taste in literature, the arts, law, and education, sometimes so closely that there is no clue to indicate an American origin in a particular creation.

Collectively these characteristics point to a Southern intellectual tradition that differed from that of the other continental colonies. Davis disagrees strongly not only with those who feel little intellectual creativity occurred south of the Mason-Dixon Line, but also with those who feel a single American, or Puritan, mind set dominated the colonial world.[18] Such a stance places him clearly at odds with Edmund S. Morgan, who argues that a "Puritan Ethic" dominated colonial culture from the Bay of Fundy to Okefenokee Swamp, thereby placing Cotton Mather and William Byrd, Samuel Adams, and Charles Carroll of Carrollton in the same camp. Well before Davis's book, Professor Morgan's prize-winning essay drew criticism from C. Vann Woodward, who felt that it failed to account for the regional distinctiveness of the South. Woodward feels Morgan ascribed to the term *Puritan* values that were common to Western culture, or at least to the British strain of it. Woodward develops the equivalents of Davis's religious, hedonistic, and agrarian characteristics as parts of a "Southern Ethic." But like the historian he is, rather than the student of literature that Davis is, Woodward concentrates mostly on the socioeconomic peculiarities of the South, such as slavery and "an aristocratic, antibourgeois spirit with values and mores emphasizing family and status, a strong code of honor," which produced "the patriarchal tradition, the caste system, the martial spirit, the racial etiquette, the familial charisma" typical of the Southern mind. All of these characteristics "deserve attention from the historian of the Southern Ethic," concludes Woodward.[19]

Whatever peculiar characteristics one ascribes to a Southern Ethic, Thomas Cradock clearly embodied most of those described by Davis and Woodward. He was deeply religious, somewhat hedonistic, supportive of the agrarian myth, devoted to the classics, and always an Anglophile. A reading of the "Maryland Eclogues" and his sermons will lead to the conclusion that he had a pervading sense of a social caste system and of distinctive places in society for the various orders of man, that he had a strong code of honor and a martial spirit, and that he lived by a racial etiquette.

In at least one way, however, Cradock differed from the norm ascribed by both Lemay and Davis to eighteenth-century Chesapeake litterateurs. Lemay argues, and Davis accepts, that even among immigrant writers there developed a tradition of American literary nationalism—the *transatio studii* motif, the idea of the westward movement of arts.[20] While Cradock's contemporary, the Reverend James Sterling (1701–63), easily adopted his Irish nationalism to America, the vicar of the Garrison Church did not write poetic images on the future glory of America. More than many of his contemporary men of letters, Cradock remained a Briton. Nowhere in the "Maryland Eclogues" is there an image of America as a future center of intellectual activity. The praise is rather of Britain and English ideals and institutions. For instance, Maryland parsons were "such Clods of Clay" that they "resemble those at Home no more,/ Than Saints of Modern Days do Saints of yore" (1. 29, 33–34). Cradock's America was part of a wider British empire, not an emerging community in its own right, much in the same manner that his native Staffordshire was part of the greater glory that was Augustan London.

What is clear from the studies of Davis and Lemay is that Thomas Cradock was part of a widespread Chesapeake intellectual community. Moreover, the Anglican clergy, despite Cradock's disdain for the ethical conduct of many of them, constituted a leading force in the intellectual life of the region. Eighteenth-century Maryland was, writes Lemay, "an age when clergymen dominated literature and society."[21] As schoolmasters, philanthropists, preachers, and litterateurs, these parsons added an important dimension to provincial culture.

Central to the cultural life of Maryland was the Tuesday Club of Annapolis. The Anglican clergy were mainstays in its activities. Among the more regular members of the club were the Reverends Alexander Malcolm, Thomas Bacon, James Sterling, and John Gordon. Others frequently attending included Parsons Henry Addison,

William Brogden, and Thomas Cradock. Bacon composed musical works esteemed in Ireland, England, and America. Malcolm wrote a standard musical treatise. Bacon played the violin and Malcolm the flute in a small Tuesday Club ensemble that regularly performed for its members and the public. Sterling authored plays and poems in Ireland and America, of which his *An Epistle to the Hon. Arthur Dobbs, Esq.* (Dublin, 1752) was a major piece of eighteenth-century American poetry. Bacon was the most widely published author in colonial Maryland, most conspicuous for his often-reprinted sermons on behalf of Christianizing the slaves and expanding educational opportunities. He climaxed a productive career with a condification of the *Laws of Maryland* (Annapolis, 1765).[22] Collectively the Maryland clergy comprised an exceptional intellectual community that brought the larger world of fine arts and bellestristic literature to His Lordship's province. As such they were merely imitating their British contemporaries, rural clergy creating a poetic genre that has only recently received serious appraisal.[23] This tradition extended to the highest levels of eighteenth-century literature, where novelists like Laurence Sterne, poets like Jonathan Swift, and philosophers like George Berkeley were also men of the cloth.

From Thomas Bray to Jonathan Boucher, Maryland's established church contained many ministers who served well as preachers, teachers, missionaries, and cultural leaders. When one uses the analytical benchmark of the London metropolis that they sought to imitate, we find that the Anglican clerics were remarkably successful in developing a humanistic colonial culture in this outpost of empire. Even though James Sterling was no Alexander Pope, nor Thomas Cradock a John Wesley, these Maryland clergy contributed significantly to the transfer of British cultural patterns to the New World.

In his sermons and poetry Cradock provides an opportunity to examine both the personal values and the amount of intellectual activity that occurred along the Chesapeake shores. We know that he lived in a time of great economic and intellectual dysfunctionalism that saw the erosion of internal social cohesion in many colonial communities.[24]

Through his sermons and poetry, Cradock propagated the traditional values of his church and nation. He strove to achieve social peace and unity through homiletics, devotional verse, satiric poetry, and moralistic drama. He called for a reinvigoration of the clergy and for a revival of conventional piety and morality among the laity. Seeking not to chart new paths but rather to traverse traditional routes to salvation, Cradock advocated a pattern of virtuous behavior requiring an abiding commitment to the golden mean. He idealized standards of conduct of the good Christian—sincere piety, personal morality, generous benevolence, sensible conviviality, honest work in a God-given social hierarchy, prudent use of each talent, and fair treatment of all of God's creatures whether they be rich or poor, husband or wife, master or servant, Indian or slave. This adoption of the Horatian ideal of the *via media* became part of the Southern self image that lasted until the Civil War.

In such a world the institution of chattel slavery had a role as part of the natural order of an hierarchial society and a necessary component to the maintenance of the delicate balance between racial groups. In the mechanistic values of the Great Chain of Being, slavery constituted a reasonable institution for the continuation of the social equilibrium. Nowhere in his writings did Cradock express moral outrage at slavery, and in fact he even owned a few slaves. Cradock expressed disgust at the mistreatment of servants and slaves by their masters and mistresses. He was repulsed by sexual promiscuity between the races. He expected blacks to be converted to Christianity, but he never adopted a stance of moral indignation at one man owning another man. In this manner Cradock represented the conventional values of his time and place.[25] His concern was with the immortal soul of men, not the temporary mortal social status in which they found themselves.

Before the Revolution, few people made the connection between freedom for some men and freedom for all. Far more important than the eradication of social inequality was the salvation of souls. Therefore Cradock sought to encourage others to follow Christ's path and personally tried do even more. He created an image of self-control that exemplified the Christian life-style and attracted attention from Annapolis to Philadelphia. To Trentham came students from the best families of Maryland's western shore. In effect, Cradock's life became a mirror for those who sought the virtuous and cultured life.

Only one letter to Cradock survives. In it the Reverend Thomas Barton of Lancaster, Pennsylvania, pled for the Maryland rector to visit him: "Positively you must come to see me; for I have so often boasted the Gentlemen here, that Mr. Cradock was my friend, that I am afraid they will think me a Man of no Consequence if you should disappoint me."[26] Similar testimonials to his reputation came with his death. On his tombstone was inscribed a verse probably composed by his longtime friend, Dr. Randle Hulse:

No pompous Marble, to thy Name we raise,
This humble Stone, bespeaks deserving Praise,
When e're we view'd Thee, o're the sacred Page,
Thy Words pervasive, did our Hearts engage,
Parental Fondness did thy Life attend,
The tender Husband; and the warmest Friend;
The Good, the Just with Thee alone could vie,
Who court not Life, nor yet afraid to die,
Faith, Virtue, Honour, did in Thee combine,
Happy the Man, who leads a Life like thine.[27]

Although such effusions were common in eighteenth-century graveyard poetry, this Cradock elegy is another example of how he exemplified the individual values and social imperatives of his day. While his English birth and education meant that he brought to his parish a somewhat different perspective than that from a native Marylander, his marriage into a local family and his long residence in a frontier community undoubtedly encouraged the acquisition of local values. That he internalized those values may be impossible to determine, but in an age of Presbyterian, Baptist, and Methodist evangelism in the back country, no dissenting churches arose in Saint Thomas' Parish during his twenty-five-year pastorate. Certainly there was no formal rejection of those religious values for which he argued. That he personified the idealized values to the satisfaction of his contemporaries may be seen in a broadside eulogy that declared that Cradock "was universally allowed to be a sincere Christian, a polish Scholar, an elegant and persuasive Preacher"[28] who for a quarter of a century captured the attention of a growing congregation on the colonial frontier. He left them with a legacy of piety, scholarship, homiletics, and verse that exemplified in practice a Christian faith that few could imitate.

NOTES

1. Carl Bridenbaugh, *Myths and Realities: Societies of the Colonial South* (Baton Rouge: Louisiana State University Press, 1952), p. 53; Daniel J. Boorstin, *The Americans: The Colonial Experience* (New York: Knopf, 1958), p. 306. David Bertelson, *The Lazy South* (New York: Oxford University Press, 1967), alleges that the region's cultural vacuum reflected a lack of moral commitment among southern colonists.

2. Louis B. Wright, *The First Gentlemen of Virginia: Intellectual Qualities of the Early Ruling Class* (San Marino, Calif.: Huntington Library, 1940); Louis B. Wright and Marion Tinling, eds., *The Secret Diary of William Byrd of Westover, 1709–1712* (Richmond, Va.: Dietz Press, 1941); Wright and Tinling, eds., *William Byrd of Virginia: The London Diary (1717–1721) and Other Writings* (New York: Oxford University Press, 1958); Wright, ed., *The Prose Works of William Byrd of Westover: Narratives of a Colonial Virginian*

(Cambridge, Mass.: Harvard University Press, 1966). Additional material emerged in Maude H. Woodfin, ed., and Tinling, trans., *Another Secret Diary of William Byrd of Westover, 1739–1741: With Letters & Literary Exercises, 1696–1726* (Richmond, Va.: Dietz Press, 1942), and Tinling, ed., The Correspondence of the Three William Byrds of Westover, Virginia, 1684–1766, 2 vols., Virginia Historical Society Documents, vols. 12–13 (Charlottesville: University Press of Virginia, 1977). See also Wright, "Literature in the Colonial South," *Huntington Library Quarterly* 10 (1947): 297–315.

3. Pierre Marambaud, *William Byrd of Westover, 1674–1744* (Charlottesville: University Press of Virginia, 1971). Carl Dolmetsch, "William Byrd of Westover as an Augustan Poet," *Studies in Literary Imagination* 9 (1976–77): 69–77; Dolmetsch's review of Marambaud's book in "William Byrd II, The Augustan Writer as 'Exile' in His Own Country," *Virginia Quarterly Review* 48 (1972): 145–49; Robert D. Arner, "Westover and the Wilderness: William Byrd's Images of Virginia," *Southern Literary Journal* 7 (Spring 1975): 105–23; Arner, "Style, Substance, and Self in William Byrd's Familiar Letters," in J. A. Leo Lemay, ed., *Essays in Early Virginian Literature Honoring Richard Beale Davis* (New York: Burt Franklin, 1977), pp. 101–19; Richard Beale Davis, "William Byrd: Taste and Tolerance," in Everett E. Emerson, ed., *Major Writers of Early American Literature* (Madison: University of Wisconsin Press, 1972), pp. 151–77; Michael Zuckerman, "William Byrd's Family," *Perspectives in American History* 12 (1979): 255–311, represent the continuation of Byrd studies since Marambaud's work.

4. Richard Beale Davis, ed., *The Colonial Virginia Satirist: Mid-Eighteenth Century Commentaries on Politics, Religion, and Society* (American Philosophical Society *Transactions*, N.S., vol. 57, pt. 1 [Philadelphia, Pa., 1967]); Davis, ed., *Collected Poems of Samuel Davies, 1723–1761* (Gainesville, Fla,: Scholars' Facsimiles and Reprints, 1968); Davis, ed., "James Reid, Colonial Virginia Poet and Moral and Religious Essayist," *Virginia Magazine of History and Biography* 79 (1971): 3–19; J. A. Leo Lemay, ed., *A Poem by John Markland of Virginia* (Williamsburg, Va.: The William Parks Club, 1965); Lemay, ed., "Hamilton's Literary History of the *Maryland Gazette*," *William and Mary Quarterly* 23 (1966): 273–85; James A. Servies and Carl Dolmetsch, eds., *The Poems of Charles Hansford,*Virginia Historical Society Documents, vol. 1 (Chapel Hill: University of North Carolina Press, 1961); Jack P. Greene, ed., *The Diary of Colonel Landon Carter of Sabine Hall 1752–1778,* 2 vols, Virginia Historical Society Documents, vols. 4–5 (Charlottesville: University Press of Virginia, 1965); John Gwilym Jones, ed., *Goronwy Owen's Virginia Adventures: His Life, Poetry, and Literary Opinions with a Translation of His Virginian Letters,* Botetourt Bibliographical Society Publications, No. 2 (Williamsburg, Va.: The Society, 1969); Jack P. Greene, ed., "A Mirror of Virtue for a Declining Land: John Camm's Funeral Sermon for William Nelson" in Lemay, ed., *Essays in Early Virginian Literature,* pp. 189–201; Edward Miles Riley, ed., *The Journal of John Harrower: An Indentured Servant in the Colony of Virginia, 1773–1776* (Williamsburg, Va.: Colonial Williamsburg, 1963); William Eddis, *Letters from America,* ed. Aubrey C. Land (Cambridge, Mass.: Harvard University Press, 1969); Hunter Dickinson Farish, ed., *Journal & Letters of Philip Vickers Fithian, 1773–1774: A Plantation Tutor of the Old Dominian* (Williamsburg, Va.: Colonial Williamsburg, 1957).

5. Parke Rouse, Jr., *James Blair of Virginia* (Chapel Hill: University of North Carolina Press, 1971); Rodney M. Baine, *Robert Munford: America's First Comic Dramatist* (Athens: University of Georgia Press, 1967); George William Pilcher, *Samuel Davies, Apostle of Dissent in Colonial Virginia* (Knoxville: University of Tennessee Press, 1971); Craig Gilborn, "Samuel Davies' Sacred Muse," *Journal of Presbyterian History* 41 (1963): 63–79; Barbara A. Larson, "Samuel Davies and the Rhetoric of the New Light," *Speech Monographs* 28 (1971): 207–16; J. A. Leo Lemay, "Robert Bolling and the Bailment of Colonel Chiswell," *Early American Literature* 6 (1971): 99–142; Robert A. Bain, "The Composition and Publication of *The Present State of Virginia and the College,*" ibid., pp. 31–54; Bain, "A Note on James Blair and the Southern Plain Style," *Southern Literary Journal* 4 (1971–72): 68–73; Edward H. Cohen, "The Elegies of Ebenezer Cooke," *Early*

American Literature 4 (1969): 49–72; Cohen "The 'Second Edition' of the Sot-Weed Factor," *American Literature* 42 (1970): 289–303; Robert D. Arner, "Clio's Rhimes: History and Satire in Ebenezer Cooke's 'History of Bacon's Rebellion,'" *Southern Literary Journal* 6 (1973–74): 91–106; Arner, "Ebenezer Cooke's *The Sot-Weed Factor:* The Structure of Satire," *Southern Literary Journal* 4 (1971–72): 33–47; Arner's perceptive review of Cohen's *Ebenezer Cooke: The Sot-Weed Canon* (Athens: University of Georgia Press, 1975), "Ebenezer Cooke: Satire in the Colonial South" *Southern Literary Journal* 8 (1975–76): 153–64; Arner, "The Quest for Freedom: Style and Meaning in Robert Beverley's *History and Present State of Virginia,*" *Southern Literary Journal* 8 (1975–76): 79–98; R. M. Myers, "The Old Dominion Looks to London: A Study of English Literary Influences on the *Virginia Gazette,* 1736–1766," *Virginia Magazine of History and Biography* 54 (1946): 195–217; A. O. Aldridge, "Benjamin Franklin and the *Maryland Gazette,*" *Maryland Historical Magazine* 44 (1949): 177–89; a series of articles (1939–43), by Joseph Towne Wheeler that conclude with "Literary Culture in Eighteenth-Century Maryland, 1700–1776: Summary of Findings," *Maryland Historical Magazine* 38 (1943): 273–76; essays by J. A. Leo Lemay, Homer D. Kemp, and A. R. Riggs in Lemay, ed., *Essays in Early Virginia Literature,* pp. 107–88; 211–28.

6. The best bibliography on art and architecture in the two provinces is found in Richard B. Davis, *Intellectual Life in the Colonial South, 1585–1763* (Knoxville: University of Tennessee Press, 1978) 3: 1658–60, 1663–64. See particularly Henry C. Forman, *Tidewater Maryland Architecture and Gardens* (New York: Architectural Book Publishing Co., 1956); John W. Reps, *Tidewater Towns: City Planning in Colonial Virginia and Maryland* (Williamsburg Va.: Colonial Williamsburg, 1972); Rosamond R. Beirne and John H. Scarff, *William Buckland, 1734–1774, Architect of Virginia and Maryland* (Baltimore: Maryland Historical Society, 1958); J. Hall Pleasants, *Two Hundred and Fifty Years of Painting in Maryland* (Baltimore, Md.: Baltimore Museum of Art, 1945). For the sciences see Edmund and Dorothy Smith Berkeley, eds., *The Reverend John Clayton, A Parson with a Scientific Mind: His Scientific Writings and Other Papers,* Virginia Historical Society Documents, vol. 6 (Charlottesville, Va.: University Press of Virginia, 1965); the Berkeleys, *Dr. John Mitchell: The Man Who Made the Map of North America* (Chapel Hill: University of North Carolina Press, 1974) and Davis's bibliography, *Intellectual Life,* 2: 1073–82.

7. J. A. Leo Lemay, *Men of Letters in Colonial Maryland* (Knoxville: University of Tennessee Press, 1972), p. 183.

8. Elaine G. Breslaw, "Wit, Whimsy and Politics," *William and Mary Quarterly* 32 (1975): 295–306; Breslaw, "The Chronicle as Satire," *Maryland Historical Magazine* 70 (1975): 129–48; Breslaw, "Dr. Alexander Hamilton and the Enlightenment in Maryland," Ph.D. diss., University of Maryland, 1973; James R. Heintze, "Alexander Malcolm: Musician, Clergyman, and Schoolmaster," *Maryland Historical Magazine* 73 (1978): 226–35; Reppard Stone, "An Evaluative Study of Alexander Malcolm's *Treatise of Music:* Speculative, Practical and Historical," Ph.D. diss., Catholic University of America, 1974; Jerritus Boyd, "The Golden Age of Maryland Culture, 1750–1770," M.A. thesis, University of Maryland, 1967; David Curtis Skaggs, "Thomas Cradock," *William and Mary Quarterly* 30 (1973): 93–116. For the text of Hamilton's famous description of the club's proceedings see: Robert Micklus, ed. "Dr. Alexander Hamilton's *The History of the Tuesday Club,*" Ph.D. diss., University of Delaware, 1980.

9. Anne Y. Zimmer, *Jonathan Boucher: Loyalist in Exile* (Detroit, Mich.: Wayne State University Press, 1978); James F. Vivian and Jean H. Vivian, "The Reverend Isaac Campbell: An Anti-Lockean Whig," *Historical Magazine of the Protestant Episcopal Church* 39 (1970): 71–89; Thomas O'Brien Hanley, *Charles Carroll of Carrollton: The Making of a Revolutionary Gentleman* (Washington, D.C.: Catholic University of America Press, 1970); Robert L. Morton, "The Reverend Hugh Jones: Baltimore's Mathematician," *William and Mary Quarterly* 7 (1950): 107–15.

10. *Maryland Gazette,* June 20, 1763.

11. The essay was published in *Virginia Magazine of History and Biography* 78 (1970): 131–43, and reprinted in Richard B. Davis, *Literature and Society in Early Virginia: 1608–1840* (Baton Rouge: Louisiana State University Press, 1973), pp. 149–67.

12. Davis, *Literature and Society,* p. 149.

13. Ibid., p. 149.

14. Ibid., pp. 151–52.

15. Davis, *Intellectual Life,* 2: 629.

16. Ibid., 3: 1649.

17. Ibid., 1: xxx.

18. See for instance, ibid., 2: 612–15, 687, 1030, 1031, 1087.

19. Edmund S. Morgan, "The Puritan Ethic and the American Revolution," *William and Mary Quarterly* 24 (1967): 3–43; C. Vann Woodward, "The Southern Ethic in a Puritan World," *William and Mary Quarterly* 25 (1868): 362–65. For an argument that a distinctive ethic arose in the Middle Colonies, see Frederick B. Tolles, "The Culture of Early Pennsylvania," *Pennsylvania Magazine of History and Biography* 81 (1957): 119–37; Patricia U. Bonomi, "The Middle Colonies: Embryo of the New Political Order," in Alden T. Vaughan and George A. Billias, eds., *Perspectives in Early American History: Essays in Honor of Richard Morris* (New York: Harper and Row, 1973), pp. 63–92; Milton M. Klein, "Shaping the American Tradition: The Microcosm of Colonial New York," *New York History* 59 (1978): 173–97; Douglas Greenberg, "The Middle Colonies in Recent Historiography," *William and Mary Quarterly* 36 (1979): 396–428.

20. Lemay, *Men of Letters,* pp. xi, 131–32, 191, 257, 296, 299, 303, 307, 311.

21. Ibid., p. 191. J. B. Bell, "Anglican Quill-Drivers in Eighteenth-Century America," *Historical Magazine of the Protestant Episcopal Church* 44 (1975): 23–45, does not appreciate the role of Southern clerics in intellectual developments and concentrates on the New York and Philadelphia ministers. Carol Lee van Voorst, "The Anglican Clergy in Maryland, 1692–1776," Ph.D. diss., Princeton University, 1978, provides the most comprehensive analysis of the provincial clergy available although she rather lightly treats cultural contributions, pp. 292–97.

22. Lemay, *Men of Letters,* pp. 188–89, 245–342; Davis, *Intellectual Life,* 2: 743–44, 3: 1260–61; Breslaw, "Wit, Whimsy, and Politics," pp. 295–306; Breslaw, "The Chronicle as Satire, pp. 29–35; Breslaw, "Dr. Alexander Hamilton and the Enlightenment in Maryland," pp. 139–99; Heintze, "Alexander Malcolm," pp. 226–35.

23. Pat Rogers, *The Augustan Vision* (New York: Barnes and Noble, 1974), pp. 110–15, 129–31.

24. Jack P. Greene, "The Social Origins of the American Revolution: An Evaluation and Interpretation," *Political Science Quarterly* 88 (1973): 1–22; Kenneth A. Lockridge, "Social Change and the Meaning of the American Revolution," *Journal of Social History* 6 (1973): 403–39; Joyce Appleby, "Social Origins," *Journal of American History* 64 (1977–78): 935–58.

25. Winthrop D. Jordon, *White over Black: American Attitudes toward the Negro, 1550–1812* (Chapel Hill: University of North Carolina Press, 1968); David Brion Davis, *The Problem of Slavery in Western Culture* (Ithaca, N.Y.: Cornell University Press,, 1966); Edmund S. Morgan, "Slavery and Freedom" The American Paradox," *Journal of American History* 59 (1972–73): 5–29; Breslaw, "Dr. Alexander Hamilton," pp. 249–57; May, *Enlightenment in America,* pp. 133–35.

26. Barton to Cradock, August 10, 1759, Cradock Papers.

27. The inscription is still readable in Saint Thomas' Churchyard, Garrison, Maryland, but the capitalization and punctuation above comes from a manuscript signed "R.H." in the Cradock Papers.

28. A copy of the broadside appears in Skaggs, "Thomas Cradock," *William and Mary Quarterly* 30 (1973): opposite p. 116.

6
The Manuscripts and Editorial Method

Most of the Cradock Papers are housed in two collections in the Maryland Historical Society, Baltimore. The first is the Maryland Diocesan Archives of the Episcopal Diocese of Maryland, which contains five sermons collected from the Cradock family in the mid-nineteenth century by the Reverend Dr. Ethan Allen, then historiographer of the diocese. To these were added in 1971 approximately 100 manuscript sermons given by the Reverend Thomas Cradock Jensen, who inherited Trentham from the last of Parson Cradock's descendants to own the home. Because Cradock suffered a paralysis in 1763 that plagued him the rest of his life, he dictated some of his compositions to an amanuensis. This explains the variety of hands in which the sermons were written and makes positive attribution of many virtually impossible. The facts that they remained at Trentham over these years and that many of them bear notations such as "Preached at St. Thomas's June 1768" cause one to suspect that many were by Thomas Cradock. The vast majority are clearly in Cradock's hand, assuming that the 1753 "Church Governance" sermon, Titus 1:5, is indeed written by him. The titles given the sermons are mine, but each sermon is also identified by reference to the scriptural text used to begin each address. The Maryland Diocesan Archives collection contains Cradock sermons, not poetry.

The second collection is the Cradock Papers, MS 196, housed in the Manuscripts Division of the Maryland Historical Society. This collection is the gift of Arthur Cradock (1869–1960), the last of Thomas's descendants to own Trentham. Donated in 1953, this collection contains a variety of family papers, mostly from the nineteenth and twentieth centuries. But in Box 6, Miscellany, are found two Cradock sermons (one a typescript copy of a missing manuscript) and all of the manuscript poetry included in this volume. Here are located the "Maryland Eclogues," *The Death of Socrates*, "Trifles," "A Fragment," and "Crurulia." The penmanship of all of these, except "A Fragment" and "Crurulia," appears to be Cradock's. The latter are ascribed to him primarily because of their religious content and their obvious reference to mid-eighteenth century personalities like General James Wolfe and Jeffrey Amherst. It is assumed they were written after his paralysis. It could have been that others in the Trentham circle composed them. These included Dr. Randle Hulse, who wrote Cradock's tombstone epitaph, Cradock's son Arthur, and his daughter, Anne. Some examples of their poetry survive in this same box. None of it appears to be of the caliber of "Crurulia." Also included in this box of miscellany are a few commonplace books, probably kept by his students, and a few other documents relative to his career. There is only one letter to Cradock in the Cradock Papers, MS 196, and no letters from him are known to survive.[1]

Two other Cradock manuscripts remain in the collection of Saint Thomas' Parish, Owings Mills, Maryland. These include the Fast Sermon delivered in memory of the victims of the Lisbon earthquake and the rules for a Methodist-like society that Cradock apparently organized during his pastorate.

The editorial method used in the poetic texts attempts to create a clear-text edition that limits the editorial intrusions in the lines of poetry and that attempts to establish the final authorial intention as far as can be determined. Because in the "Maryland Eclogues" Cradock used his own notation system, my notations incorporate these authorial comments and add editorial commentary where necessary. In the "Eclogues" all comments are Cradock's unless enclosed in brackets. Elsewhere the few Cradock notations receive special editorial comment and all other notations are mine.

As far as possible, the poetry appears in its original form with Cradock's irregularities, inconsistencies, punctuation, capitalization, and misspellings. Because of my desire to provide a clear text containing final authorial intent, I have omitted editorial apparatus from the lines of poetry, but not from the prose in Cradock's notations. Obviously the author's cancellations, or his superscript insertions over original words in a line, or his additions of words or letters to a line are of interest to those concerned with the process of composition. For this reason a section including authorial variations and entitled "Textual Notations" is appended to the end of this volume.

Like that of most historians, my editorial methodology has been influenced by Julian P. Boyd's famous "Editorial Method" essay that began *The Papers of Thomas Jefferson.* However, Boyd's expanded text system has been modified by the criticisms of G. Thomas Tanselle of *The Writings of Herman Melville* series and by the editorial principles enunciated by Fredson Bowers. Because Cradock's poetic efforts are of interest to literary scholars as well as historians, Tanselle's more sophisticated procedures are followed for the most part.[2] Since there is a second version of the fourth eclogue, the variants from the one in the booklet of eclogues are included in the "Textual Notations."

Cradock's punctuation, capitalization, grammar, and spelling are retained throughout without the use of *sic* to indicate such deviations from modern convention. Thus "it's" to indicate the possessive form of "it" is retained, despite modern usage. Editorial insertions in the manuscript are enclosed in square brackets, such as "Ch[ri]stian." Cradock's use of a tilde over certain consonants usually doubled in English and Latin orthography are silently expanded, i.e. "gammon." Where the tilde is omitted the expansion is done by brackets—"gam[m]on." Abbreviated names of speakers in the eclogues and the play are expanded without comment. Also expanded are such abreviations as "yr" for "your," "wch" for "which," "wth" for "with," and "wd" for "would." The thorn, widely used in Cradock's orthography, has been converted to the intended "th," rather than the "y" sometimes used in printing. In most instances such abbreviations utilized a procedure of elevating the last letter or letters in the manscript. This allows distinguishing between "the" and "ye," since in the latter the "e" is not a superscript letter. Elisions in the Latin texts of the eclogue notations are expanded without comment since Cradock had special symbols to shorten double vowels such as "ae," "oe," or "ue."

On the other hand, the ampersand is not expanded to "and." Word shortenings like "shou'd" and "wou'd" and contractions are retained as in the original since they are often used for lyric effect.

Where determination of Cradock's intent is unclear, his normal procedure in similar situations is followed. If there is no precedent, then modern usage is adopted. Such problems generally occur relative to capitalization—particularly with the letters "s" and "j"—and to whether a comma, semicolon, or period is intended.

Another issue concerns Cradock's notations to the "Maryland Eclogues." The Latin text appears in the left page of the text with no indication as to exactly where the imitation is intended. The superscript numbers are inserted in the text at what appears to be the end of the appropriate bucolic passage. The Latin text follows Cradock's peculiar variations from modern editions; obviously his original was Anglicized using "j" and "y" in modern usage.
Often I have added in square brackets additional Latin, which allows a clearer understanding of the following translations.

Cradock's English notations in the eclogues were obviously added after the Latin ones. They are often interlined with the Vergilian poetry. For the purposes of this text the Latin and English notes are separated into distinctive footnotes. Cradock used a superscript "X" in the text to designate the place commented upon. Usually this "X" appears before the word intended. I have followed modern convention and placed elevated numbers after the selected word to indicate location of the comment.

To determine the final authorial intention, I have used what appears to be the last modification of Cradock. Usually it consists of a word or words inserted above a canceled word or words. However, Cradock often failed to cancel, thus indicating indecision as to final intent. Sometimes there are two or three variants in particular lines. To comprehend the earlier versions the reader is referred to the "Textual Notations."

Cradock regularly underlined proper names. These are represented by italics. Occasionally he used underlining to represent an omitted word—"Lord B____" for "Lord Baltimore." More often, since omitted letters were in proper names, he would underline the included and excluded letters, and represent the latter with a dash or dashes to indicate the missing letters "Ch——" for "Christ." Whenever the intent to underline is clear, the missing letters enclosed in brackets will be italicized; when an underlining intent is unclear, the letters are inserted in roman type.

In the "Textual Notations" words identified as written "above" or "below" other words are interlined, while words written "over" other words cover the reading they supplant. A word identified as being inserted "between" two words indicates that with or without a caret, it is clear these words are added to a line and are not supplanting any that may lie below them. If a word is described as being inserted "after" another, it means no interlineation has occurred.

Square brackets—"[are]"—indicate an editorial insertion while angle brackets—"⟨made up of a⟩"—denote a canceled passage. Except for the "Maryland Eclogues" and the two notations in *The Death of Socrates,* all line numbers are an editorial device.

Documentation has been reduced to a minimal essential level. Identification and clarification are provided where necessary, but no attempt has been made to assay the historical significance of particular phrases or events. All annotation utilizes the conventional superscript numbers rather than the single notation at the end of each piece that Boyd often uses with the Jefferson papers.

The editorial objective is a critical edition for use by both literary scholars and historians that pursues and recovers the author's full intentions and presents them in an easily usable printed form. Only with such a presentation will the writings of Thomas Cradock receive the wider audience they deserve.

KEY TO SYMBOLS

[word]	editorial remark
[illegible]	illegible text
⟨word⟩	Cradock's cancellation
⟨illegible⟩	illegible cancellation
[. . .]	blank space left by Cradock or torn MS.

NOTES

1. Avril J. M. Pedley, comp., *The Manuscript Collections of the Maryland Historical Society* (Baltimore, Md.: The Society, 1968), p. 79; David C. Skaggs and F. Garner Ranney, "Thomas Cradock Sermons," *Maryland Historical Magazine*, 67 (1972): 179–80; catalog description, Manuscripts Division, Maryland Historical Society, Baltimore.

2. Julian P. Boyd, editor, *The Papers of Thomas Jefferson* (Princeton, N.J.: Princeton University Press, 1950), 1: xxv–xxxix; G. Thomas Tanselle, "The Editing of Historical Documents," *Studies in Bibliography* 31 (1978): 1–56; Tanselle, "The Editorial Problem of Final Authorial Intention," *Studies in Bibliography* 29 (1976): 167–211; Fredson Bowers, "Transcription of Manuscripts: The Record of Variants," *ibid.*, 212–64; Bowers, ed., *The Dramatic Works in the Beaumont and Fletcher Canon*, (Cambridge, Eng.: At the University Press, 1966), 1: ix–xxv; Bowers, ed., *The Dramatic Works of Thomas Dekker* (Cambridge, Eng.: At the University Press, 1953), 1: ix–xviii. Also providing considerable editorial assistance was: Frank Anderson, Michael B. Frank, and Kenneth M. Sanderson, eds., *Mark Twain's Notebooks and Journals (1875–1873)* (Berkeley: University of California Press, 1975), 1: 575–84.

Bibliography

PRIMARY SOURCES

1. Manuscripts

Bedford Office, London, England.
Bedford Manuscript Letters
Robert Butcher Papers

Guildhall Library, London, England.
J. S. Horne, "Matthew Cradock" (typescript, ca. 1937)

Hall of Records, Annapolis Maryland.
Baltimore County Records:
Debt Books
Deeds
Patents
Wills

John Work Garrett Library, Johns Hopkins University, Baltimore, Maryland.
Alexander Hamilton, "Record Book of the Tuesday Club"

Library of the Representative Church Body, Christ Church Cathedral, Dublin, Erie.
J. B. Leslie, "Fasti of Christ Church Cathedral, Dublin" (typescript)

Maryland Diocesan Archives, Maryland Historical Society, Baltimore, Maryland.
Cradock Papers and Sermons
Ethan Allen, "History of St. Thomas Parish, Baltimore County, Maryland" (manuscript, ca. 1840)

Maryland Historical Society, Baltimore, Maryland.
Cradock Papers
Alexander Hamilton, "History of the Ancient and Honourable Tuesday Club"

Public Record Office, London, England.
Probate Records

Saint Thomas' Parish, Owings Mills, Maryland.
Thomas Cradock, "Fast Sermon, Joel 1:14–15"
Thomas Cradock "Rules for the Society in St. Thomas' Parish in Baltimore County"

Somerset Record Office, Taunton, England.
Saint Cuthbert Parish, Wells:
Baptisms and Burials, 1740 to 1787

Marriages, 1740 to 1754
Overseers Accounts, 1728–51

Staffordshire Record Office, Stafford, England.
Collecting Rentals for the Manor of Trentham
Court Rolls, Manor of Trentham
Leveson-Gower Papers

2. *Published Materials*

Anderson, Frank; Frank, Michael B., and Sanderson, Kenneth M.; eds. *Mark Twain's Notebooks and Journals (1855–1873).* Berkeley: University of California Press, 1975.

Beresford, John, ed. *The Diary of a County Parson: The Reverend James Woodforde, 1758–1781.* 5 vols. Oxford: Oxford University Press, 1926–31.

Berkeley, Edmund, and Berkeley, Dorothy Smith, eds. *The Reverend John Clayton, A Parson with a Scientific Mind: His Scientific Writings and Other Papers.* Virginia Historical Society Documents, vol. 6. Charlottesville: University Press of Virginia, 1965.

Boethius. *The Consolation of Philosophy.* Introduction: by Irwin Edman. New York: Modern Library, 1943.

Bowers, Fredson, ed. *The Dramatic Works in the Beaumont and Fletcher Canon.* Cambridge, Eng.: At the University Press, 1966.

———. *The Dramatic Works of Thomas Dekker.* Cambridge, Eng.: At the University Press, 1953.

Boyd, Julian P., ed. *The Papers of Thomas Jefferson.* Vol. 1. Princeton, N.J.: Princeton University Press, 1950.

Browne, William Hand, et al. *The Archives of Maryland.* 71 vols. Baltimore: Maryland Historical Society, 1883–1971.

Butt, John, ed. *The Poems of Alexander Pope.* New Haven, Conn.: Yale University Press, 1963.

The Calvert Papers, No. 2. Maryland Historical Society, Fund Publication No. 34. Baltimore, Md.: The Society, 1894.

Canby, Courtlandt, ed. "Robert Munford's *The Patriots.*" *William and Mary Quarterly* 6 (1949):437–503.

Cradock, Thomas. *A Poetical Translation of the Psalms of David from Buchanan's Latin into English Verse.* London: R. Ware, 1754.

———. *A New Version of the Psalms of David.* Annapolis, Md.: Jonas Green, 1756.

———. *Two Sermons with a Preface Shewing the Author's Reasons for Publishing Them.* Annapolis, Md.: Jonas Green, 1747.

Davis, Richard Beale, ed. *Collected Poems of Samuel Davies, 1723–1761.* Gainesville, Fla.: Scholars' Facsimiles and Reprints, 1968.

———. *The Colonial Virginia Satirist: Mid-Eighteenth-Century Commentaries on Politics, Religion, and Society.* American Philosophical Society *Transactions,* new series, vol. 57, pt. 1 (Philadelphia, Pa., 1967).

———, C. Hugh Holman, and Louis D. Rubin, Jr., eds. *Southern Writing, 1585–1920*. New York: Odyssey Press, 1970.

Eddis, William. *Letters from America*. Edited by Aubrey C. Land. Cambridge, Mass.: Harvard University Press, 1969.

Edmonds, J. M., ed. *Elegy and Iambus . . . with the Anacreontea*. 2 vols., Cambridge, Mass.: Harvard University Press, 1931.

———, trans. *The Greek Bucolic Poets*. Cambridge, Mass.: Harvard University Press, 1912.

Farish, Hunter Dickinson, ed. *Journal & Letters of Philip Vickers Fithian, 1773–1774: A Plantation Tutor of the Old Dominion*. Williamsburg, Va.: Colonial Williamsburg, 1957.

"A Friendly Character of the Late Rev'd. Thomas Cradock . . . " London: Thomas Worrall, 1770? (Personal collection of late Rev. Thomas C. Jenson, Owings Mills, Maryland.)

Greene, Jack P., ed. *The Diary of Colonel Landon Carter of Sabine Hall, 1752–1778*. 2 vols., Virginia Historical Society Documents, vols. 4–5. Charlottesville: University Press of Virginia, 1965.

Hubbell, Jay B., and Adair, Douglass, eds. "Robert Munford's *The Candidates*." *William and Mary Quarterly* 5 (1948):217–57.

Jones, John Gwilym, ed. *Goronwy Owen's Virginia Adventures: His Life, Poetry, and Literary Opinions with a Translation of His Virginia Letters*. Botetourt Bibliographical Society Publications, No. 2. Williamsburg, Va.: The Society, 1969.

Lemay, J. A. Leo, ed. "Hamilton's Literary History of the *Maryland Gazette*." *William and Mary Quarterly* 23 (1966):273–85.

———, ed. *A Poem by John Markland of Virginia*. Williamsburg, Va.: The William Parks Club, 1965.

Martialis, Marcus Valerius. *Epigrams*. Translated by Walter C. A. Kerr. 2 vols. Cambridge, Mass.: Harvard University Press, 1947.

Maryland Gazette, Annapolis, Maryland, 1745–1770.

Page, T. E., ed. *P. Vergili Maronis Bucolica et Georgia*. London: Macmillan, 1910.

Papenfuse, Edward C., ed. "An Undelivered Defense of a Winning Cause: Charles Carroll of Carrollton's 'Remarks on the Proposed Federal Constitution.'" *Maryland Historical Magazine* 71 (1976):220–51.

Riley, Edward Miles, ed. *The Journal of John Horrower: An Indentured Servant in the Colony of Virginia, 1773–1776*. Williamsburg, Va.: Colonial Williamsburg, 1963.

Servies, James A., and Dolmetsch, Carl, eds. *The Poems of Charles Hansford*. Virginia Historical Society Documents, vol. 1. Chapel Hill: University of North Carolina Press, 1961.

Skaggs, David Curtis, ed. "Thomas Cardock's Sermon on the Governance of Maryland's Established Church." *William and Mary Quarterly* 27 (1970):630"3.

Tinling, Marion, ed. *The Correspondence of the Three William Byrds of Westover,*

Virginia, 1684–1766. 2 vols. Virginia Historical Society Documents, vols. 12–13. Charlottesville: University Press of Virginia, 1977.

Trentham Parish Register. Staffordshire Parish Register Society, *Publications* 28 (Stafford, Eng., 1906).

Woodfin, Maude, ed. *Another Secret Diary of William Byrd of Westover, 1739–1741: With Letters & Literary Exercises, 1696–1726*. Translated by Marion Tinling. Richmond, Va.: Dietz Press, 1942.

Wright, Louis B., ed. *The Prose Works of William Byrd of Westover: Narratives of a Colonial Virginian*. Cambridge, Mass.: Harvard University Press, 1966.

———, and Tinling, Marion, eds. *The Secret Diary of William Byrd of Westover, 1709–1712*. Richmond, Va.: Dietz Press, 1941.

———, *William Byrd of Virginia: The London Diary (1717–1721) and Other Writings*. New York: Oxford University Press, 1958.

SECONDARY SOURCES

1. Articles And Books

Aldridge, A. O. "Benjamin Franklin and the *Maryland Gazette*." *Maryland Historical Magazine* 44 (1949):177–89.

Allen, Ethan. "Sketches of the Colonial Clergy of Maryland: Thomas Cradock." *American Church Review* 7 (1854):308–11.

———. *The Garrison Church: Sketches of the History of St. Thomas' Parish, Garrison Forest, Baltimore County, Maryland, 1742–1852*, ed. by Hobart Smith. New York: James Pott & Co., 1898.

Appleby, Joyce. "The Social Origins of American Revolutionary Ideology." *Journal of American History* 64 (1977–78):935–58.

———. "Ideology and Theory: Tensions between Political and Economic Liberalism in Seventeenth-Century England." *American Historical Review* 81 (1976):499–515.

Arner, Robert D. "Clio's *Rhimes:* History and Satire in Ebenezer Cooke's 'History of Bacon's Rebellion.'" *Southern Literary Journal* 6 (1974):91–106.

———. "Ebenezer Cooke: Satire in the Colonial South." *Southern Literary Journal* 8 (1975–76):153–64.

———. "Ebenezer Cooke's *The Sot-Weed Factor:* The Structure of Satire." *Southern Literary Journal* 4 (1971):33–47.

———. "The Quest for Freedom: Style and Meaning in Robert Beverley's *History and Present State of Virginia*." *Southern Literary Journal* 8 (1976):79–98.

———. "Westover and the Wilderness: William Byrd's Images of Virginia." *Southern Literary Journal* 7 (1975):105–23.

Bain, Robert A. "The Composition and Publication of *The Present State of Virginia and the College*." *Early American Literature* 6 (1971):31–54.

———. "A Note on James Blair and the Southern Plain Style." *Southern Literary Journal* 4 (1971):68–73.

Baine, Rodney M. *Robert Munford: America's First Comic Dramatist.* Athens: University of Georgia Press, 1967.

Baker, Thomas. *History of the College of St. John the Evangelist.* Edited by John E. B. Mayor. 2 vols. Cambridge, Eng., At the University Press, 1869.

Barrell, John, and Bull, John, eds. *A Book of English Pastoral Verse.* New York: Oxford University Press, 1975.

Baumann, Roland P. *George Stevenson (1718–1783): Conservative as Revolutionary.* Cumberland County Historical Society Publications, vol. 10, no. 1. Carlisle, Pa.: The Society, 1978.

Beirne, Rosamond R., and Scharff, John H., *William Buckland, 1734–1774: Architect of Virginia and Maryland.* Baltimore: Maryland Historical Society, 1958.

Bell, James B. "Anglican Quill-Drivers in Eighteenth Century America," *Historical Magazine of the Protestant Episcopal Church* 44 (1975):23–45.

Bercovitch, Sacvan. *The American Jeremiad.* Madison: University of Wisconsin Press, 1978.

Berkeley, Edmund, and Berkeley, Dorothy Smith. *Dr. John Mitchell: The Man Who Made the Map of North America.* Chapel Hill: University of North Carolina Press, 1974.

Bertelson, David. *The Lazy South.* New York: Oxford University Press, 1967.

Boas, Frederick S. *An Introduction to Eighteenth Century Drama, 1700–1780.* Oxford, Eng.: Clarendon Press, 1953.

Bonomi, Patricia U. "The Middle Colonies: Embryo of the New Political Order," pp. 63–92, in Alden T. Vaughan and George A. Billias, eds., *Perspectives in Early American History: Essays in Honor of Richard B. Morris.* New York: Harper and Row, 1973.

Boorstin, Daniel J. *The Americans: The Colonial Experience.* New York: Knopf, 1958.

Bowers, Fredson. "Transcription of Manuscripts: The Record of Variants." *Studies in Bibliography* 29 (1976):212–64.

Breslaw, Elaine G. "The Chronicle as Satire: Dr. Hamilton's History of the Tuesday Club." *Maryland Historical Magazine* 70 (1975):129–48.

———. "Wit, Whimsy and Politics: The Uses of Satire by the Tuesday Club of Annapolis." *William and Mary Quarterly* 32 (1975):295–306.

Bridenbaugh, Carl. *Myths and Realities: Societies of the Colonial South.* Baton Rouge: Louisiana State University Press, 1952.

Brinton, Crane. *The Shaping of Modern Thought.* Englewood Cliffs, N.J.: Prentice-Hall, 1963.

Bullitt, J. M. *Jonathan Swift and the Anatomy of Satire.* Cambridge, Mass.: Harvard University Press, 1953.

Cavenagh-Mainwaring, J. G. "The Mainwarings of Whitmore and Biddulph in the County of Stafford." *Staffordshire Historical Collections,* 3d series (1933), part 2:1–212.

Carroll, Charles Michael. "A Classical Setting for a Classical Poem: Philidor's *Carmen Saeculare*," *Studies in Eighteenth-Century Culture* 6 (1977):97–111.

Clive, John, and Bailyn, Bernard, "England's Cultural Provinces: Scotland and America." *William and Mary Quarterly* 9 (1954):200–213.

Cohen, Edward H. "The Elegies of Ebenezer Cooke." *Early American Literature* 4 (1969):49–72.

———. "The 'Second Edition' of the Sot-Weed Factor." *American Literature* 42 (1970):289–303.

Cohen, Ralph. "The Augustan Mode in English Poetry." *Eighteenth-Century Studies* 1 (1967–68):3–32.

Commager, Henry Steele. "The American Enlightenment and the Ancient World: A Study in Paradox." *Proceedings of the Massachusetts Historical Society* 83 (1972):3–15.

Cooper, John Gilbert. *The Life of Socrates, Collected from the Memorabilia of Xenophon, and the Dialogues of Plato, and Illustrated Farther by Aristotle, Diodorus Siculus, etc.* 3rd ed., London: R. Dodsley, 1750.

Cragg, Gerald R. *Reason and Authority in the Eighteenth Century*. Cambridge, Eng.: At the University Press, 1964.

Crane, R.S. "Suggestions toward a Genealogy of the 'Man of Feeling.'" *Journal of English Literary History* 1 (1934):205–30.

Crawford, Richard. "An Historian's Introduction to Early American Music." *Proceedings of the American Antiquarian Society* 89 (1979):261–98.

———. "Watts for Singing: Metrical Poetry in American Sacred Tunebooks, 1761–1785." *Early American Literature* 11 (1976):139–46.

Curtis, Lewis P. *Anglican Moods of the Eighteenth Century*. New Haven, Conn.: Archon Books, 1966.

Daniel-Rops, H. *The Church in the Eighteenth Century*. Translated by John Warrington. New York: E. P. Dutton, 1964.

Davis, Herbert J. *The Satire of Jonathan Swift*. New York: Macmillan, 1947.

Davis, Richard Beale. *Intellectual Life in the Colonial South, 1585–1763*. 3 vols. Knoxville: University of Tennessee Press, 1978.

———. "James Reid, Colonial Virginia Poet and Moral and Religious Essayist." *Virginia Magazine of History and Biography* 79 (1971):3–19.

———. *Literature and Society in Early Virginia: 1608–1840*. Baton Rouge: Louisiana State University Press, 1973.

Davis, Thomas M., and Davis, Virginia L. "Edward Taylor's Metrical Paraphrases of the Psalms." *American Literature* 48 (1976–77):455–70.

Dolmetsch, Carl. "William Byrd II: Comic Dramatist?" *Early American Literature* 6 (1971):18–30.

———. "William Byrd II, The Augustan Writer as 'Exile' in His Own Country." *Virginia Quarterly Review* 48 (1972):145–49.

———. "William Byrd of Westover as an Augustan Poet." *Studies in Literary Imagination* 9 (1976):69–77.

Dombree, Bonamy. *English Literature in the Early Eighteenth Century.* Oxford, Eng.: Clarendon Press, 1959.

Ehrenpreis, Irvin. *Literary Meanings and Augustan Values.* Charlottesville: University Press of Virginia, 1974.

———. "Meaning: Implicit and Explicit," pp. 117–55, in Phillip Harth, ed., *New Approaches to Eighteenth Century Literature: Selected Papers from the English Institute.* New York: Columbia University Press, 1974.

Elder, William V. III. "Bloomsbury, a Cradock House in the Worthington Valley," *Maryland Historical Magazine* 53 (1958):371–75.

Elliott-Binns, L. E. *The Early Evangelicals: A Religious and Social Study.* Greenwich, Conn.: Seabury Press, 1953.

Emerson, Everett E., ed. *Major Writers of Early American Literature.* Madison: University of Wisconsin Press, 1972.

Forman, Henry C. *Tidewater Maryland Architecture and Gardens.* New York: Architectural Book Publishing Co., 1956.

Gay, Peter. *The Enlightenment: An Interpretation—The Rise of Modern Paganism.* New York: Knopf, 1966.

Gilborn, Craig. "Samuel Davies' Sacred Muse." *Journal of Presbyterian History* 41 (1963):63–79.

Gohdes, Clarence, ed. "Old Virginia Georgics." *Southern Literary Journal* 9 (1978–79):44–53.

Greenberg, Douglas. "The Middle Colonies in Recent Historiography." *William and Mary Quarterly* 36 (1979):396–428.

Greene, Donald. "Augustinianism and Empiricism: A Note on Eighteenth-Century English Intellectual History." *Eighteenth-Century Studies* 1 (1967–68):33–68.

Greene, Jack P. "Search for Identity: An Interpretation of Selected Patterns of Social Response in Eighteenth-Century America." *Journal of Social History* 3 (1969–70):189–220.

———. "The Social Origins of the American Revolution: An Evaluation and Interpretation." *Political Science Quarterly* 88 (1973):1–22.

Greenslade, M. W., ed. *A History of the County of Stafford (Victoria History of the Counties of England).* Vol. 3. London: University of London Press, 1970.

Gribbon, William. "Rollin's Histories and American Republicanism." *William and Mary Quarterly* 29 (1972):611–22.

Halsband, Robert. *The Life of Lady Mary Wortley Montagu.* London: Oxford University Press, 1956.

Hampden, John. *Eighteenth-Century Plays.* New York: E. P. Dutton, 1961.

Hanley, Thomas O'Brien. *Charles Carroll of Carrollton: The Making of a Revolutionary Gentleman.* Washington, D.C.: Catholic University of America Press, 1970.

Hardy, S. M., and Baily, R. C. "The Downfall of the Gower Interest in the Staffordshire Boroughs, 1800–30." *Staffordshire Historical Collections,* 3d series (1950–51):267–301.

Heintze, James R. "Alexander Malcom: Musician, Clergyman, and Schoolmaster." *Maryland Historical Magazine* 73 (1978):226–35.

Humphreys, A. R. *The Augustan World: Life and Letters in Eighteenth-Century England.* 2d ed. London: Methuen and Co., 1964.

———. "Literature and Religion in Eighteenth Century England." *Journal of Ecclesiastical History* 3 (1952):152–90.

Johnson, James W. "The Meaning of 'Augustan.'" *Journal of the History of Ideas* 19 (1958):507–22.

Jordan, Winthrop D. *White over Black: American Attitudes toward the Negro, 1550–1812.* Chapel Hill: University of North Carolina Press, 1968.

Keith, Charles P. *Chronicles of Pennsylvania from the English Revolution to the Peace of Aix-la-Chapelle, 1688–1748.* 2 vols. Philadelphia: Privately Printed, 1917.

Kettle, Ann J. "The Struggle for the Lichfield Interest, 1747–68." *Staffordshire Historical Collections,* 4th Series, 6 (1970):115–35.

Klein, Milton M. "Shaping the American Tradition: The Microcosm of Colonial New York." *New York History* 59 (1978):173–97.

Klingberg, Frank J. "The Expansion of the Anglican Church in the Eighteenth Century." *Historical Magazine of the Protestant Episcopal Church* 16 (1947):292–301.

Kraus, Michael. *The Atlantic Civilization: Eighteenth-Century Origins.* Ithaca, N.Y.: Cornell University Press, 1949.

Kropf, C. R. "Libel and Satire in the Eighteenth Century." *Eighteenth-Century Studies* 8 (1974–75):153–68.

Larson, Barbara A. "Samuel Davies and the Rhetoric of the New Light." *Speech Monographs* 28 (1971):207–16.

Leach, Eleanor Winsor. *Vergil's Eclogues: Landscapes of Experience.* Ithaca, N.Y.: Cornell University Press, 1974.

Le Gates, Marlene. "The Cult of True Womanhood in Eighteenth-Century Thought." *Eighteenth-Century Studies* 10 (1976–77):21–39.

Lemay, J. A. Leo. *A Calendar of American Poetry in the Colonial Newspapers and Magazines and in Major English Magazines through 1765.* Worcester, Mass.: American Antiquarian Society, 1972.

———, ed. *Essays in Early Virginia Literature Honoring Richard Beale Davis.* New York: Burt Franklin, 1977.

———. *Men of Letters in Colonial Maryland.* Knoxville: University of Tennessee Press, 1972.

———. "Robert Bolling and the Bailment of Colonel Chiswell." *Early American Literature* 6 (1971):99–142.

Lewis, C. Day. *The Eclogues and Georgics of Virgil.* Garden City, N.Y.: Doubleday, 1964.

Litto, Frederic M. "Addison's *Cato* in the Colonies." *William and Mary Quarterly* 23 (1966):431–49.

Lockridge, Kenneth A. "Social Change and the Meaning of the American Revolution." *Journal of Social History* 6 (1973):403–39.

Lounsberry, Barbara. "Sermons and Satire: Anti-Catholicism in Sterne." *Philological Quarterly* 55 (1976):403–17.

Lovejoy, Arthur O. *The Great Chain of Being: A Study in the History of Ideas.* Cambridge, Mass.: Harvard University Press, 1936.

May, Henry F. *The Enlightenment in America.* New York: Oxford University Press, 1976.

Marambaud, Pierre. *William Byrd of Westover, 1674–1744.* Charlottesville: University Press of Virginia, 1971.

Mills, Frederick V. "Anglican Expansion in Colonial America, 1761–1775." *Historical Magazine of the Protestant Episcopal Church* 39 (1970):315–24.

Montagu, Mary Wortley. *The Letters and Works of Lady Mary Wortley Montagu edited by her Great-Grandson Lord Wharncliffe with Additions and Corrections. . . . by W. May Thomas.* 2 vols. London: Swan Sonnenschein and Co., 1893.

Moorman, J. R. H. *A History of the Church in England.* 3d ed. London: Adam and Charles Black, 1976.

Morgan, Edmund S. "The Puritan Ethic and the American Revolution." *William and Mary Quarterly* 24 (1967):3–43.

Myers, R. M. "The Old Dominion Looks to London: A Study of English Literary Influences on the *Virginia Gazette,* 1736–1766." *Virginia Magazine of History and Biography* 54 (1946):195–217.

Namier, Lewis. *The Structure of Politics at the Accession of George III.* 2d ed. London: Macmillan, 1957.

Nitchie, Elizabeth. *Vergil and the English Poets.* New York: AMS Press, 1966.

Nussbaum, Felicity A. "Pope's 'To a Lady' and the Eighteenth-Century Woman." *Philological Quarterly* 54 (1975):444–56.

Olson, Alison Gilbert. "The Commissaries of the Bishop of London in Colonial Politics," pp. 109–24, in Alison Gilbert Olson and Richard Maxwell Brown, eds. *Anglo-American Political Relations.* New Brunswick, N. J.: Rutgers University Press, 1970.

Ormsby-Lennon, Hugh. "Poetic Standards on the Early Augustan Background." *Studies in Eighteenth-Century Culture* 5 (1976):253–80.

Overton, John H., and Relton, Frederick. *The English Church from the Accession of George I to the End of the Eighteenth Century (1714–1800).* London: Macmillan, 1906.

Pennington, D. A. "County and Country: Staffordshire in Civil War Politics, 1640–1644." *North Staffordshire Journal of Field Studies* 6 (1966):12–24.

Petrakis, Byron. "Jester in the Pulpit: Sterne and Pulpit Eloquence." *Philological Quarterly* 51 (1972):430–47.

Pilcher, George William. *Samuel Davies, Apostle of Dissent in Colonial Virginia.* Knoxville: University of Tennessee Press, 1971.

Pleasants, J. Hall. *Two Hundred and Fifty Years of Paintings in Maryland.* Baltimore, Md.: Baltimore Museum of Art, 1945.

Pocock, J. G. A. "The Classical Theory of Deference." *American Historical Review* 81 (1976):516–23.

Price, Jacob M. "One Family's Empire: The Russell-Lee-Clark Connection in Maryland, Britain, and India, 1707–1857." *Maryland Historical Magazine* 72 (1977):165–225.

Putnam, Michael C. J. *Virgil's Pastoral Art: Studies in the Eclogues.* Princeton, N. J.: Princeton University Press, 1970.

Rankin, Hugh F. *The Theater in Colonial America.* Chapel Hill: University of North Carolina Press, 1965.

Reps, John W. *Tidewater Towns: City Planning in Colonial Virginia and Maryland.* Williamsburg, Va.: Colonial Williamsburg, 1972.

Richey, Russell E. "Effects of Toleration on Eighteenth-Century Dissent." *Journal of Religion* 8 (1975): 350–63.

Rightmyer, Nelson W. "The Character of the Anglican Clergy of Colonial Maryland." *Maryland Historical Magazine* 44 (1949):229–50.

———. *Maryland's Established Church.* Baltimore: Diocese of Maryland, 1956.

Rollin, Charles. *The Ancient History of the Egyptians, Carthaginians, Assyrians, Medes, and Persians, Grecians, and Macedonians.* 2 vols. Cincinnati, Ohio: Applegate and Co., 1856.

Rouse, Parke, Jr. *James Blair of Virginia.* Chapel Hill: University of North Carolina Press, 1971.

Scott, Robert F. *Admissions to the College of St. John the Evangelist in the University of Cambridge.* 4 vols., Cambridge, Eng.: At the University Press, 1882–1931.

Skaggs, David Curtis. "The Great Chain of Being in Eighteenth-Century Maryland: The Paradox of Thomas Cradock." *Historical Magazine of the Protestant Episcopal Church* 45 (1976):155–64.

———. "Thomas Cradock and the Chesapeake Golden Age." *William and Mary Quarterly* 30 (1973):93–116.

———, and Hartdagen, Gerald E. "Sinners and Saints: Anglican Clerical Conduct in Colonial Maryland." *Historical Magazine of the Protestant Episcopal Church* 47 (1978):177–95.

———, and Ranney, F. Garner. "Thomas Cradock Sermons." *Maryland Historical Magazine* 67 (1972):179–80.

Sykes, Norman. "The Sermons of a Country Parson: James Woodforde in His Pulpit." *Theology: A Monthly Review* 38 (1939):97–106, 341–52.

———. *Church and State in England in the XVIIIth Century.* Cambridge, Eng.: At the University Press, 1934.

Tanselle, G. Thomas. "The Editing of Historical Documents." *Studies in Bibliography* 31 (1978): 1–56.

———. "The Editorial Problem of Final Authorian Intention." *Studies in Bibliography* 29 (1976): 167–211.

Taylor, A. B. *Socrates: The Man and His Thought.* Garden City, N.Y.: Doubleday, 1953.

Tillotson, Geoffrey. *Augustan Studies.* London: Athlone Press, 1961.

Tolles, Frederick B. "The Culture of Early Pennsylvania." *Pennsylvania Magazine of History and Biography* 81 (1957): 119–37.

Traherne, John Montgomery. *Historical Notices of Sir Matthew Cradock, Knt. of Swansea in the Reigns of Henry VII and VIII*. Llandovery, Wales: W. Rees, 1840.

Turner, Maxine. "Three Eighteenth-Century Revisions of the *Bay Psalm Book*." *New England Quarterly* 45 (1972): 270–72.

Vivian, James F., and Vivian, Jean H. "The Reverend Isaac Campbell: An Anti-Lockian Whig." *Historical Magazine of the Protestant Episcopal Church* 39 (1970): 71–89.

Wallace, Paul A. W. *Conrad Weiser, 1696–1760, Friend of Colonist and Mohawk*. Philadelphia: University of Pennsylvania Press, 1945.

Walton, Joseph S. *Conrad Weiser and the Indian Policy of Colonial Pennsylvania*. Philadelphia: George W. Jacobs, 1900.

Ward, A. W., and Waller, A. R., eds. *From Steele and Addison to Pope and Swift*. The Cambridge History of English Literature, vol. 9. Cambridge, Eng.: At the University Press, 1913.

Ward, Kathryn Painter. "The First Professional Theater in Maryland and Its Colonial Setting." *Maryland Historical Magazine* 70 (1975): 29–44.

Warne, Arthur. *Church and State in Eighteenth-Century Devon*. New York: Augustus M. Kelley, 1969.

Wedgwood, Josiah C. "Staffordshire Parliamentary History." *Staffordshire Historical Collections*, 3d series (1919–20).

Wheeler, Joseph Towne. "Books Owned by Marylanders, 1700–1776." *Maryland Historical Magazine* 35 (1940): 337–53.

———. "Literary Culture in Eighteenth-Century Maryland, 1700–1776: Summary of Findings." *Maryland Historical Magazine* 38 (1943): 273–76.

Williams, John Rogers, comp. "A Catalogue of the Books in the Library of 'Councillor' Robert Carter of Nomini Hall, Westmoreland County, Virginia." *William and Mary Quarterly*, 1st series, 10 (1901–2): 232–41.

Woodward, C. Vann. "The Southern Ethic in a Puritan World." *William and Mary Quarterly* 25 (1968): 343–70.

Worcester, David. *The Art of Satire*. Cambridge, Mass.: Harvard University Press, 1940.

Wright, Louis B. *The Cultural Life of the American Colonies, 1607–1763*. New York: Harper and Row, 1957.

———. *The First Gentlemen of Virginia: Intellectual Qualities of the Early Ruling Class*. San Marino, Calif.: Huntington Library, 1940.

———. "Literature in the Colonial South," *Huntington Library Quarterly* 10 (1947): 297–315.

Zimmer, Anne Y. *Jonathan Boucher: Loyalist in Exile*. Detroit, Mich.: Wayne State University Press, 1978.

Zuckerman, Michael. "William Byrd's Family," *Perspectives in American History* 12 (1979): 255–311.

2. Reference Works

Dictionary of American Biography, Edited by Allen Johnson and Dumas Malone. 20 vols. New York: Charles Scribner's Sons, 1928–37.

Dictionary of National Biography. Edited by Leslie Stephen and Sidney Lee. 66 vols. London: Oxford University Press, 1885–1901.

Foster, Joseph, comp. *Alumni Oxonienses: The Members of the University of Oxford, 1715–1886*. Vol. l. London: Parker and Co., 1882.

A General and Heraldic Dictionary of the Peerage and Baronetage of the British Empire. London: J. Burke, 1837.

Pedley, Arvil J., comp. *The Manuscript Collections of the Maryland Historical Society*. Baltimore, Md.: The Society, 1968.

Venn, John, and Venn, J. A., comps. *Alumni Cantabrigienses . . . Part 1 . . . to 1751*. 4 vols. Cambridge, Eng.: At the University Press, 1922–27.

3. Theses, Dissertations, and Papers

Black, Mary Childs. "The Theatre in Colonial Annapolis." M.A. thesis, George Washington University, 1952.

Boyd, Jerritus. "The Golden Age of Maryland Culture, 1750–1770." M.A. thesis, University of Maryland, 1967.

Breslaw, Elaine. "Dr. Alexander Hamilton and the Enlightenment in Maryland." Ph.D. diss., University of Maryland, 1973.

Micklus, Robert. "Dr. Alexander Hamilton's *The History of the Tuesday Club*." Ph.D. diss., University of Delaware, 1980.

Stone, Reppard. "An Evaluative Study of Alexander Malcom's *Treatis of Music:* Speculative, Practical and Historical." Ph.D. diss., Catholic University of America, 1974.

van Voorst, Carol Lee. "The Anglican Clergy in Maryland, 1692–1776." Ph.D. diss., Princeton University, 1978.

Welsh, William Jeffrey. "The Rhetoric of Thomas Cradock, 1744–1770: A Study in the History of Ideas." MA thesis, Bowling Green State University, 1977.

A watercolor of the original St. Thomas' Church used to illustrate Ethan Allen *The Garrison Church: Sketches of the History of St. Thomas' Parish, Garrison Forest, Baltimore County, Maryland, 1742–1852*, edited by Hobart Smith (New York, 1898) and reprinted therefrom.

Part II
Cradock's Poetry

Who can thy great beneficence express,
The various gifts which thy mercies bless?
E'en while with gratitude thy love he sings,
Man rests beneath the shadow of thy wings.
On him thou nameless bounties dost bestow;
To him the rivers of thy pleasures flow;
From thee life's fountain springs; from thee a ray
The mind illumes, and spreads eternal day.

Thomas Cradock, *A New Version of the Psalms of David* (1756), Psalm 36

7
Devotional Poetry

To *Thyrsis*[1]

While *Vice* triumphant lords it o'er the plain,
And holds o'er abject man her tyrant-reign;
While poor dejected *Virtue* hangs her head,
Her dictates quite despis'd, her influence dead;
While hoary *Age* forgets its wonted lore,
And lives a pattern of good deeds no more;
While *Youth*, no more by modest duty bound,
Of vice or folly runs one constant round;
In fine, while almost all their bane pursue,
Nor have one gen'rous God-like aim in view;
Dear *Thyrsis*, scorn the listless, impious, throng,
And harken to the precepts of my song.
Observe the muse that tempts the moral lay,
And boldly follow, where she leads the way;
With me be brave in virtue's injur'd cause,
Gain thou from heav'n, if not from men, applause.

First then, to *Him*, who bad the first *to be*,
Th' all-good, all-wise, all pow'rful *Deity*;
With humblest awe, thy faithful pray'r address,
To guide thee thro' this *thorny Wilderness*.
For Oh! without his providential care,
How vain our most important projects are?
The man, who travels life's uncertain way,
And fondly cries, *I will not err to Day*,
Deceives himself; for, mortal, canst thou tell,
How oft thou swervest ev'n from *thinking* well?

O *Thought*! from *thee* what anxious griefs arise:
How great the pain, to labour to be wise?
What various triffles will the heart amuse,
And stagger all her pow'rs, ere we can chuse?
And in the choice, how oft do we prefer
What's more absur'd to what is just and clear,
Cherish *Ideas* wandering, low and gay,
And cast each serious, useful thought away.
How fatal the result! - my friend beware,

And fall not heedless in the baneful snare.
Ah! let not *Wit* profane thy heart engage;
Read ev'ry moral, ev'ry sacred page.
To *Reason's* strength call *Revelation's* aid,
Nor be by too presuming *Self* betray'd;
By *Both* assisted, soon thou'lt gain the field,
Without the aid of *Both* as soon wilt yield.
Then passions plead, and prejudice has sway,
And poor insulted *Virtue* dies away.

And now the *Tongue* demands thy utmost care,
'Tis wise, the mischiefs of the *Tongue* to fear.
How oft are schemes the noblest, closest laid,
By one unthinking, guardless word betray'd?
What guilt, what shame in loose expression lies?
And yet how few can be in silence wise?
Ah friend! the silly rant of fools defy,
The nauseous ribaldry, the senseless lie;
The hideous blasphemy, the envious sneer;
The killing scandal and the biting jeer.
Why should you blush at what yourself have said?
Why blushes stain the face of *that fair Maid*?
Why will you thus, where nought can tempt, offend?
Why shame your wife, your father or your friend?
Why anger heav'n without a *seeming Cause*?
Or why affront great nature's purest laws?
Why, lastly, hurt his character and fame,
Whom, tho' you scarcely know, but by his name,
Yet for mere folly's sake, you censure and condem?
In prudent silence, rather seek to shine,
And pay your offrings at *her* sacred shrine.
She heaps applause, if you her rules obey,
Gives you a temper sweet, serene and gay,
And chases all chagrin, and all remorse away.

A just regard to *Action* next succeeds:
Foul *Thoughts*, foul *Words* are bad, but worst foul *Deeds*.
The maid deflour'd, the easy friend deceiv'd;
The helpless orphan of his rights betray'd;
The pow'r divine disclaim'd, the breach of troth;
The *Midnight* revel, and the *Mid-day* sloth
The *Poor* neglected, and the *Villain* fed;
Religion with her *institutes* betray'd———
O what a scene of guilt! How wretched *He*

O'er whelm'd with half this load of infamy!
And yet look round———such is the hideous face
Of things *below*———————————
But turn thine eyes——a different prospect view,
And the blest path now pointed out pursue.
And firm regard to *Heav'n* devoutly paid;
His pow'r acknowledg'd, and implor'd *his* aid;
The *Parent's, Sov'reign's, Reason's* laws
observ'd;
The *Naked* cloath'd, the *Fainting* soul preserv'd;
The duties of each station well perform'd,
And in her strongest holds *vice* bravely storm'd;
Goodness, by pattern more than precept, taught;
And *Wisdom's* awful rules for ever fought——
These, these have charms——*these, these* pursue, my
friend!
On *these* e'en here the surest joys attend;
And *these* will give thee bliss, which ne'er shall end.

Maryland, Baltimore County, written in the year 1744.

Note

1. *American Magazine or Monthly Chronicle for the British Colonies* 1 (1757-58):605-7. "To Thyrsis" is ascribed to Cradock in J. A. Leo Lemay, *A Calender of American Poetry in the Colonial Newspapers and Magazines and in the Major English Magazines through 1765* (Worcester, Mass.: American Antiquarian Society, 1972), p. 206. Thyrsis is the shepherd in the first bucolic poem of Theocritus and may signify a pastoral innocent to whom the poet is giving advice. In the original, *Thyrsis* in the title and in line 11 is printed in small capital letters rather than in italics.

A POEM[1]

Sacred to the Memory of Miss Margaret Lawson, Miss Elizabeth Lawson, Miss Dorothy Lawson, and Miss Elizabeth Read.

As whilom roving o'er the lonely Plain,
Pensive and sad, my Soul distract with Grief
For unexpected woes; yet still intent
My Thoughts on Thee, O God, and on thy Ways,
Thy deep mysterious Ways with mortal Man;
Struck with thy various Dispensations, long
In humble Adoration lost, I stood.
"Surely (I said), the God that's just and wise,
"And good and pow'rful needs must act aright:
"And who shall say, *What dost thou?* *to what end?*"
Yet still, when anxious, I presum'd to scan
His late tremendous Act; t'explore the Cause,
Why sweetest Innocence and loveliest Youth,
Fell such an early Sacrifice to Death:
Why beauteous *Margaretta*, peerless Maid!
The two *Elizas*, faultless both as fair,
And gentle *Dorothea*, heav'nly Child!
So sudden left us, left us, to bewail
Beauties and Graces, that with Rapture long
We'ad view'd perfection op'ning; Thought
Was in Amazement sunk, I look'd astound,
And all was *Chaos* round me: Like the Sage,
Who, when exploring great Creation's Laws,
Finds Difficulties not to be explain'd,
And owns his Reason's dim short sighted Pow'rs.
Strait I cried out; "Inscrutable thy Ways,
"Thy Counsels and thy Will, O sov'reign Lord!"
Long in the dark Perplexity my Soul
Was not involv'd; I onward bent my Way,
And to yon *Empyrean* lift my eyes,
Tho' dubious, yet adoring; when behold!
The Face of Heav'n was chang'd; the gloomy Clouds
Divided and stream'd out a shining Light,
Radiance, as is a Summer's Sun at Noon.
Surpriz'd I stopp'd and contemplated strait
The blest Appearance, when a heav'nly Form
Broke forth, and stood before me; such her Charms
"As make Expression dumb;" her Voice, her Mien

Spoke Margaretta; but, tho' lovely she
When mortal, yet a thousandth thousandth Part
She had not of the Beauties that beam'd forth
Now from her Face celestial; nobler Sweets
Than or Arabia, or the spicy Isles
E'er boasted, from her breath'd; she look'd, she smil'd,
As Angels Look and Smile, to some good Man
On happy errand sent. I stood entranc'd
In speechless Rapture, while the Charmer spoke
(Such Sounds none surely but Immortals hear),
She spoke, and fill'd me with ecstatic Joy.
"O thou, my Father's Friend, and therefore mine,
"To thee I'm sent, to teach thee how to chear
"The drooping Hearts of those, whose Parent-Love
"Strikes them with bootless Grief, and fills their Eyes
"With streaming Sorrows for their dear beloved.
"Alas! why mourn they? Mourn they not for them,
"Who to Eternity are blest? For them,
"Who tread you happy heav'nly Plains, where reign
"Immortal Peace and Pleasure? Joy is there,
"Such Joy as mortal Eye ne'er yet as seen,
"Nor mortal Tongue exprest, nay more; the Heart
"Of Man, will ne'er conceive, 'till they, like us
"Thereto have blest Admittance. Oh! that thou,
"Or that my Father, or that honour'd Dame,
"Who bore me in the Womb, who train'd me up
"From Infancy, in Virtue's heav'nly Road;
"O that you knew, what Joy celestial struck
"Our ravish'd Senses, when advanced first
"To what we now possess! From your dull Earth
"Short was our Passage, and but slight our Pain,
"Death's a mere Bug-bear, which, because untried,
"Vain Man thinks all that's horrible and dire.
"Far, far from this;—to those, who like Ourselves
"Walk in the Ways of Pleasantness and Peace,
"In Wisdom's Ways, he is the kindest Friend.
"Scarce had we felt the Danger that you mourn'd
"When from our Bodies mounted blithe our Souls,
"And flew to light, so lively that we soon
"Reach'd the desired goal; as soon forgot
"The idle World we 'ad left behind, and blest
"The Means that disengag'd us from our Clay:
"But this is nought to the ecstatic Bliss

"We prov'd, when to the bright Assembly join'd
"Of just Men perfect made; when 'mid a Host
"Of Cherubim and Seraph we approach'd
"The King of Kings, in Glory bright array'd,
"And join'd in Allelujahs to the Lamb
"That sat by him enthron'd. Omnipotence
"And Majesty and Holiness divine,
"And boundless Wisdom, Justice, Goodness, Love,
"Are now the Theme of our eternal Songs.
"This, this the Happiness, for which we've left
"Your nether World; and say, tho' Children ne'er
"Enjoy'd from Parents a sincerer Love,
"Can we regret the blessed Change? Ah, no!
"Tho' dear unto us still, yet wou'd we not
"For all then thousand Worlds like yours can yield
"Quit yon blest Plains, to tread with them again
"Your sordid Earth. Your Message then be this:
"Tell them to sigh no more for us; our God
"In kind Compassion to themselves hath call'd
"The darling Objects of their Souls away.
"Of us depriv'd, they now must surely know
"The Vanity of earthly Bliss, and feel,
"Sensibly feel, that they must seek for Joy
"In other Worlds, in Worlds where only Joy
"Is to be found: Their best Affections then
"Set they on Things above; and soon shall we
"In Heaven's due time to yon immortal Shores
"Hail them arriv'd: Their happy Daughters there
"Again shall they behold; and with them live
"Eternal Ages, never more to part."

T. CRADOCK

Note

1. Maryland Gazette (Annapolis), March 15, 1753. This piece is reprinted in Richard B. Davis, C. Hugh Holman, and Louis D. Rubin, Jr., eds., Southern Writing, 1585–1920 (New York: Odyssey Press, 1970), pp. 203–5. In the original each of the girls' names in the title is printed in small capital letters.

Seven Hymns[1]

Hymn for Christmas

1

Rejoice, ye servants of the Lord:
Be this great name ador'd:
Exalt your voices high:
For lo! He comes; the Godhead comes;
Our nature to His own assumes,
That he for us may die.

2

This blessed day, glad Earth receives
The Prince of Peace: a Virgin gives
The Savior to the light:
Angelic hosts the wonder sing;
The Shepherds haste to hail their King,
And bless the awful sight.

3

And see, the Magi from afar,
Directed by a radiant star,
To where their Maker lay;
Offer, with mingled joy and fear,
Their gold, frankincense, and their myrrh,
And adoration pay.

4

And shall not we, with equal fear,
With equal warmth and joy revere,
His great and glorious name!
And shall not we in loftiest hymns,
With Seraphs and Cherubims,
The Saviour God[2] proclaim!

Notes

1. In "Sketches of the Colonial Clergy of Maryland, No. I—Rev. Thomas Cradock," American Church Review 7 (July 1854): 308-311, the Rev. Ethan Allen published the first four hymns. He copied all but "Hymn for Christmas" in a manuscript history of the

parish and added "Hymn for Ascension," "Funeral Hymn," and "On Viewing the Grave of Arthur Cradock" to this manuscript. These three handwritten verses have no punctuation at the end of the lines. That utilized here has been added by the editor. Dr. Allen reported the existence of hymns for Easter and Good Friday, but they appear not to have survived. Allen, "History of St. Thomas Parish, Baltimore County, Maryland," 17-18, Maryland Diocesan Library, Maryland Historical Society, Baltimore, Md.

2. God is in small capital letters in the original.

Hymn for Whitsunday

1

Thou Holy Ghost; mysterious power!
 To thee we fly for aid;
Teach us, on wings of Faith to soar,
 Our inmost hearts purvey'd.

2

O still, as erst Thou didst inspire,
 The chosen of the Lord,
When first they felt the Sacred fire,
 Instruct me in Thy Word.

3

With wonder, heard the mingled throng!
 They saw and were amazed!
The rushing wind, the cloven tongues—
 They trembled as they gazed.

4

But what astonishment was theirs!
 Who can their joy unfold!
While each, in his own language hears
 Th'important tidings told.

5

This wond'rous work, all clement power,
 Didst then for man ordain!

That sin, and death, and hell, no more
Might hold their hated reign.

6

Therefore, our gratitude to Thee,
Breaks forth in hymns of joy;
And thus, thro' all eternity,
May we our tongues employ.

Sacremental Hymn

1

The feast's prepared; the table's set;
The chosen of the Lord are met.
Blest visitants! how happy all,
Who haste to obey the gracious call.

2

Hark! 'tis the Saviour Who invites!
Such condescension, sure excites
Each fervent heart to join the feast;
Who would not be the Saviour's guest?

3

Haste then, with ardor to your bliss!
"O taste and see how good He is!"
Feast your glad souls, in what will prove
Sweet earnest of your bliss above.

Resignation[1]

1

What e'er, all-clement God,
Thy justice shall ordain;
I'll bow, submissive to thy rod,
And never will complain.

2

Though ills, successive fall,
On my devoted head,
With patient heart, I'll bear them all,
And to thy mercy plead.

3

For well, I know, the cause
Of thy consuming wrath;
Too long I've disobey'd thy laws,
I've merited my death.

4

I know, whate'er I feel,
The Saviour suffer'd more;
And man's distempered heart to heal,
Severest tortures bore.

5

Hear this! my soul, thou'lt say,
Since God's such tender love,
I'll bear life's sorrows as I may,
My gratitude to prove.

Note

1. Allen believes this poem was written by Cradock upon the death of his son Arthur in 1770. Allen, "Sketches," American Church Review 7 (July 1854): 311.

Hymn for Ascension

1

He springs, he rises from the ground
He cleaves the yielding sky.
Then Earth, the heavens with joy resound,
That Savior mounts on high.

2

O Wondrous proof of power divine
The God, the God ascends;
With what a lustre does he shine,
And what a train attends.

3

The cherubim & seraphim
Crowd thick his azure way;
And hark in one continued hymn
Their duteous homage pay.

4

Hear this ye nations and adore;
The Era is begun,
When time and death—their ravage o'er—
Lie vanquished by the Son.

5

Again he'll in the clouds appear;
When—all-tremendous thought—
For what we've live & acted here,
Shall be to judgement brought.

6

The wicked in the depths of hell,
To wail eternal woe;
The righteous with their Lord to dwell,
Where joys immortal flow.

Funeral Hymn

1

Fruitless the toils which harrass man;
His anxious cares for wealth or pow'r;
Life's longest period's but a span,
And soon he meets his destined hour.

2

Death strikes! fell tyrant! less he lies,
And those that loved him round him mourn;
But vain their tears & vain their sighs,
For life once fled has no return.

3

And is there nothing that can boast,
Its various ills to make us bear?
Is all in disappointment lost,
Without one prospect worth our care?

4

Yes, there's a brighter, a heavenly prize
Deserves our care, our utmost pains;
You blooming fields above the skies,
Where Seraphs sing, where Jesus reigns.

5

With these in view & these our aim,
Life's deepest woes we can support.
And immortality our claim,
Who'll dare to say that life is short?

On Viewing the Grave of Arthur Cradock

1

In the dark Earth his body lies—
    Deep hid from mortal sight;
Clos'd, ever clos'd, those beaming eyes—
    That gave me such delight.

2

Cold as the turf that covers him—
    He whom the parent mourns;
Corruption triumphs o'er each limb—
    And dust to dust returns.

3

O with what rapture viewed we all—
    His sweet, his manly form;
Ah, could we think so soon he'd fall—
    A victim to the worm.

4

And yet that body cloth'd a mind—
    That with devotion glow'd;
And could no solid pleasure find—
    But in the love of God.

5

And yet those eyes so mildly bright—
    Trac'd out creation's laws;
And guided by celestial light—
    Discern'd th'Almighty Cause.

6

And yet that form display'd a Soul—
In every grace complete;
Which every passion could control—
Serene, sublimely great.

7

Is then my dear loved son no more?—
Ah yes! he lives above;
No longer then, fond heart, deplore—
The loss of filial love.

A Fragment[1]

Blest is the Man who's free from publick Cares;
Who no Man envies, and who no Man fears,
Whose Heart, a Stranger to the Ways of Sin,
Gives him true Joy, true Happiness within.
X X X X X X X X[2]
With his own Hands he ploughs that native Field,
His Father, Grandsire, and their Grandsires till'd.
Under those Oaks they found a cool Retreat
When spent with Labour in the Midday Heat,
He throws Him down: The Rooks, whose Sires before
Lull'd his Forefathers with their cawing Lore,
On him like Tribute gratefully bestow.
Tis all they have to give, tis all the Rent they owe.
Though small his Income, though his Household great,
The Poor unpitty'd never leave his Gate.
To them a Little of his Little's given.
Did I say, given? no; that is lent to Heaven.
On Sundays seated in his wicker Chair,
His Wife, his Children, Friends and Neighbours near,
He from the sacred Text a Chapter reads,
Comments, explains each verse as he proceeds:
Not to corrupt, but to apply the Word,
Not make his Hearers Casuists, but good.
When in the Markett with his Team he stands,
The Rich, the Great will take him by the Hand.
Though he no Pensions grants, no Bribes bestows,
Virtue will meet Respect where'evr She goes.
Among his Neighbours if Disputes arise,
The injur'd Party straight to him applys.

He hears both Sides, determines soon the Cause;
For He has Sense, though unskill'd in the Laws.
And Who has Sense with Honesty combin'd,
Him make thy Judge, if such one Thou canst find.
X X X X X X X X X X
When Death prepares his Being here to end,
Celestial Angels round his Couch attend;
Who wait impatient till the Stroke be given,
Eager to waft his honest Soul to Heaven.
X X X X X X X X X X

Notes

1. This poem is clearly neither in Cradock's hand nor in that of his daughter or his friend Dr. Randall Hulse, whose poems are also found in the Cradock Papers. Yet it seems to represent sentiments regularly displayed in Cradock's writings and may be written in honor of his father, Arthur Cradock of Trentham, Staffordshire. The reference to European birds and to ancestral lands seems to indicate a non-American subject matter.
2. These "Xs" in the original indicate space where the author expected to insert new lines in a final draft.

Crurulia

Part the 2d

The Check

1

But why, my soul, so mournfully complain?
The crime of base ingratitude beware;
Has Heav'n no mercies mingled with thy pain?
Dost thou no blessings from thy Maker share?

2

Oh yes! they're countless—hourly on my head—
(For which his glorious name be still ador'd)

Has he the bounties of his goodness shed,
Like gladning rains on thirsty pastures pour'd.

3

Various indeed his mercies—nor forget,
My soul, his blest benificence to praise,
Never oh never thou'lt discharge the debt,
Tho' to his will devoted all thy days:

4

Blest in th'affection of a tender wife
Whose constant joy's my wayward heart to please;
Who seeks to smooth the rigours of my life,
And ne'er is happy, but when I have ease:

5

Blest is my children who with duteous eye
Wait ev'ry motion of their father's will;
Whose infant hearts with filial simpathy,
Young as they are, their father's anguish feel:

6

Blest in the genuine friendship of the Few,
Whose worthy souls, from servile meanness free,
Firmly the rigid paths of truth pursue,
And scorn the dupes of modern modes to be:

7

Blest in my country's welfare which no more
Mourns battles badly fought & basely lost,
But with her fleets insults the hostile shore,
Cou'd late a Wolfe, can yet an Amherst boast:

8

Blest in my faith, which wanders not abroad
After the wild fanatick's idle schemes,
But makes it only rule the book of GOD,
Clear from the taint of superstition's dreams:

9

But all above, blest in the glorious hope,
That, when I die, I shall not total die,

But Heav'n will give my soul her amplest scope,
To climb yon bright etherial worlds on high.

10

Lo! these are blessings of the noblest kind;
And can I then ungratefully complain
For trifling ills?—for shame, my dastard mind,
The coward's weak unmánly moan disdain,

11

Be thy own self—thy origin respect;
The ways of Heav'n, it's kind intension scan;
On what thou art design'd for, calm, reflect;
And bravely act the *Christian* & the *Man*.

2

Afflictions mercies

1

Yes; well the sacred page informs my soul,
That our severest evils mercies prove;
The force of sensual passion to controul,
Inflicted on us by Almighty love.

2

I find it so; for now my humbled heart
Melts with the dread of that tremendous hour,
When I from earth & all its ties must part,
And see the glories of the sun no more.

3

Now ev'ry word and ev'ry action's weigh'd;
Now the minutest thought I strickly poise;
That I to him whose blood my ransome paid,
May yet present a welcome sacrifice.

4

Yet not my soul, thou of perfection boast;
Alass! I feel how very frail I be;
How weak my virtue, where I struggle most
How wondrous hard, from folly to be free:

5

That still my mind a motley-mixture shews,
Where *grace* & *passion* have by turns their pow'r;
As in the mass, wherein the bullion glows,
Dull worthless earth is blended with the ore.

6

But as that ore is by the fire refin'd,
Purg'd from it's dross, & render'd bright & pure;
So is my hope, that my afflicted mind
Will whiten thro' it's pains, & Heav'n secure:

7

And is it thus? and will that Heav'n be mine?
By means of blest affliction shall I see
My Maker's face? kind source of bliss divine!
That thus conducts me to eternity!

8

Eternity, thou no more dreadful thought!
My only prospect, and my only aim!
In pain's hard school the wholsome lesson taught,
For thee I labour, & tis thee I claim.

9

Let princes vain fantastick hopes pursue
And wade thro' blood & carnage to a crown;
I scorn their low ambition; thou my view,
With pity on a *Bourbon* I look down.

3

The Resolve

1

The royal shepherd in his songs of woe,
When noisome ulcers o'er his body ran,
And he no respite from his pains cou'd know,
Determin'd on his wise religious plan:

2

That if high Heav'n him to his health restor'd,
His voice in hymns of gratitude he'd raise,

Duely attend the temple of the Lord,
And make his life one constant act of praise.

3

And shall not I, by his example led,
Sweet health returning to my weaken'd frame,
Thus rescued from the confines of the dead
Adore my gracious God & bless his name:

4

Taught by his chastning, yet supporting hand,
My duty and true interest to know,
The pleasant ways, the paths to peace regain'd
With the bright flame of heavenly zeal to glow?

5

Yes, O my God, thy praise I'll ever sing,
Thou heard'st me in the direful hour of pain,
Didst kind relief in all my sad anguish bring,
And gav'st me to behold the sun again.

6

To thee I'll dedicate my future days;
Subject my ev'ry passion to thy will;
And, while my tongue shall grateful hymn thy praise,
My soul shall joy thy precepts to fulfill.

7

The lures of pleasure & charms of sence
Shall cheat my now-awaken'd heart no more;
But a new Era I'll of life commence
Devoted solely to thy gracious power.

8

I stand resolv'd and thou all-clement God,
Benignly these my resolutions aid,
On me be thy effectual grace bestow'd,
That I, prepar'd, may ev'ry sin evade:

9

Firmly that I the ways of truth may tread,
And follow close the precepts thou hast given,

From virtue still to virtue by thee led,
Till I have reach'd at length my destin'd Heav'n.

10

Then I'll rejoice, affliction has been mine,
That I have felt thy kind correcting rod;
Thus fully prov'd the son of Love divine,
Of Thee, my Lord, my Saviour, & my God.

4

The Relapse

1

Vain empty efforts of humanity!
And is it thus I've kept the solemn vow?
Thus sudden from my resolutions fly?
The wretch I was alate, the same I'm now——

2

Base dastard as I am, I quit the field
To boist'rous passions leave my soul the prey;
E'en at the first assault supinely yield,
A rebel, where I bound my heart t'obey.

3

Thus when the shaggy tirant of the waste
Falls on the scatter'd flocks, the caitiff-swain
Deserts his fleecy charge with all his haste,
And leave the bestial master of the plain.

4

What tho' my soul they unexpected storm'd
And pour'd upon her with impetuous rage?
The noble resolutions she had form'd,
Had arm'd her sure their fury to assuage!

5

Fool! to forget the scared promise made
Of firm obedience to all-righteous Heav'n!
Fool! to forget, how ardently I pray'd,
To have my crimes & errors past forgiven.

6

And can I hope his goodness will assist
The enormous wretch who thus deserts his post
Who acts just as his lordly passions list,
In the wild whirl of impious anger lost.

7

Ah no! I feel the heavy weight of sin,
That if I'd conquer, I must sorely strive,
My faithful monitor forewarns, within,
Incessant contest, if with God I'd live.

8

And yet how hard!—too vainly we essay
To check our passions, in their full career;
Our poor weak hearts too suddenly given way,—
And lose their fortitude when danger's near.

9

So, in a tempest's rage, with headlong force
The torrents, rushing from the mountains, roar.
Mounds, dams & banks in vain oppose their course,
On all around they desolate pour.

10

Delusive plea, & indolent excuse!
Passions must be controul'd, if Heav'n we'd win;
The gates of mercy entrance will refuse
If we approch them, laden with our sin.

5

The Recovery

1

Delightful change! my heart again has peace
I feel my soul now to her God return;
The terrors of impenitence decrease
Again with bright celestial zeal I burn.

2

Wild passions now no more distort my frame:
Their base pernicious influence is o'er;

My soul now glowing with devotion's flame,
I bend beneath their tiranny no more.

3

Religion waits me with her lovely train;
The sister virtues all around me shine.
And now, a votary to my God again,
I cease to tremble at the wrath divine.

4

Rapt into prospects of sublimest joys
Which by his blood my Saviour for me won,
E'en Pleasure's gaudy lures and gilded toys,
Firmly, I scorn, and can with horror shun.

5

How great soever their attractions prove,
Let them their trophies & their conquests boast,
Thanks to me my God and his afflicting love
On me their flatt'ring, fatal charms are lost.

6

So to the wisest of the kings of Greece,[1]
As by their dangerous shore the Heroe past,
The Sirens sung; in vain—the song they cease;
They see they gain not on his guarded breast.

7

Yes, O my God, to thee with humbliest awe,
With earnest love, I'll dedicate my days;
The rule of all my actions is thy law,
The sweet employment of my tongue—thy praise;

8

Thy grace conducting me, I look above
The narrow limits of this lower sphere,
The seats of light, the scenes of heav'nly love
My only mark for thou, O Lord, art there.

9

Sincerest thanks to thy correcting hand
That led thro' pain, thro' anguish to my bliss;
Strengthen'd by thee I now collected stand,
And fix my views on endless happiness.

6

The Prospect

1

What glorious vision breaks upon my eyes?
What heav'nly prospect charms my raptur'd mind?
What wondrous beauties sudden round me rise,
As if to dissipate my doubts design'd?

2

Sure Heav'n now opens to my longing heart,
And gives a prelude of those future joys,
Which it's high Monarch will to all impart,
Who strive to win the great eternal prize.

3

So to the weary swain, who travels long
A miry road, the verdant plains appear,
Whose flow'ry glades & breezy groves among,
He hopes his harast, panting soul to cheer.

4

Now are forgot the labours that are o'er,
His many toilsome steps in dreary ways;
A sweet continued prospect lies before,
His ravish'd sight, and tunes him all to praise.

5

O what a view of bliss? in transport lost,
I can't my wonder, my surprise express?
Sure these the shining fields, that joyous coast,
Where ever blooms celestial happiness.

6

Greece, boast no more thy fond ideal plains
Oh joys, Elysian, where Immortals throng—
Tis here, full in my view, that pleasure reigns
Which far exceeds the scenes thy *Homer* sung.

7

What rapture, O my soul! the minstrelsy
Of *Seraph* & of *Cherub* strikes my ears;

Amid the tuneful choir I seem to be,
And listen to the musick of the spheres.

8

Lo! what a flood of piercing light pours down
Thro' the *Immense*, & brightens all around!
This sure th'effulgence from th'Eternal's
throne
On them who're with his mighty favour crown'd.

9

I see them all—O what a countless train!
Myriads & Myriads number not their bands;
Who'd tell the *Blest* that in these regions
reign,
Might count in the extended oceans
glitt'ring sands.

10

And does my God this place for me prepare?
And will these heavenly pleasures all be mine?
Shall I the glories of Immortals share?
O blest benificence of love divine!

11

Strive, O my soul, with all thy efforts strive
To please that Saviour—God who to provide
These bright rewards; his precious blood did give;
His life thy pattern and his law thy guide.

Notes

1. Ulysses or Odysseus, King of Ithaca, is the hero of Homer's *Odyssey* who in one episode resists the temptations of the Sirens who song beckoned his ship to destruction.
2. *Harast* is presumably a poetic variation of *harassed*.

8
Maryland Eclogues in Imitation of Virgil's

By Jonathan Spritly, Esqr.

Formerly a Worthy Member of the Assembly

Revis'd & Corrected by his

Friend Sly Boots

SPLIT-TEXT

Eclogue 1st.

Argument

Crape, a Virginian Clergyman, being turn'd out of his Living for Misdemeanours, comes to the House of Split-text in Maryland, where Split-text's happy Situation & Crape's Misfortune naturally beget the following Dialogue.

Crape, Split-text

Crape:

Beneath the Shade of these wide-spreading Trees,
Dear Split-text. You can smoke your Chunk[1] at Ease;
I hapless Wretch! must bid such joys Adieu;
Strip't of my Credit, & my Income too;
Must leave my Glebe, which all my Bacon[2] fed,
(Bacon, my rich repast so often made)
While you, while chearful, Plenty round you dwells,
Can talk with D——y,[3] how Tobacco sells.[4]

Split-text:

Yes, Brother Crape—a gen'rous Chief bestow'd
On me these Blessings—all to him I ow'd.
For which I'll ne'er forget, each Sabbath-Day,
With hearty Zeal for my good Lord to pray:
He[5] made me Parson here; & bids me fill
My Pipe & Bowl, as often as I will.[6]

Crape:

I envy not your Bliss, but wonder much
Their[7] Hate for Pray'rs & Parsons here is such!
Poor I am forc'd on this lank jade to ride,
Which often alate with hunger lik'd to 've died:
But yesterday she tumbled in the Dirt,
And 'gainst a white oak[8] Stump my Forehead hurt,

Fool! that I was!—I might have known my Fate;
But Man is conscious of his Faults too late;
My Vestry[9] told me oft, they'd bear no more,
And now at length have turn'd me out of Door.
—But say how you have all this Favour got?[10]

Split-text:

Assurance & Good Luck:—what will they not?
A—[11] by Birth, I came a School to teach;
But little thought (God knows) I e'er should preach;
I found the Parsons here such Clods of Clay,
That soon to my Ambition I gave Way:
Why might not I, I said, harangue as well
As W——n or Wh——r or D-ll?[12]
For we resemble those at Home no more,
Than Saints of Modern Days do Saints of yore.[13]

Crape:

And pray, what made you to this Country come?[14]

Split-text:

Faith! Poverty—I shou'd have starv'd at Home.
Soon as the Down 'gan on my Chin t'appear;[15]
I quite grew weary of my country Fare.
Oatmeal & Water was too thin a Diet,
To keep my grumbling Guts in peace & Quiet;
So Fear of Starving, Hope of living better,
Made me have Heart enough to cross the Water.[16]

Crape:

I was surpris'd, that tho' you liv'd so well,[17]
Your Carcase was so lank, you Phiz so pale;
The Cause is plain[18]—your native, hungry Food
So gain'd th'Ascendant o'er your youthful Blood,
You look, as, if no meat cou'd do you good.

Split-text:

Twas Time then to some other place to roam,
And seek for better Fare than was at home;

Here then I came—but soon went back again,
The B[i]sh[o]p's Blessing, & my L[or]d's[19] to gain
Soon both I got—I saw that noble P[ee]r,
For whom our Church puts up each week a Pray'r.[20]
He bad me come, he bad me preach & pray,
And, if the Planters wou'd not, make 'em pay.[21]

Crape:

O happy Brother; happy is Thy Plight;[22]
Happy in all that can thy Soul delight;
Sure of the Forties,[23] Whate'er Loss betide
The Planter's Toil; since they must be supply'd.
O happy Brother—By this purling Rill
These shady Locusts,[24] & that pleasant Hill,
What dost thou not enjoy?—the fanning Breeze
Comes sweetly breathing on thee thru the trees;
That busy Swarm with lulling sound compose
Thy wearied Soul to gentle, soft Repose;
Thy Negros, chanting forth their rustick Loves,
The melancholy Musick of the Doves;
The feather'd Choir, which, while they skim along
The liquid Plain, regale thee with a Song;[25]
All, all conspire to heighten ev'ry Bliss,
And make theee taste sincerest Happiness.

Split-text:

Planters Tobacco shall forget to smoke,
Hogs to love Mast and Peaches, Frogs to croak,
The Indians range, where flows the princely Thames,
And Duchess live nigh Potomack's[26] Streams,
'Ere from my Heart that smiling Mien I lose[27]
With which the gen'rous[28] Lord his Gifts bestows.

Crape:

But I alass![29] no more my Glebe must view,
But to my once-lov'd Dwelling bid Adieu,
Go preach the Gospel in some Indian's Ear,[30]
Who'll mind my Preaching, like your Planters here?
And must a Stranger—Parson rule the roost,
And Glean the Harvest I so stupid lost?[31]
What has my Guzzling & my Folly done?

Go, *Planters*, go, your *quondam* Parson shun;[32]
No more shall I with you rant, drink & smoke;
Toast baudy Healths, or crack a smutty joak;[33]
No more in Bumbo, or in Cyder swill;[34]
Faith! all's o'er now—I may go where I will.

Split-text:

To night howe'er with me you'll foul a Plate;
A juicy fat Gammon & a Chick we'll get;
Wine I have none; Good Bumbo[35] & small Beer,
Clean, tho' coarse Linnen, will be all your Fare.
This year of Cyder I but made one Stoup,[36]
One Night the *Planters* came & drank it up,
Walk in—the Chimney's Smoke's more plainly seen;
And Giant Shadows cross the dewy Green;[37]
In louder Musick sing the marshy Frogs;[38]
—Sambo, go, pen the Turkies, feed the Hogs.

Author's Notations

1. A small Planter's Pipe which some of the Clergy don't disdain to make use of.

2. The chief Food of the Marylanders. [A *glebe* is land owned by an Anglican parish, often farmed by the rector.]

3. A numerous Family in the Province [Dulany?]

4. Tityrus

Ecloga 1ma
Meliboeus, Tityrus

Mel:
Tityre, tu patulae recubans sub tegmine fagi
Silvestrem tenui Musam meditaris avena;
Nos patriae finis et dulcia linquimus arva;
Nos patriam fugimus; tu, Tityre [lentus in umbra]
Formosam resonare doces Amaryllida
Sylvas [lines 1-5]

[Tityrus, here you loll, your slim reed-pipe serenading
The woodland spirit beneath a spread of sheltering beech,
While I must leave my home place, the fields so dear to me.
I'm driven from my home place: but you can take it easy
In shade and teach the woods to repeat "Fair Amaryllis."

Latin corrections and additions and English translations from C. Day Lewis, The Ecologues and Georgics of Virgil (Garden City, N.Y.: Doubleday, 1964). The letters and words in brackets are Latin omitted by Cradock.]

5. Too just an Insinuation, that the true merit of a Clergyman is not considered here in his Promotion.

6. Tit:
O Meliboe[e], Deus nobis hoc otia fecit
[namque erit ille mihi semper deus,] illius aram
Saepe tener nostris ab obilibus imbuet agnus
Ille meas errare boves [ut cernis] et ipsum
Ludere quae vellem calamo permisit agresti [lines 6-10]

[O Meliboeus, a god has given this ease—
One who will always be a god to me, whose altar
I'll steep with the blood to many a tender lamb from my sheep-folds.
It's by his grace, you see, that my cattle browse and I
Can play whatever tunes I like on this country reed-pipe.]

7. The name of a Clergyman [is] almost scandalous here; which proceeds from two Causes: the ill Conduct of some of them & the vast numbers of Roman Catholicks & Quakers, who, however wide in their Points of Belief & doctrine, both of them heartily join in aspersing the Teachers and Members [of the] Church of England. [Teachers possibly Preachers.]

8. A particular kind of oak very plentiful in this Province.

9. The Vestries in Virginia have it in their Pow'r, if the minister behaves ill, to get rid of him; which the Maryland Vestries have not.

10. Mel:

Non equidem invideo, miror magis; undique totis
Usque adeo turbamur agris
Protinus aeger ago; hanc etiam vix, Tityre, duco
Hic inter densas corylos modo manque gamellos
Spem gregis, ah! silice in nuda connixa reliquit.
Saepe malum hoc nobis, Si mens non laeva fuisset,
De caelo tactas memini praedicere quercus.
Saepe sinistra cava praedixit ab ilice ornix
Sed tamen ille Deus qui sit, da, Tityre, nobis [lines 11-18]

[Well, I don't grudge you that: but it amazes me, when
Such a pack of troubles worry us countrymen everywhere.
On and on, sick-hearted, I drive my goats: look, this one
Can hardly move—in that hazel thicket she dropped her twin kids,
The hope of my flock, but she has to leave them upon bare flint.
Times enough, I know it, I was forewarned of this,
When lightning struck the oaks—my wits must have been addled.
But tell me about god of yours, my friend: who is he?]

11. What Countryman my friend means, I can't exactly tell; however, am of opinion he had no Intention of aspersing any Country. [Many Chesapeake clergy were discredited because of their Scottish ancestry.]

12. These really are Gentlemen that bring a great discredit on their Funtion. [Probably they were Stephen Wilkinson, Nathaniel Whitaker, and Thomas Dell (or Dill).]

13. Tit:
Sic canibus catulos similis, [sic matribus haedos]
Noram [sic parvis componere magna solebam.
verum] Haec tantum alias inter caput extulit urbes
Quantum lenta solent inter viburna
cupressi. [lines 22-25]

[Thus I came to know how dogs resemble puppies,
Goats their kids, and by that scale compare large things with small.
But Rome carries her head as high above other cities
As cypresses tower over the tough wayfaring tree.]

14. Mel:
Et quae tanta fuit Romam tibi causa
videndi? [line 26]

[What was the grand cause of your setting eyes on Rome, then?]

15. Ti:
Libertas, quae sera tamen respexit inertem.
Candidior postquam tondenti barba
cadebat [lines 27-28]

[Freedom gave me a look—oh, long-delayed it was.
And I apathetic; my beard fell whiter now as I clipped it—]

16. Nec spes libertatis erat, nec cura
peculi. [line 32]

[I had no chance of freedom, no attention to spare for savings:]

17. Me:
Mirabar quid maesta Deos, amarylli,
vocares; [line 36]

[I used to wonder why Amaryllis called so sadly]

18. The philosophy of this I don't pretend to assert; but I think Experience is plainly on our Side.

19. Lord B[altimore,] Proprietary of Maryland, who has all the Livings in his own Gift.

20. A very just Satyr I think on our Clergy for putting his lordship in our Pray'rs on a par with the Royal Family.

21. Tit:
[Quid facerem?] neque servitio me exire licebat,
Nec tam praesentis alibi cognoscere divos.
Hic illum vidi juvenem, Meliboe[e], quotannis
Bis senos cui nostra dies altaria fumant.
Hic mihi responsum primus dedit ille pententi;
Pascite boves boves, pueri; submittite
tauros. [lines 40-45]

[What was I to do? There was no way out from my slavery.
Nowhere else could I find a divine one ready to help me.
At Rome, Meliboeus, I saw a young prince in whose honour
My altar shall smoke twelve times a year. At Rome I made
My petition to him, and he granted it readily saying, "My lads,
Pasture your cattle, breed from your bulls, as you did of old."]

22. Mel:
Fortunate senex ergo tua rura manebunt; [line 46]

[Fortunate old man!—so your acres will be yours still.]

23. The Clergy's Income is by forty Pound W[eigh]t of Tobacco a Head; & indeed little enough for those that are worthy of it; tho' occasion is taken from the Ill behaviour of some to represent their Income as a great Burthen on the Country.

24. A wood that grows by the Waterside, remarkable for its Hardness & it's long Continuance so that it is made use of much in their Gardens &c.

25. Nec Mala vicini pecoris contagia laedent.
Fortunate senex; hic inter flumina nota
Et fontes sacros frigus captabis opacum.
Hinc tibi, quae semper vicino ab limite saepes
Hyblaeis apibus florem depasta salicti;
Saepe levi somnum suadebit inire susurro
[hinc alta sub rupe] canet frondator ad auras,
Nec tamen interea raucae [tua cura] Palumbes
Nec gemere aeria cessabit turtur ab ulmo [lines 50-58]

[And there's no risk of their catching disease from a neighbour's flock.
Ah, fortunate old man, here among hallowed springs
And familiar streams you'll enjoy the longed-for shade, the cool shade.
Here, as of old, where your neighbour's land marches with yours,
The sally hedge, with bees of Hybla sipping its blossom,
Shall often hum you gently to sleep. On the other side
Vine-dressers will sing to the breezes at the crag's foot;
And all the time your favourites, the husky-voiced wood pigeons
Shall coo away, and turtle doves make moan in the elm tops.]

26. A fine large River, that divides Virginia & Maryland, tis reckond twenty miles wide at it's Mouth. [*Mast* in line 72 is an archaic term for the fruit of forest trees used as a food for swine.]

27. Tit:
Ante leves ergo pascentur in aethere cervi,
Et freta destituent nudos in littore pisces;
Ante pererratis amborum finibus ex[s]ul
Aut Ararim Parthus bibet aut Germania Tigrim,
Quam nostro illius labatur pectore vultus. [lines 59-63]

[Sooner shall lightfoot stags go grazing on thin air;

Or the sea contract, leaving its fishes high and dry;
Sooner shall the Germans and the Parthians, migrating
Across each other's frontiers, drink of each other's broad
Rivers, than I'll forget the look the young prince gave me.]

28. Gen'rous indeed, since his Church Favours fall without Distinction, on any that ask for them.

29. Mel: At nos hinc &c. [line 64]

[But the rest of us . . .]

30. Ten to one! a great deal more Purpose; tho' tis observable all over America, Christianity makes very small Progress among the Indians, which is owing no doubt to the scandalous Lives of it's pretended Professors among them .

31. Impius haec tam cultra novalia miles habebit
Barbarus has Segetes En quo discordia civis
Perduxit miseros [lines 70-73]

[To think some godless soldier owning my well-farmed fallow,
A foreigner reaping these crops! To such a pass has civil
Dissension brought us . . .]

32. Ite, meae, felix quondam pecus, ite capellae; [line 74]

[Move onward, little she-goats, onward, once-happy flock!]

33. Carmina nulla canum; non, me pascente Capellae
Florentem Cytisum & salices carpetis amaras. [lines 77-78]

[No more singing for me, no taking you to browse,
My little goats, on bitter willow and clover flower.]

34. I'm sorry to say, the Satyr here too just. Indeed Ecclesiastical Authority is much wanted here; & till proper measures are taken, there will be some among the Clergy, whose Lives will be a Scandal to the rest.

35. Rum, Water and Sugar without Acid.

36. Cider very plentiful in this Country: but tis observable that the Trees bear but ev'ry other Year. We must suppose this then to be the scarce year.

37. Tit:
Hic tamen ha[n]c mecum poteras requiescere nocte[m]
[fronde super viridi:] Sunt nobis mitia poma
Constaneae molles et pressi copia lactis;
Et jam summa procul villarum culmina fumant
Majoresque cadunt altis de montibus
umbrae [line 79-83]

[Yet surely you could rest with me tonight and sleep
On a bed of green leaves here? You're welcome to taste my mellow
Apples, my floury chestnuts, my ample stock of cheese;
Look over there—smoke rises already from the rooftops
And longer fall the shadows cast by the mountain heights.]

38. The frogs here <have various notes> are of various Kinds & have notes as various, which on a summer's Ev'ning make a musick not disagreable.

DAPHNE

Eclogue 2d.

Argument

Pompey, a Negro Slave, is in Love with Daphne, a fellow Slave that has gained the good Graces of her Master—He therefore in this Eclogue complains of her Cruelty, says all he can in his own Favour, & importunes her to come & live with him; till at last perceiving the Vanity of her Pretensions, he acknowledges his Folly, & is resolv'd to Trouble himself no more about her.

For Daphne's Charms did hapless Pompey[1] burn,
In vain, She scorn'd to make him a Return;
The planter lov'd too well the coal-black Maid,[2]
Joy of his Eyes, & Partner of his Bed:
The gloomy Woods were all the Slave's Relief,
His toil once o'er, he'd solace there his Grief;
To echoing hills wou'd tell his piteous Tale,
And grumble to the trees—without Avail.[3]

O cruel Daphne, must I die indeed,
Nor thou my Songs, my Cares, my Passion heed?
Our fleecy Flocks the breezy Cool enjoy;
Secure midst bushy Brakes the Lizards lie,
Kind Nell delicious Huomine[4] prepares
For weary Cesar, & for lusty Mars.
But I, pursuing charming Thee in vain,
Constant with chirping Grashopper complain.

The haughty Airs of proud Mulatto Bess,
Was't not enough to bear—without redress?
True; she was yellow;—lovely black art thou;
Yet both coneur my Wonted Peace t'undo.
Trust not too much, my Tyrant, to thy Charms;
The whites are sometimes welcome to our Arms:
My Mistress oft invites me to her Bed,[5]
And, if thou'rt cruel still, she'll sure succeed.[6]

Daphne, indeed you shun you don't know who;
A thousand Things at your Command I'll do.
Fullrich am I in Poultry, Turkies, Geese;
Cotton I gather, white as any Fleece;
Potatoes sweet shall be thy Winter-Fare,
And most delicious Fruits thy Summer's Share.
I sing as well as ever Negro sung.
Nor Sambo has a Banjar[7] better strung.[8]

Nor am I so deform'd—alate I stood,
And view'd my shape in Choptank's[9] Silver Flood
My Master's self, tho' we were judg'd by thee,
Can't boast a Body, Shape, or Limbs like me.[10]

O might this humble Hut thy Charms receive;
With me the Piggies to their Accorns drive.
Our haughty Lord, tho' now so wondrous great,[11]
Once on Tobacco, & on Hogs did wait:
First toil'd like me, was next an Overseer;
So by Degrees grew what you've found him here.
Nor think it Scorn to use this gentle Hoe;
Once in his Life, twas more than he wou'd do.[12]

Besides, within the Woods I lately found
Two lovely Fawns,[13] with White all Spotted round,
These have I kept for thee—Nell oft in vain
Has beg'd 'em of me; she'll her Suit obtain,
Since thou the Giver & the Gift disdain.[14]

Come beauteous Girl—For thee each Brother slave
A Garland, mint of fairest Flow'rs shall weave,
For thee myself will Nuts & Peaches[15] get,
And Apples sweeter than thou'st tasted yet,
The Cedars too, their fragrant Boughs shall lend,
Thee from the Summer's Heat, or Winter's Cold
to fend.[16]

Ah, Pompey! she thy scoundrel—Presents scorns;
Thy Lord with nobler Gifts her Love returns;
What wou'd I have?—how wretched is my Lot?
The Hogs into my Cotton Patch have got.[17]
Surely our Huts you scorn'st not; lest you're mad;
Our Master's self at first no better had.[18]

The Wolf with greedy Eyes the Lamb pursues,
The Gentle Lamb the Glade with rapture views.
I follow thee, My Daphne; thee alone;
All follow that they want to make their own.
See my returning Mates—their Toil is done,
The Shadows now attend the setting Sun:
Yet I'm burnt up with Love—What yet could prove
Sufficient Guard against the Flames of Love.

Ah Pompey, say! thy Mind what Frenzy sways?
And yet no Boughs support thy drooping Peas:
Why rather does thou not those Things prepare
Which both for thy wants & ease more needful are?
Another court, since thou must do without her;
Make no more Rant, nor vex thyself about her.

Author's Notations

1. The Planters generally give to their Negroes the names of the greatest men of old, which I can't help thinking is doing a great outrage to the Heroes of antiquity.

2. Tis very well known both Planters & their Wives have transgrest this Way.

3. Alexis
Ecloga 2da

Formosum pastor Corydon ardebat Alexin,
Delicias Domini; nec quid Speraret habebat.
Tantum inter densas, umbrosa cacumina, fagos
Assidue veniebat[.] ibi haec incondita solus
Montibus et silvis studio jactabat inani [lines 1-5]

[A shepherd, Corydon, burned with love for his master's favourite,
Handsome Alexis. Little reason had he for hope;
But he was always going into the beech plantation
Under whose spires and shades, alone was his futile passion,
He poured forth words like these, piecemeal, to wood and hill:]

4. The negro's Food in the Winter, made of Indian corn and Beans boil'd in salt & water; & eat generally with Hog's fat.

5. See note a. [Cradock meant the second note, indicating he inserted the first note in the text at a later time or else he forgot it when writing this one. None of the notations have superscript designations in the text except for an "X" to denote the location for Cradock's English comments.]

6. O crudelis Alexi, nihil mea carmina curas;
Nil nostri miserere; mori me denique coges:
Nunc etiam pecudes umbras & frigora captant,
Thestylis & rapido fessis messoribus aestu
Nunc viridis etiam occultant spineta lacertos,
Allia serpyllumque herbas contundit olentis.
At mecum raucis, tua dum vestigia lustro,
Sole sub ardenti resonant asbusta cicadis.
Nonne fuit satius tristes Amaryllidis iras
Atque superba puti fastidia? [nonne Menalcan,]
Quamvis ille niger, quamvis tu candidus esses.
O formose puer, nimium ne crede colori,
Alba liqustra cadunt. Vaccinia nigra
leguntur. [lines 6-18]

["Cruel Alexis, can my sad airs mean nothing to you?
No pitty for me? One day you'll drive me to my death.
Even the cattle now are making for the cool shade,
Even the green lizards are hiding in thorn thickets,
And Thestylis prepares a pottage of savoury herbs,
Garlic and thyme, for harvesters whom the fierce heat has wearied.

But I trail in your footsteps under the blazing sun
While copses thrum with my hoarse voice and the cicada's.
I have done better to bear the sulks and rages, the insolent
Disdain of Amaryllis, or to make do with Menaclas,

Swarthy though he is, compared with your dazzling fairness
Don't bank too much on your complexion, lovely boy—
Pale privet-blossom falls, no less than the dark-toned hyacinth.]

7. A Negro Instrument, something like a Bladder.

8. Despectus tibi sum, nec, qui sim, quaeris, Alexi.
Quam dives pecoris, nivei quam lactis abundans.
Mille meae Siculis errant in montibus agnae
Lac mihi non aestate, novum non frigore desit
Canto quae solitus [si quando armenta vocabat,]
Amphion Dircaeus———————— [lines 19-24]

['Alexis, you look down at me; you never think
What I am—how rich in livestock, in wealth of snowy milk.
A thousand lambs of mine roam the Sicilian hills;
I never have run short of fresh milk, summer or winter.
I sing as, on a time, Amphion used to sing,
Call his cattle home . . .]

9. A River on the Western Shore of the Chesapeak. [Actually, it is on the Eastern Shore.]

10. Nec sum adeo informis: nuper me in litore vidi,
Cum pacidum ventis staret mare; non ego Daphnim
Judice te, metuam [si numquam fallit imago.] [lines 25-27]

[I'm not so ill-favoured, either: the other day on the shore,
When sea's face was unfretted, I saw myself; if that mirror
Tells true, I could compete with Daphnis and win your verdict.]

11. Nothing more common than for the Convits that go over, if they prove anything careful, to get a handsome Livelihood; & buy Slaves themselves; which they are sure to use cruelly enough.

12. O tantum libeat mecum tibi sordida rura
Atque humilis habitare casas, [et figere cervos,]
Haedorumq[ue] gregem viridi compellere hybisco.—
Mecum una in sylvis imitabere Pana canendo.
Pan primus calamos cera conjungere plures.
Instituit—[Pan curot ovis oviumque magistros.]
Nec te paeniteat calamo trivisse labellum
Haec eadem ut Sciret, quid non faciebat Amintas? [lines 28-35]

['How wonderful it would be to live together in these
Rough fields, in a homely cottage, hunting the deer with our bows,
Herding a flock of kids with green marsh-mallow switches!
Here with me in the woodlands, you'd rival Pan for music.
Pan invented the shepherd's pipes, waxing a handful
Of reeds together: Pan looks after sheep and shepherd.
You'd never regret chafing your lip upon the pipes—
Thing what Amyntas gladly suffered to learn the art.]

13. Deer range here in great Plenty, & anyone that will, may destroy them, tho now [they are] scarcer, especially in the more cultivated Part of the Country, than they were in the author's Time.

14. Praeterea duo nec<t> tuta mihi valle reperti
Capreoli, sparsis etiam nunc pellibus ambo
[bina die siccant ovis ubera;] quos tibi servo
Iam pridem a me illos abducere Thestylis orat:
Et faciet; quoniam sordent tibi munera nostra.
Huc Ades, O formose puer Tibi &c. [lines 40-45]

[What's more, I have two roes which I found in a dangerous combe—
Their hids have not lost the white markings: twice a day now
They're milking a ewe dry. I'm keeping them for you.

Thestylis has been beggin for ages, to take them off me;
And she can have them, as you turn up your nose at my presents.
'Handsome boy, come here!]

15. Peaches are surprisingly plentiful here, so that in the Season they feed their Hogs with them.

16. Ipse ego cana legam tenera langugine mala
Castaneasq[ue] nuces [mea quas Amaryllis amabat;]
Addam cerea pruna, & honos erit huic quoque Malo.
Et vos, O lauri, carpam, & te, proxima myrte
Sic positae quoniam suavis miscetis odores. [lines 51-56]

[Myself will gather you quinces of pale and velvety bloom
And chestnuts Amaryllis loved when she was mine;
Waxy-looking plums too—that fruit shall have its due;
And I'll cut branches of laurel, and of myrtle that grows near it—
Sweet is their fragrance when they are put together.]

17. Ev'ry Planter allows his Negro a little spot of ground to raise some little Truck [barter] for himself, such as Cotton, Potatoes, Negro Peese, &c.

18. Rusticus es, Corydon: nec munera curat Alexis;
Nec si muneribus certes, concedat Iol[l]as.
Ehue! [hue] quid volni misero mihi Floribus Austrum
Perditus & liquidis immisi fontibus Apros.
Quem fugis ah! demens! habitarunt di quoque sylvas
Dardaniusque Paris. [lines 56-61]

['Bumpkin! as if Alexis cared two pence for your offerings!
And anyway, Iollas could beat you at present-giving.
Poor fool that I was, to have such day dreams. Now in my folly

I've let the wind get at my flowers, the boars
muddy my spring.
Who are you running from, you crazy man? Why, Trojan
Paris, and even gods, have lived in the woods like
me.]

19. [The other version of this eclogue has line 63 read: "The gentle Lamb as Greedily the browze."]

20. Lupis ipse capellam
Florentem cytisum sequitur lasciva capella
Te Corydon, O Alexi; Trahit sua quemque voluptas.
Aspice, aratra jugo referunt suspensa juvenci,
Et Sol crescentes decendens duplicat umbras:
Me tamen urit amor—quis enim modus adsit
Amori? [lines 63-68]

[Fierce lioness goes after the wolf, wolf after
goat,
The wanton goat goes after the flowering clover,
and I
Go after you, Alexis—each towed by his own fancy.
'Look, ploughs feather the ground as the
ox-teams draw them home,
And a declining sun enlarges the lengthening
shadows:
Yet love still scorches me—love has no lull, no
limit.]

21. Good advice truly; & follow'd by the Generality of the Province, for from the Counsellor to the Slave, there was never an instance of true gen'rous Courtship; The Refinement of that noble Passion being what they are wholly Strangers to.

22. Ah Corydon, Corydon! quae te dementia cepit?
Semiputata tibi frondosa vitis in ulmo est.
Quin tu aliquid saltem potius, quorum indiget usus,
Viminibus mollique paras detexere junco.
Invenies alium, si te hic fastidit,
Alexim. [lines 69-73]

["Ah Corydon, Corydon, what is this lunacy you're
possessed by?

You've left your vines half-pruned, and the leafy
elms they grow on.
Why not, instead of moping, get down to something
useful,
Weaving from reeds and withies some article that
you need?
If you're brush off by this Alexis, you'll find
another."]

SHOAT

Ecloga 3

Argument

After a Squabble, as too usual among Convicts, Scape-Rope & Cutpurse challenge one another to sing, & make their Shipmate Shoat Judge of the Performance.— If the Poetry of this Eclogue seems in some Places worse than ordinary, you must consider how hard it is, to make such Persons Speak in Character.

Scape-Rope, Cut-Purse, Shoat

Scape-Rope:

Ho! Cutpurse, say, whose starveling Kine are these?

Cutpurse:

My Master Foists;—They brousing on the Trees.

Scape-Rope:

Ay, so it seems, while any slut he'll court,
Who picks his Pocket, & laughs at him for't
You, Scoundrel as you are, his Corn destroy,
And the few Cows he has with Hunger die.

Cutpurse:

Good Words become you; or I'm much mistaken;
Who late was caught a filching Dobson's Bacon?

Scape-Rope:

Rascal! I did not kill my Neighbour's Trees;
They're Rogues like you, that play such Pranks as these.

Cutpurse:

Not you, be sure—poor Hodges best can tell;
'Cause he his Master pleas'd & serv'd him well;
A Jacket his Reward—You, envious Wight!
To Pieces tore it, purely out of Spite.

Scape-Rope:

Sirrah! I caught thee late—thou know'st, I did.
The Dog betray'd thee—in the Bushes hid;
And when I cried; Beward the Turkies,[1] ho!
Aside the Rails you scamper'd—Is't not so?

Cutpurse:

The Turkey's mine; twas by a Song I won it;
And tho' he kept it from me, Bumpkin own'd it.

Scape-Rope:

Heigh! thou pretend to sing—sure never yet
Cou'd Voice like thine one Tart by singing get,
Tis true, thou scar'st the Wild-Cats by thy yell;
For thy shrill Roar's enough to frighten Hell.

Cutpurse:

Ha! darst thou try, which of us best can sing?
This Dog I prize 'bove any earthly Thing;
Better than ought of thine—yet this I'll lay—
Tis plain, thou dar'st not—dar'st thou, Scoundrel, ha!

Scape-Rope:

Dogs I have none; My Mistress well you know
To Dogs e'er since her Loss has been a Foe;
By them her hapless Lover was betray'd,
And thro' her Husband's Rage an Eunuch made;
And now she hates them with the utmost Spite,
And the least Howl still puts her in a Fright.[2]
But since thou art resolv'd the Fool to play;
The only Thing I have, I'm free to lay:
This Knife, last Instance of that nimble Art,

Which liked to have plac'd me in the fatal Cart
This I have valued long—& yet I'll stake it,
And if thou win'st it from me, thou must take it.

Cutpurse:

And I've a Spoon too, Sukey to me gave,
That last sad Day we took our parting Leave;
O keep it for my Sake, she fondly cry'd,
While round her neck the Noose the Hangman tied,
Yet tho' I value't much, you see, I stake it,
And if you win it from me, you must take it.

Scape-Rope:

Agreed!—I'll make thee own thy Folly soon,
And to my Knife will add thy Sukey's Spoon
See Shoat, that grinning Knave does trudge this Way,
Let him be judge, who sings the better song.

Cutpurse:

Begin then Strait, thy very awkward Song;
I promise, not to be behind thee long.
Come neighbour Shoat, tis not of little Weight;
Mind which of us sings best; & judge aright.

Shoat:

Ay, ay, My Lads; begin; so cold's the Day,
No Danger that your Cows too far will stray;
Or if they do, they'll come to feed at night.[3]
Come make a Fire, & let us all sit by't;
You, Cutpurse, first; then you, in answer sing;
And I'll soon tell which merits most the String.

Cutpurse:

Be Rum[4] 'bove ev'ry Earthy Thing my Choice;
Rum makes me work & animates my Voice.

Scape-Rope:

To me good Cyder's the more welcome Draught;
If I've enough of that, I'm thankful for't.

Cutpurse:

'Tis me black *Juno* pats, the wanton Queen;
Then hides herself, & twitters to be seen.

Scape-Rope:

But Jenny oft aside with me has gone;
Myself not to my Cows am better known

Cutpurse:

Ribbons to *Juno*, fine Ones I design;
Ribbons I'll buy her, when the money's mine.

Scape-Rope:

Kerchiefs to Jenny I've already given;
Tho' yet she 'as had but three, I'll make 'em even.

Cutpurse:

O what kind Whispers from the Slut I've heard;
Tho! lest her Dame shou'd catch her, much afraid.

Scape-Rope:

When on poor Jenny's Hide the Lash I hear;
Her Smart's not less, tho' I the Torment Share.

Cutpurse:

Soon shall I have my Dues; ye Lasses, come
And Jovial Lads; I'll glut you all with Rum.[5]

Scape-Rope:

I shall in Time be free—Arriv'd the Day;
Ye Lads & Lasses, we wll sing & play.

Cutpurse:

My Overseer I've oft a Cuckold made,
And his Wife tells me, I'm a clever Lad.

Scape-Rope:

And dost thou brag of that; thou silly Elf;
My Master out, I kiss my Dame herself.[6]

Cutpurse:

My Master loves to hear My Fecund Song,
For this I work with Pleasure all Day long.

Scape-Rope:

My Master sings himself; so glad's his Heart,
That in each drunken Catch he'll bear a Part.

Cutpurse:

Who loves the honest Planter, may he swill
In Bumbos[7] & in Cyder, when he will.

Scape-Rope:

And he who likes the man that sings unwell;
Let him d[a]mn'd & Anthems chant in Hell.

Cutpurse:

Ha! Rascals, while you lurk to steal all Night
Take Care you do not get a Whipping by't.

Scape-Rope:

Forbear my Lads, in Time, & be not mad;
For I now suffer for the filching Trade.

Cutpurse:

Ho! Sambo, drive those oxen from the Spring;
Myself will Time enough their Fodder bring.

Scape-Rope:

Lads, feed the Cows; if they Shou'd once go dry;
Milk wou'd be wanting to our Huomini.[8]

Cutpurse:

L-as! see yon butting Bull is wondrous lean;
Love makes the Herdsman & the Herds look thin.

Scape-Rope:

That's not the Cause the Yearlings are so poor;
They're sure bewitch'd by some old ugly Whore.

Cut-Purse:

Tell us the reason when we at home again,
We yet our itching Fingers can't restrain.[9]

Scape-Rope:

Say, when the Girls with eating Chalk are pale,
Say, what will make them ruddy fresh & hale.

Shoat:

You've both perform'd so ill, I can't say which
Doest most deserve the Honours of the Switch.
Might I advise, who first of you shall sing,
Shall make his Exit in a hempen String.
For shame! ha' done—I ne'er heard such before;
And Heav'n forefend, I e'er should hear you more.

Author's Notation

1. Turkies [are] surprisingly plentiful & the best I ever eat in my Life.

2. A true story, & just as it is related here.

3. There is no tending of Cattle in the summer after April, but they range at Liberty, where they will; And about the middle of November they begin to feed them night & morning; at which Time the Season begins to grow cold.

4. Rum [is] suppos'd to destroy as many here for the number of the People, as Spirits of all Kinds do at Home.

5. When the Convicts have serv'd out their seven years they have certain dues allow'd them by an Act of Parliament; which they very commonly spend in an Entertainment on their Friends.

6. A Case common among the lower Tribe of Planter's wives. Nay indeed, not twenty years ago the major Part of a whole Bench of justices in a Certain County were <made up of a> not only open adulterers <themselves>, but as remarkable Cuckolds!

7. A common Word in Maryland.

8. Hominee of two Sorts; the Small Hominee eat with Milk.

9. Tis been observed that even those Convicts that have Liv'd honestly here, & have prov'd good and faithful Servants to their masters, have, when they have gone Home, either been hang'd or return'd, in a short Time; & I myself have known two or three, who had a good character of their masters, & who have sold the dearest from that Character, a third Time brought into the Country.

THE M[*ARYLAN*]D-D[*IVIN*]E

Ecloga 4th

Argument

The Satyr here is on those of the Clery, who, after they have try'd in vain, to get a gentile Maintenance in another Profession, fly to the Church as their last Refuge, & are too apt (as Experience sadly shews) by their imprudent Behaviour to bring a Disgrace upon their Office.

Ye *Severn*[1] Nymphs, attempt a nobler song;
Tho' meaner Themes delight the vulgar Throng,
Slaves, Convicts, scoundrel Subjects please not all;
Sublimer Minds for loftier Numbers call.
Such then I'll sing, wou'd *Baldus*[2] lend an Ear,
As *Baldus*' self wou'd not disdain to hear.

Now, now's arrived the long expected Time
Old Hoeus had foretold in tuneful Rhime.
Now M[arylan]d a Set of Priests[3] can boast
To slavish Principles of Truth not lost:
Whose golden Tongues true Freedom shall restore
And make those cease to pray, who pray'd before.
And so the Doctrines of our Faith explain,
As serves make th' Observance of 'em vain.
Caress them, Baldus, great to them thy Debt;
For faith! thyself & they are nicely met.
To thy auspicious Rule all Bliss we owe,
And *Epochas* of Blessings wait us now.
Our Leader thou; if any Marks remain
Of blind Subjection to the Priestly Chain,
These deep Divines the Darkness shall remove,
In Freedom's Cause *Hiberno's* self shall prove;
Thomaso's Genius shall their Breasts inspire,
And fill them with his own persuasive Fire.
O happy Priest! Your *Forties* shall be paid,
And old *Hybernio* too, shall give his Aid,
Hybernio who at Parsons long has growl'd,
And rail'd at Bishops like an errant Scold.

But make a jest of Jesus & his Laws,
And he without a Fee will plead you Cause.
To you the Fair in Clusters shall repair,
The glorious Doctrines that you teach to hear.
E'en all the Church & Parson shall entoll;
And why, 'cause now twill be no Church at all.

Now *Tindal's* System's ev'ry where received,
And *Collins*, *Morgan*, *Whoolstan* all believ'd,
Now sits great Sh[aftesbury] on each Heart enthron'd,
And *Mandevil*'s with highest Honour's crown'd.[4]
Some few Remains of Truth howe'er shall be,
Some stubborn Souls won't with these Schemes agree,[5]
Will own a Saviour, & will think him *God*.
Of honest Faith will Still endure the Load:
Will think the Sacraments art awful Things,
And great the Transports true Religion brings.
In short, in Spite of all these Sons of Reason,
Will still be *Godly*, tho' tis out of Season.

No more than *Britain* need our Parsons come,
Enough we have, that better know at Home.[6]
No more the beardless Boy Damnation fears,
But at such *Old Wive's Fables* nobly sneers;
The tim'rous Girl that wont to fear an Oath,
And trembled at the Thought of Breach of Troth,
Now smiles at Perjuries—the Reason's plain
By Gospel-Laws who wou'd themselves restrain?[7]
They socrn, with self-sufficient Wisdom fraught,
By *Bibles* or by *Parsons* to be taught.
Thus spoke they to each other; 'now's the Time,
'Let's to the Honours of the Forties climb;
'Tho 'tis a Trade, tis yet a gainful Trade;
'Better help on the Cheat, than not have Bread,
'Both Law & Physick Starves, too well we know,
'And tho' we've hardly common sense, twill do.'

O had I strength but equal to my will,
These glorious Wights shou'd be my Subject still;
Nor shou'd e'en L[ewi]s poor, unhappy Bard,[8]
Be read with more Delight or more Regard.
L[ewi]s, on whom the Muse her Favours Shed
And yet to Want her Favourite betray'd.
Nay, M[arylan]d, Spite of herself, Shall own,

Their Preaching by my Poetry out done;
I'd paint them out, just in the Light I ought;
And shew the wondrous Lessons they have taught.

Go on; as yet you hardly know your Pow'r;
Harangue 'gainst sacred Doctrines ev'ry Hour;
With Love of Truth, with Love of Freedom fill'd,
To moral Systems bid the Bible yield;
So shall his fav'rite Priests great Baldus make ye;
And to his inmost Soul & Counsels take ye.

Author's Notations

1. Severn, a River on the mouth of which Annapolis the Metropolis of Maryland is built; & this Eclogue seems to have a particular Eye on sev'ral Places to that polite Place.

2. Baldus—This & the other names in this Ecologue have much puzzled me; but I presume they are Gentleman, which sometimes or other have distinguish'd themselves in the Author's Company: Baldus especially appears to be one of extra-ordinary note. [Baldus was apparently Charles Calvert, fifth Lord Baltimore (1699–1751).]

3. This must not be understood of them all; for there are really sev'ral of them that have done Honour to their Profession, & tis observ'd the Gentleman that come over alate, have had more Learning & Piety too that their Predecessors [Old Hoeus, 1.8, was Horace whose 16th Epade call for a Roman migration to establish a new Golden Age and against which Vergil wrote his 4th Ecologue.]

4. I myself have heard these Gentlemen's Systems approv'd by some of the Clergy. [Matthew Tindal (1657–1733), Anthony Collins (1676–1729), Thomas Morgan (d. 1743), Thomas Woolston (1669–1733), Anthony Ashley Cooper, third earl of Shaftesbury (1671–1713), and Bernard Mandeville (1670?–1733) were all leading deists or attackers of orthodox Christian doctrines.]

5. There are indeed some worthy Gentlemen, who, spite of the Politeness that prevails, still think the Truths in that exploded Book the Bible serious, & fashion their Lives according to the Rules it gives us.

6. The common Cant of a great many of the polite Marylanders.

7. This has an Eye to the mercenary Temper of the young Girls, who after the most solemn Promises to one Lover, never scruple to marry another that is richer, & has the approbation of the generality for it.

8. A Gentleman who had a pretty Vein in Poetry, & like other sons of Parnassus, was very poor; he was also a fine Gentleman, & laught at Religion with the rest. [Richard Lewis of Annapolis was colonial Maryland's most famous poet and schoolmaster.]

TOSS-POT

Eclogue the 5th

Argument

Love-Rum & *Ever-Drunk*, two planters, meeting together, to take a Morning's Draught, resolve to divert one another with a Song; But think none so proper, as what relates to their old Companion, *Toss-pot*, whose Worth, the Loss they receive by his Death, & his Admission into the happy Shades of honest Topers they merrily sing.

Love-Rum, Ever-Drunk

Love-Rum:

Since, Everdrunk, we're here so nicely met
Beneath these Trees let's take a Morning's Wet;
And as we're both old Dabsters at a Song,
A merry Catch won't make it seem too long.[1]

Ever-Drunk:

Agreed—We two such boon Companions are,
If you once bid me sing, I can't forbear:
Say, shall we sit beneath these shady Boughs,
Or wou'd you rather walk into the House?[2]

Love-Rum:

I think in all our Country there's but one,
Can sing with you, & that is *Boozy John*.[3]

Ever-Drunk:

Why; e'en at church he makes so great a roar,
The Clerk declares he'll sing the Psalm no more.

Love-Rum:

Begin then First; No Love-song have you got
'Bout *Nancy's* Charms? the brave & valiant Scot,
Or bouncing *Nell* most woundily wou'd please—
—*Cato*, I see, is cropping round the Trees.—[4]

Ever-Drunk:

I'll give you then a Song I lately made;
From *Boozy John*, a *Better* you ne'er had. [5]

Love-Rum:

Pho! Man; he sing with you; I'd think as soon,
Twas lighter far at Midnight than at Noon;
Or that a Weevil's[6] larger than a Mouse.[7]

Ever-Drunk:

Enough, old Lad—Come, walk into the House—
—When Tosspot died, Lord! What a do we made;
The planters round lamented, he was dead:
While 'bout his Clay-cold cor[p]se poor Susy hung,
And sigh'd so deep, she cou'd not use her Tongue.[8]
None now our Guts with Ham & Chicken fill;
Nor can we in our much-lov'd *Bumbo* swill;
Toss-pot, there's not an honest Lad alive,
But t' have thee here again, his Soul wou'd give.
Toss-pot wou'd make the wisest Man a Fool,
And give new Life, if we were e'er so dull;
Wou'd make us drink, till we cou'd drink no more,
But cover'd with our Carcases the Floor.[9]
As of all Liquors *Rum* delights the best,
And 'midst all Food, good *Ham* excels the rest;
So 'mongst us Planters there was none became,
So well the Business, or deserv'd the name.
His Death of all our fud[d]ling Bouts bereft us,
Sober, we've gone to Bed, since he has left us.
Where wont the Silver Tankard to be brought,
With Nutmeg'd Cyder for a Morning's Draught,[10]
Now can we scarce regale on thin small Beer,
And Ten to One! that's dead—& never clear.
For the full Bowl, Obedient to our Call,

Alass! What meet us now? Faith! nought at all.
Come, Brother Planters, dance we round his Grave;
Such Honours fit it is our Friend shou'd have;
Each bring his Song & Bowl & toss 'em off;[11]
Our Value, our great Regard, we can't shew enough,[12]
His Influence still shall warm us, when we meet,
And, tipsy, we shall think, we have him yet.[13]

Love-Rum:

As, when confounded drunk, a Nap to take
Makes me quite gay and spritely when I wake;
As in the Morning—Drunkards then are dry—
Small-Beer does e'en a grateful Draught supply:
So does thy well-made Song delight me now;
Nor e'er a better have I heard, I vow.[14]
But I must have my Song, as well as you,
And I've a good One—'Tis on *Tosspot* too—
The honest Fellow lov'd me, as his Life—
—I'm sure, much better than he did his Wife.[15]

Ever-Drunk:

You can't oblige me more—Friend *Rumps* declar'd,
A feater Song than yours he never heard;
And well poor *Toss-pot* merited our Lay's,
Since 'Twas his continual care his Friends to
please.[16]

Love-Rum:

When *Toss-pot's* Spirit left his breathless Clay,
And to more solid Pleasures wing'd away;
Where he, with happy Topers, gone before,
Might swallow Nectar, & more nobly roar;
With joy ourselves & Mates all gather'd round
And all our sorrows in our Bumpers drown'd:[17]
Our *Negroes* all their Hardships quite forgot,
Our Overseers the *Seasons* heeded not;[18]
Toss-pot lov'd Ease & Indolence—So we
To go the Road he led us, all agree.
With *Toss-pot's* Name the neighbouring Woods resound,
And distant Mountains eccho back the Sound:
A *Saint* we've made him & his constant Task's

To hover o'er the Punch-Bowls & the Flasks.
For which we'll yearly Honours to him pay,
For his sake drink our very souls away.[19]
As oft as boozy thy old Friend shall be,
My Catches, Toss-pot, shall be all of Thee;
With soaking Tom, & toping Hodge I'll join,
And make thy mem'ry & thy Fame divine.
Yes while in Woods fell Wolves shall chuse to rove,
While Humming-Birds[20] & Bees sweet Blossoms love,
Thy name, thy Praise, thy Honour shall remain,—
Gad! if they don't I'll ne'er get drunk again.[21]

Ever-Drunk:

What does thy Song deserve? A North-West Wind
In Summer's Heat can't better Welcome find;
Not yon green Waves, that grumble 'gainst the Shore,
Nor that smooth murm'ring Stream, delight me more.[22]

Love-Rum:

This, 'Baccostopper first do thou receive;[23]
The same I thought t'our Parson once to give;
But faith! I think it better here bestow'd,
And I'll assure it made of stoutest Wood.

Ever-Drunk:

And here's a Gourd the neatest of the Sort,[24]
Old jerom Crump bad me a Shilling for't,
Tho', being an Assembly-man his wound is great,[25]
I'd rather you the Triffle wou'd accept.

Author's Notations

1. Daphnis; Ecloga 5ta

Menalcas, Mopsus

Me:

Cur-non, Mopse, boni quoniam convenimus ambo,
Tu calamos inflare leves, ego dicere versus,

Hic corylis mixtas inter consedimus
ulmos. [lines 1-3]

[Good-day to you, Mopsus. Now we have met here, both of us experts
—You are playing the light reed-pipe, and I at singing—
Let us sit down together in this grove of elm and hazel.]

2. Mo:

Tu major; tibi me est aequum parere, Menalca
Sive sub incertas Zephyris motantibus umbras,
Sive antro potius succeedimus— [lines 4-6]

[You were the elder, Menalcas: it's for me to fall in with your wishes.
Shall we go under the trees, where light airs stir the shadows
Or would you prefer a cave?—]

3. Mo:

Quid si idem certet Phoebum superare
canendo? [line 9]

[No singer in these hills but Amyntas dares to challenge you.]

4. Me:

Incipe Mopse prior, si quos aut Phillidus ignes,
Aut alconis habes laudes aut jurgia Codri.
[Incipe]—Pascentis servabit Tityrus
haedos. [lines 10-12]

[Lead off with a song then, Mopsus—"The Loves of Phyllis," or
"In Alcon's Praise," or "Quarrelsome Condrus"—any you know.
Lead off, and Titrus here will look after our grazing kids.]

5. Mo:

Im[m]o haec, in virdidi nuper quae cortice fagi
Carmina descripsi—[et modulans alterna notavi,]
Experiar; tu deinde jubeto [ut] certet
Amintas. [lines 13-15]

[I'd rather try a song which I wrote the other day
On a green beech trunk, and set to music for voice
and pipe
Antiphonally: let Amyntas improve on this, if he
can.]

6. A very small Insect that does great damage to Corn & Bread.

7. Me:

Lenta salix &c. [quantum pallenti cedit olivae,
puniceis humilis quantum saliunca rosetis,]
judicio nostro tantum tibi cedit
Amintas. [lines 16-18]

[Well, in my view Amyntas compares with you no more
Than a dejected willow with the olive's silvery
sheen,
Or the unassuming flower of valerian with red
roses.]

8. Mo:

Sed tu desine plura, [puer;] successimus antro.
Ex[s]tinctum Nymphae crudeli funere Daphnim
Flebant—[(vos coryli testes et flumina Nymphis),]
Cum complexa sui Corpus miserabile nati;
Atque deos atque [astra] vocat crudelia
Mater. [lines 19-23]

[But here we are in the cove, my lad, so sing away.

Mopsus

Daphnis died. The nymphs bewailed his death—
rivers and hazels heard them weeping:

"Cruel stars and gods!" his mother cried,
    clasping the poor corpse close in her arms.]

9. Daphni, tuum Poenos etiam in gemuisse leones
Interitum [montesque feri silvaeque loquuntur.]
Daphnis & Armenias curru subjungere tygres
Instituit; Daphnis Thiasos inducere Baccho,
Et foliis lentas intexere Mollibus hastas.
Vitis ut arboribus &c. [lines 27-32]

[Even Afric lions roared their grief,
    forest and hill keened Daphnis dead.
Daphnis first enwreathed our wands with leaves,
    Daphnis was first to harness tigers,
Daphnis led the revellers through a dance—
    all for the Wine-god's festival day.
Vines grace elms, and grapes the vine,
    bulls grace herds and corn the joyous tillage.]

10. Tu decus omne tuis. Postqu[a]m te fata tulerunt
Ipsa Pales agros, atque ipse reliquit Apollo
Grandi saepe &c. [quibus mandavimus hordea
    sulcis,] [lines 34-36]

[Daphnis graced all nature—when he died
    Corn-god and Song-god left us too.
Where we sowed our champion barley seed,]

11. Spargite humum Foliis &c. [line 40]

[Scatter leaves and shade the springs,]

12. For him we ne'er can show Regard enough.
[Presumably a later version for this line.]

13. Formosi pecoris custos, formosior ipse. [line 44]

[Lovely my flocks was, lovlier I.]

14. Me:

Tale tuum carmen nobis, [divine poeta,]
Quale Sopor fessis in Gramine, quale per aestum

Dulcis aquae saliente Sitim restinguere
rivo. [lines 45-47]

[What an inspired poet you are! To me, your
singing
Is as a sleep on the grass to a tired man, or a
draught of
Fresh water from a dancing brook when the noonday
parches
One's throat.]

15. Nos tamen haec quocunque mod tibi nostra vicissim
Dicemus, Daphninque tuum tollemus ad astra.
———amavit nos quoque Daphnis. [lines 50-52]

[Still, I'll do what I can to make you some return
By way of this song, extolling your Daphnis to the
stars
. . . for Daphnis loved me too.]

16. Mo:

An quicquam nobis tali sit munere majus;
Et puer ipse fuit cantari dignus, & ista
jam pridem stimicon laudavit carmina
nobis. [lines 53-55]

[Nothing you could give me would please me more
than that,
For Daphnis, if any, deserved elegies; and besides,
Stimichon often has praised to me this song of
yours.]

17. Me:

Candidus insuetum &c. [miratur limen Olympi
Sub pedibusque videt nubes et sidera Daphnis.]
Ergo alacris silvas & cetera rura voluptas
Panaque postoresque tenet, Dryadasque
puellas. [line 56-59]

[Daphnis shines at heaven's dazzling gate,
under his feet sees clouds and planets,

Shepherds, nymphs and Pan are glad for this,
forest and champaign quickened with joy.]

18. Times for the managing of Tobacco, which can never be medled with, but in the rain.

19. Ipsi laetitia voces [ad sidera iactant]
[. . .] Deus, Deus ille, [Menalca]
Sis bonus O felixque tuis En quat[t]uor aras
[ecce duas tibi, Daphni, duas altaria Phoebo.]
Pocula bina &c. [lines 62, 64-67]

[Wooded hills, crags, orchards cry to heaven
. . . A god is he!
Bring us luck, good Daphnis! Here are two
altars for you, and two for Phoebus,
. . . two cups . . .]

20. Very small and a very beautiful Bird that is seen all over America in the Summer; flying and humming about the flow'rs.

21. Cantabunt mihi Damoetas & Lyctius Aegon.
Dum juga montis aper,—
Dumque thymo pascentur apes—
Semper honos nomenque tuum laudesque
manebunt. [lines 72, 76-78]

[These shall be your rites . . .
Long as boars love heights . . .
Long as bees suck thyme—will you remain
praised and famed, our yearly vows receiving.]

22. Mo:

Quae tibi, quae tali reddam pro carmine dona?
Nam neque me tantum venientis Sibilus Austri
Nec percussa juvant fluctu tam littora, nec quae
Saxosas inter decurrunt flumina
valles. [lines 81-84]

[What, oh what can I do to reward you for such
singing?
Sweeter it was to me than a south wind's rising
murmur

Or the rhythmic drumming of waves on a beach; more sweet than the music
Rivulets make as they scamper down through rocky glens.]

23. Me:

Hac te os fragili donabimus ante cicuta. [line 85]

[But I will give you a present first—this delicate reed-pipe.]

24. Gourds here grow very large; & of great use; on various accounts, the great ones, to keep Fat, Flow'r, &c., the less, for water.

25. Mo:

At tu sume pedum, quod me cum Saepe rogaret
Non tulit Antigenes (et erat tum dignus amari[)]
_____.

[And you shall have this beautiful crook, evenly studded
With bronze. Antigenes often asked me for it (and he was
lovable then), . . .]

CELSUS

Eclogue 6th

Argument

The great Progress of Infidelity gives rise to this Poem; & I can hardly call it even an Imitation of the Eclogue.[1] I cou'd wish there was no Occasion for the Satyr in it; & am sorry to say some very great men make the important Truths of our holy Religion the daily Subjects of the wanton Raillery! The Author will venture to affirm, That nothing is here suppos'd to be said by Celsus, but what he has actually heard often & vehemently maintained in common Conversation.

The first was I, who thought it worth my while,
Of Mary-Land to Speak in any Style;
Nor bless'd my Muse—a modest girl you'll say—
Her wondrous[2] Sons to sing in rustick Lay—
Assembly Men, & Counsellors, & jars[3]
In highflown Numbers thought I to rehearse;
No; she reply'd;—too ventrous are the Themes;
Nor dare you triffle with those glorious Names.
What Worth they have, deserving nobler Rhimes,
Some, tuneful Bard shall sing in blither Times.
Thy humbler Verse of Celsus' Worth shall tell,
Celsus, who is Himself's own Parallel;
Celsus, whose large capacious Soul's too great,
Things sacred with the least Regard to treat:
He keeps with W——n, M——n[4] strict Alliance,
And holds Priests, Prophets, Gospels, at Defiance!
'Gainst Creeds with what persuasive Force he raves;
How scorns the Wretches Priestly, Pow'r enslaves?
Yet when, Himself his Rheth'rick flings about,
And gives 'gainst Heav'n & Ch[urch] his dictates out;
Whate'er he says, his Hearers must believe;
What he calls Truth implicitly receive.
Thus is the Wight the very Priest, he blames,[5]
And the same Track pursues that he condemns.

On then, my Muse—Once visited the Sage,
Thoughtless & Rakely, Youths of equal Age,

Of equal Warmth in Reason's mighty Cause,
Of like Invet'racy to Tyrant-Laws.
Oft had he promis'd to their longing Heart
A Schedule of his fav'rite, Scheme t'impart.
They now demand it—He with gracious Eyes
Benignly to their fond Request replies:
'Children, I'll all your doubtings joyful clear;
'just is the Boon you ask; attentive Hear.'
He said, & strait a Silence most profound,
Still as the Dead of night reign'd all around.
E'en Crab, his fav'rite Foist,[6] was quite struck
dumb,
Nor Puss has stir'd, tho' Mouse, had crost the Room.
As serious as Dan: Burgess did he look,
As grave as Nailor's were the Words he spoke.[7]

First, then he sung how this round Spacious Ball
Once on a Time, was a huge Chaos all;
Till Chance, a mighty Pow'r, but who or what,
Was far beyond this Ken—that matter'd not—
Bad Order from Confusion to arise,
And thus form'd Lands & Seas, & liquid Skies.
Next, [God] he sung, but such a [God] as shew'd[8]
He thought he very little to him ow'd;
Too great, too glorious, & too unconfin'd,
The paltry Bus'ness of our Earth to mind,
And therefore left poor Mortals to their Passions,
To do what suited best their Inclinations.

Then sacred Story was his Scoundrel-Theme,
And wondrous wisely did he now declaim:
Adam & Eve Non-Entities were made;
No Serpent yet a Woman e'er betray'd;
Noah's a Blockhead, & Cham Serv'd him right,
T'expose, His Weakness to his Brother's Sight;
Abr'ham's great Faith was nothing but a name,
And Moses cheated Israel with a Sham:
Sampson's vast Strength deserves our Ridicule,
David's a Villain, Solomon a fool;[9]
By childish whims were fill'd the Prophets all,
No more inspir'd by H[eave]n, than by Baal.
And the whole Bible's a notorious Cheat,
A Maintenance for lazy Priests to get.

The Gospel next his Eloquence commands,
And now he loudly *Ch[rist]* himself arraigns.
A pack of Sots is ev'ry Ch[ri]st[ia]n, Nation,
And gull'd the World had been, e'er since the Passion.
And they, who his Absurdities believe,
A just Pretence alone to Wisdom have.
—But hark! the Muse is shock'd[10]—She bids me cease
These Outrages against the Prince of Peace:
And to those other *glorious* Tenets haste,
Which wondrous *Celsus* to the Youths exprest.
The Sacraments he made of equal Force
To save a Ch[ri]st[ia]n, as to save a Horse:
No sacrifice of Praise did H[ea]v[e]n require,
And fruitless, needless all were *Forms* of *Pray'r*.
By *Consequence* no Need there was of Teaching,
And P[a]r[s]ons shou'd be planting, instead of preaching.[11]
In short, Religion was the Child of Pow'r,
To keep poor ign'rant Man from knowing more,
Than what their *wise* Forefathers knew before.
Hence then, this Inference he plainly drew,
Our Passions shou'd be all submitted to;
Pray why were they bestow'd if not employ'd,
And what are Blessings, that are not enjoy'd?
Come then, indulge where Humane Laws permit,
Hell, Devil defy, these *School-boy* Fears forget,[12]
Dare any Act, but what may cause you swing:
Libel your G[od], your Country & your King;
Debauch a diff'rant Fair one ev'ry Night;
The Nuptial Tie's an Imposition quite.

Go Bravely on—No After-Reck'ning fear,
With which old Dreamers frighten Children here
When Death invades, the Humane Frame's no more,[13]
Than just the empty *nought* it was before.
Souls we've no more, than has a Bug, a Mite,
And all is wrapt in one eternal Night:
No Heav'n, no Hell will be hereafter seen,
But we shall be, as tho' we' had never been.

He ceas'd—the list'ning Youths around him bow'd,
And grateful own'd what mighty Thanks they ow'd.
His fine Harangue, enraptur'd Hearts approv'd,
While *Tray* began to bark, & *puss* remov'd:

Some farther Time in friendly Converse spent,
Away well-pleas'd with Blasphemy they went!

Author's Notations

1. The Imitation so small, that I shan't think it worth my while to mark out the few Places, where I have follow'd the Poet. [In Eclogues 1, 2, and 9, the author wrote in the left side of each page the Latin verse he parodied in the eclogues. He does the same in Eclogue 5 of the first booklet but does not do so with Eclogues 3, 4, 8, or 10 of the second booklet.]

2. <A sneer, I suppose.>

3. Surely our Author is here upon the Sneer, for I never knew one Squabble they ever had that was worth a wise Man's regarding at all; or even a Bavius's making an Epigram on. ["Jar" is a variation of char or charwoman.]

4. [Probably Thomas Woolston (1669-1773) and Thomas Morgan (d. 1743), both deists, whom the poet mentions in the fourth eclogue, l. 36.]

5. This the case of too many of the Maryland Gentry, who, without any Education still fancy themselves wiser than all the great Men that went before 'em, & expect all they say to be receiv'd as Oracles.

6. Foist, a name for a little dog. [In line 105 he calls the dog "Tray."]

7. Well does our Author sneer those two Enthusiasts, for to their followers is in great measure owing the Infidelity of the Marylanders; whom having too much sense to be Quakers & too much Pride to submit to the Establish'd Church, set up for Free Thinkers & drown what Sense they have in an arrogant Self-Conceit. [Daniel Burgess (1645-1713) was a notable, witty, and enthusiastic Presbyterian divine of London during the late

Stuart period. James Nayler (1617?-60) was an emotional, mystic leader of the early Quakers who was tried by Parliament in 1656 and pilloried, whipped, and branded for alleged blasphemy.]

8. I'm afraid this may be thought treating a serious Subject in too ludicrous a Manner. Certain I am, the Author had the highest Veneration not only to the divine Being consider'd as his Creator; but with regard to ev'ry Relation he bears to us according to the Christian Scheme.

9. David in particular is sadly maul'd, & a certain —— himself have been known to call him the grandest Villain that ever liv'd: But no wonder, he meets with no better Treatment from a Common Sharper. [Craddock's note does not name David's antagonist. Originally he wrote the second clause of the first sentence, "and —— themselves have" which accounts for the use of "have" rather than "has" in this sentence.]

10. Shock'd indeed; Ev'ry serious Ear must be shock'd at the daily Conversation of our pretended Solomons.

11. The constant Part of 'em all to a Man——Indeed we are so unhappy, that not a few of our Clergy wou'd become a Hoe, better than a Pulpit.

12. Hell & Devil now are old antiquated Notions & as such Laugh'd at here, as ever they were at St. ——'s.

13. This is really the Doctrine they teach, & endeavour to persuade themselves of, in Spite of that unwelcome Monitor, their Conscience, who is always telling them quite the Reverse.

JEMIMA

[Eclogue 8th]

Argument

Jemima, forsaken by her Lover Crocus, goes to Granny, an old Midwife, famous among Planter's Wives & Daughters for her great Skill in Charms & Enchantments; where Jemima complains much of her Lover's Cruelty & Perfidiousness; & then Granny endeavours to get the disconsolate fair One another, tho' alas! for once she fails & loses her Labour.

Poor sad Jemima's[1] doleful Plaints I sing,
And the kind of Comfort Granny strove to bring:
At which grave Puss, unmindful of her Prey,
Stood so aghast, the Vermin stole away.
Nay, e'en the Fire, (if all was said, is true)
Struck with sage Granny's magick Force, burnt blue.
Thou, Celia,[2] deign to listen to the Theme,
Thou Glory of my Lays, from whence their Influence came.

By Crocus[3] long Jemina had been woo'd,
At last he'ad gain'd the Point he'ad long persued.
Her kind Consent was one—the happy Night's
Appointed to begin Connubial Rites.
When, basely treach'rous to th'expecting Maid,
He left her, a more wealthy Fair to wed;
And now he revels in Dorinda's Charms,
Forgetful of Jemima's vacant Arms.
While the poor Girl pours forth her vain Complaints,
And 'gainst the perjur'd Wretch her Curses vents.
True;—oft she'ad thus been us'd by other Men;
But thought it wondrous hard, to be so us'd again.

Twas Night; the grateful Dew carest the Glade,
When to old Granny's Hut repairs the Maid;
Granny, fam'd matron, vers'd in midnight Lore;
O'er Ghosts & Stars & Devils great her Pow'r,

Such she to whom for Ease Jemima run;
She wip'd her blubber'd Cheeks, & thus begun.

Jemima

O Chearful God of Day, restore the Morn,
While I with fruitless Love for Crocus burn:
Crocus, who soon my easy Heart deceiv'd;
Ye Pow'rs! ye know it, tho' ye've not reliev'd:
Witness you are of my Distress in vain:
Begin, my Heart, begin the Plaintive Strain.

Crocus is married to Dorinda fair,
What Lover now has Reason to despair,
Let Sc[o]ts & Buckskins[4] now together join,
And cleanly Polecats mix with cleanlier Swine;
Dorinda go; the nuptial Candle light;
Perhaps one Candle he'll allow to Night;
Too great th' Expence for him t'indulge again,[5]
Begin, my Heart, begin the Plaintive strain.

O better match'd, than thou cou'dst e'er expect,
While thus you treat me with unjust Neglect;
While thus my Face once flatter'd you despise,
And view my Features with ill-natur'd Eyes,
You think the Gods to punish you disdain;
Begin, my Heart, begin the plaintive Strain.

First, when I saw you twas with Captain Grim
Strait, strait I lov'd, you look'd so gay & trim:
Then were my years I think scarce twenty four;[6]
Happy indeed, had I ne'er seen you more.
I saw, was lost, siez'd with the raging Pain;
Begin, my Heart, begin the plaintive Strain.

I know thee, Love; a savage Life thou'st led;
In some hard Highland Rock with Crows bred;
None of our Buckskin Blood runs in thy Veins;
Begin, my Heart, begin the plaintive strains.

'Tis Love, hard-hearted Love, has oft imbrued
The mother's Hands in her poor Infant's Blood;
Such Mothers sure must bear a cruel Heart:
Yet, Cupid! Thou by far more cruel art;

To thy vile Ends such hapless nymphs to gain;
Begin, my Heart, begin the plaintive strain.

Now fly the Wolf at the young Lamb's Pursuit
Produce the knotty Oak delicious Fruit;
With tuneful Mocking-Birds[7] let Owls contend,
Their Lives let Planters thro' D-ll's[8] Preaching mend,
And free from scandal let our Priests remain;
Begin, my Heart, begin the plaintive Strain.

Ye woods, farewel; let all be Seas around;
My Sorrows soon shall in their Waves be drown'd,
My faulting Tongue no longer shall complain,
But, my Heart, cease at once the plaintive Strain.

She ceas'd—Old *Granny* pitied much her Case,
And sooth'd with sof'ning words her great Distress;
Bad her be calm, nor for one Youth run mad,
If Charms cou'd do't another shou'd be had;
Jemima beg'd that she might have one soon;
The mumping Beldam grin'd, & thus begun.

Granny

Bring Water, & this Circle sprinkle round,
With Greens & Ribbands be this Threshold burn'd,
Tho' I your former Lover can't restore,
Court the desponding Maid, one Lover more.

What wondrous Things my pow'rful Charms have done,
How oft against her Will brought down the Moon?
E'en Snakes themselves I've stiffen'd many a Score;
Court the desponding Maid, one Lover more.

This particolour'd Ribband, fair One, take,
And true Love Knots of various Fashion make;
Tie, tie 'em fast & *Venus*' Aid implore;
Court the desponding Maid, one shepherd more.

As this Wax Image melts afore the Fire,
With Love of Thee some Youth shall yet expire;
Thou want'st a Husband—all thy Wants are o'er;
Court the desponding Maid, one Lover more.

For am'rous Transports such thy wondrous Love,
That Sows themselves not greater Longings prove,[9]
When thro' the Woods they seek the foamy Boar;
Court the desponding Maid, one Lover more.

These Presents, which the faithless Lover left,
Pledges of Love, tho' of that Love bereft,
Hide deep beneath the Threshold of the Door.
Court the desponding Maid, one Lover more.

To me these Poisons an old *Negro* gave,[10]
Mighty his knowledge in them, tho' a Slave,
Strange Things with them he'as done, strange Changes made,
As if all *Hell* itself came to his Aid.
With these the very Graves can I explore;
Court the desponding Maid, one Lover more.

Within this Door, Jemima, Ashes bring,
And o'er thy Head into that Riv'let fling;
Look not behind; some shepherd thou shalt see,
If there is Truth or in my Charms or me:
Ha! Sure I am, I never fail'd before;
O Court the hapless Maid, one Lover more.

See how in vain I all my Arts have tried;
My sullen Sprites have all the Aid denied;
Ah! poor Jemima! all thy Hopes are o'er,
Die an old Maid, nor think of Lover more!

Author's Notations

1. Jemina, a name extremely common in this Country. [Henrietta Maria was a common name of Maryland girls, since that was the appellation of Charles I's consort after whom the colony was named. Note how in line 9 he first wrote "Maria" and then inserted Jemima.]

2. Any body, whom the Reader, pleases.

3. By *Crocus* one wou'd think he meant some ship surgeon, of which this Country is full, where they

administer their Poysons under the pompus name of Doctors.

4. A Name, given the Country-born [i.e., American-born] in Derision, from the great number of Deer in the Country.

5. From this & sev'ral other Hints, tis plain this Eclogue has it's Foundation on Truth.

6. A great age for an unmarried woman in Maryland.

7. A remarkable Bird, whose Musick equals any of the feather'd Choir, & has this peculiar to it, that it can imitate any other Bird it hears.

8. See Eclogue the first [line 32.]

9. I can't help owning, that this Simile, tho strong, is yet too coarse; yet if we consider the Plenty of Hogs in this Country, & how nearly allied in nature the People are to this useful animal, we shall the more readily excuse the author.

10. Negroes, especially the saltwater [African] ones, [are] remarkable for their skill in Poysons, of which they sometimes gives too fatal Instances.

Gachradidow

Eclogue the 9th

Argument

Tachanoontia, & Gachradidow, two Indians, meeting together, bewail the common Loss of their Lands, usurp'd by the English; thence are led to celebrate the Worth of Shuncallamie, one of their Chiefs; & at last, Gachradidow sings in Praise of that Liberty which in the most severe Distresses they are still resolv'd to enjoy.

Tachanoontia, Gachradidow,

Tachanoontia:

Hoa, Gachradidow, whither art thou going?[1]

Gachradidow:

To Town, to pay some Skins[2] I've long been owing.
—O Tachanoontia, see our Wayward Fate;
Strangers how Lord it, where we liv'd alate,
'Away, you Scoundrels, you've no Business here;'
Are Sounds which once we thought to hear.
Now driven far distant from our native Lands,
(So Heav'n ordains—that Heav'n, which all commands).
We live in Want, in Poverty, in Pain,
And part with all our Skins for little Gain.[3]

Tachanoontia:

Surely I've heard—if what I've heard, is true—
That by our Indian Road a Line they drew,
Which Line by Treaty was the Barrier made,
For both, all future Wranglings to evade.[4]

Gachradidow:

'Twas Truth;—But what will Treaties e'er avail

With Christian-Whites, whose Av'rice grasps at all?
As wisely might you hope, the plaintive Dove
The hungry Eagle's empty Maw might move.[5]
Soon they encroach'd upon us, kill'd our Deer
And, did they not our wild Resentment fear,
Of all our Lands we'ad quickly been depriv'd,
And must without our Venison have liv'd:
Your Gachradidow wou'd have wanted Pone,[6]
And what wou'd great Shuncallamie ha' done?[7]

Tachanoontia:

Shuncallamie? Wou'd he to Ills submit,
Whose stubborn Soul ne'er knew a Master yet?[8]
Who then should teach our brawny youth to sling
The hissing Stone, or missive Shaft to wing?
Who bid 'em, with loud chearful Cries, advance
Against the hostile Fort, in Warlike Dance?
Who sing our Warriours in melodious Strains,
How they with Villain Blood have died the Plains;
How with Katawby[9]—Furies they've engag'd,
And War unequal, tho' successful wag'd?

Gachradidow:

Or rather, who our Liberty shall sing,
Of all the joys we yet retain, the Spring?
That we have yet—& oh! while that we have,
Distresses, e'er so great; we'll nobly brave.
Tho' Swarms of Ch[ri]stian-Scoundrels round us roam,
Afraid, at least, asham'd, to stay at Home,[10]
In strains as sweet as Mocking-bird's we'll shew,[11]
Our gen'rous Hearts with Love of Freedom glow.

Tachanoontia:

So 'gainst hoary Winter's nipping Cold,
Mayst thou ne'er Match Coat[12] want, thy Limbs t'enfold;
So from the Scorching Sun's impetuous Heat
Thy Feet conduct thee to some cool Retreat:
Begin—in Freedom's grateful Theme rejoice,—
I've my Song too—They say I have a Voice—
Tho' unharmonious to a skilful Ear,
Yet oft, when Red-Birds[13] sing, the Raven's Croak
you hear.[14]

Gachradidow:

I will—nor shall my Song unworthy be
Of what we hold most dear, blest *Liberty*.
Here then, O Goddess, midst our Tribes remain;
With Us, thy faithful Race, for ever reign;[15]
Poor as we are, our wide-extended Waste,
Our Christal Streams, which yield a cool Repast,
Our lofty Forests all shall witness be,
How much we love, how greatly honour thee.
Let vile Injustice[16] & base Slav'ry sway[17]
The Christian Plans—we neither will obey—
What Wonder that these Wretches seek our Shore,
Since Wealth, not Thee, O Freedom, they explore?
Nor wou'd they come, did not each fruitful Field
Large golden Crops of our *Tobacco* yield.—
—What will not Age—My Mem'ry once was strong,
And, when a Boy the live-long Day I sung;
Now I've my Lays forgot, my Voice I've lost;
—Surely my Eyes some *Rattlesnake*[18] hath crost![19]

Tachanoontia:

Why do you rob me of Delight so soon?
You've Time enough—As yet tis scarcely Noon.
The town's not far—Besides, the Winds are still,
Without a Murmur glides this gentle Rill;[20]
Shrill sounds you Voice along this gloomy Shade—
—Or if you're of yon low'ring Cloud, afraid,
Sing as we walk—less tedious is the Road—
Sing as we walk—I'll help to bear your Load.[21]

Gachradidow:

No more—we see *Shuncallamie* to Night;
His Voice will give you more sincere Delight.[22]

Author's Notes

1. Moeris: Ecloga 9a
Lycidas, Moeris

Ly:

Quo' te, Moeri, pedes? an quo via ducit in urbem? [line 1]

[Where are you footing it to Moeris? to town? this trackway leads there.]

2. Deer Skins;—the Indians kill a great many, & sell the skins for Triffles to the Traders.

3. Mo:

O Lycida, vivi pervenimus, advena nostri,
(Quod nunq[ua]m veriti sumus) ut possessor agelli
Diceret: Haec mea sunt; veteres migrate coloni.
Nunc victi, tristes, quoniam fors omnia versat,
Hos illi [(quod nec vertat bene)] mittimus haedos. [lines 2-6]

[Oh, Lycidas, that I should have lived to see an outsider
Take over my little farm—a thing I had never feared—
And tell me 'You're dispossessed, you old tenants, you've got to go.'
We're down and out. And look how Chance turns the tables on us—
These are <u>his</u> goats (rot them!) you see me taking to market.]

4. Ly:

Certe equidem audieram, qua se subducere colles
Incipiunt &c.
Omnia carminibus vestrum servasse Menalcan [lines 7-8,10]

[Can this be true? I had heard that all the land . . .
. . . all this land had been saved by Menalcas' poetry.]

5. Mo:

Audieras & fama fuit: sed carmina tantum
Nostra valent, Lycida, tela inter Martia quantu[m]
Chaonais dicunt aguila veniente, columbas. [lines 11-13]

[So you heard. That rumor did get about. But poems
Stand no more chance, where the claims of solders are involved,
Than do the prophetic doves if an eagle swoops upon them.]

6. Bread made of Maize or Indian Corn.

7. Nec tuus hic Moeris, nec viveret ipse Menalcas

[What ever it cost, neither I nor Menalcas would be alive now.]

8. Ly:

Quis caneret Nymphas? quis &c. [line 19]

[Who would have written about Nymphs, . . .]

9. [Catawba,] A nation of Indians ever in war with the Indians of the Six Nations; who are the Borderers on Mary Land, Penn. & New York. At the last Treaty between Virg[inia] & Mar[ylan]d with the S[ix] Nat[ions], when the Virginians would have made Peace between them, our Indians said the Kat[awba] had so affronted them that they never wou'd, & had called them women & not men; whereas themselves were men & double men for they had two ________. [Poet leaves a blank line.]

10. In good Truth; the case of most of us.

11. Mo:

Im[m]o haec quae Varo [necdum perfecta] canebat
Vare, tuum nomen.
Cantantes sublime ferent ad sidera
cycni [lines 26-27,29]

[Why not these lines from a poem to Varus he's not
yet finished—
Varus, if but Mantua remains untouched . . .
Swans shall exalt your fame right up to the starry
heavens.]

12. The Indian's dress in the Winter.

13. A Bird of the Bigness of an English Sparrow—all over Red & Sings finely.

14. Ly:——

Incipe, [si quid habes] & me fecere poetam
Pierides; sunt & mihi carmina; me quoque dicunt
Vatem Pastores
[nam]Neque adhuc vario videor nec dicere Cinna
Digna, sed argutos inter strepere anser
olores [lines 32-36]

[And so let us have some poem of your own. The
muses made me
A poet too. There are songs of mine. The
shepherd folk
Call me their bard. . .
I know I cannot be mentioned in the same breath
with Cinna
Or Varius—a honking goose with silver-throated
swans.]

15. Mo:

Id quidem ago [. . .]
[. . .] neque est ignobile Carmen.
Hec ades, O Galatea [. . .]
Hic ver purpureum &c. [lines 37-39]

[I'll try then . . .
. . . I made a quite good poem:—
Come to me, *Galatea* . . .
Coloured Spring is here.]

16. Indeed it is reckon'd among the Indian Traders, no Crime to cheat an Indian; & yet these Wretches call themselves Christians.

17. Insani feriant sine littora fluctus. [line 43]

[*Let the wild waves pound the shore* . . .]

18. A Serpent illegible well known; there are sev'ral odd notions about it, & this among the rest.

19. Omina fert aetas [animum quoque] saepe ego longos
Cantando puerum memini me condere Soles.
Nunc oblita mihi tot carmina; vox quoque Moerim
Jam fugit ipsa; lupi Moerin videre priores. [lines 51-54]

[Time bears all away, even memory. In boyhood
Often I'd spend the long, long summer daylight singing.
Lost to memory, all those songs; and now my voice too
Is not what it was: the wolves ill-wished it before I could spot them.]

20. [Ly:]

Et nunc omne tibi stratum silet aequor, & omnes
[aspice,] ventosi, ceciderunt murmuris aurae [lines 57-58]

[Look how the mere lies hushed and sleek from end to end
For you: the gusty wind has died down to silence now.]

21. [. . .] tamen veniemus in urbem;
Aut si, nox pluviam ne colligat ante veremur,
Cantantes licet usque (minus via laedit) eamus;
Cantantes ut eamus, ego hoc te fasce levabo [lines 62-65]

[. . . we shall reach town, don't worry;
Or if there's a fear the night may turn rainy, we can press on,
Singing as we go; a song lightens a long road.
Give me that packs of yours, and we'll go on our way singing.]

22. Mo:

Desine plura, puer [et quod nunc instat agamus:]
Carmina tunc melius, cum venerit ipse, canemus.

[No, we have done enough, lad. To business! And Menalcas'
Songs will sound better still when he's home to hear us sing them.]

WORTHY

Ecloga the 10th

Argument

Worthy, a young Maryland Gentleman, had long courted Flavia, & was kindly receiv'd by her, so far, that he gain'd her consent, & only waited proper Time for the Ceremony. Being oblig'd the meanwhile to make a Voyage to England & a richer match offering, Flavia very prudently accepted of it & left poor Worthy to his fruitless complaints. This Poem was writ, it seems, at the very Time the affair was in agitation, Worthy being an Intimate Friend of the Authors.

This my last Labour, gentle Goddess, aid,
To Worthy due, by Flavia hapless made;
Be such the Song, that she the Bard approve,
And listen to the honest Planter's Love.
To Worthy who their Measures can refuse?
The best in Maryland deserves the Muse.
So shall thy Bard acknowledge still thy Sway,
And when thou bid'st the Song, attune the Lay.
Begin—his gen'rous Passion let us sing,
While warbling Mock-Birds usher in the Spring
Nor think the cheerful, spritely Labour vain
The waving Woods will echo back the Strain!

What Groves, my jolly Girls, your forms conceal,
When Worthy burns with Love, without Avail?
What tow'ring Hills such grateful Prospects shew,
Or what meandring Rills so sweetly flow,
Your unkind absence from the Youth t'excuse,
Not Woods themselves their gen'rous Plaints refuse;
E'en Mountains sympathize with him in Grief,
And stony Rocks can wish him kind Relief.
His faithful Overseer his Task forgets,
And every Slave at his misfortune frets:
Poor Brother Philip comes to sooth his Pains:
All kindly ask what Nymph his suit disdains.

E'en Thickscull, 'mongst his Neighbors wondrous wise,
Gives him a helping hand, & bravely cries;
'Pho Man!' why makst thou such a mighty Pother,
'Scorn the false Jade, & briskly court another.'
Kind neighbor Twanhum, by his Tresses known,
To join his honest Grief with his rides down;
Good Parson Saygrace his lov'd Bumbo leaves,
Tho' he small Comfort to the Lover gives;
Saygrace whose fiery Phiz more brightly shines,
Than Lay'rs of Gold in rich Peruvian Mines.
'Where will this end? he cries, too cruel Love,
'No skill what'er can from our Hearts remove:
'As well teach deists faith, & Lawyers Truth,
'Give Sense to Coxcombs, & to old Maids Youth.'
He sorrowful returns—Yet, gentle Swains,
In doleful Ditties sing my am'rous Pains;
Some little Ease my harrass'd Soul may feel
My hapless Tale in Rhime to hear you tell.
O that an Overseer I'ad only been,
This cruel Creature I shou'd ne'er have seen;
Some Convict-Girl full well had serv'd my Turn,
Black Bess at least with equal Flame wou'd burn;
And what tho' black she is—The Crabs[1] brave food,
Tho' it's Form's hideous, yet the meat is good:
O Flavia, by this Riv'let's purling stream,
These woods, these flow'ry Meads (thy Charms my Theme)
O blest with Thee, with that dear Shape & Face,
Be me disclaimed, Eternity might pass.
Now furious Love boils up my heated Blood,
And I cou'd revel in a purple Flood,
Cou'd feast on murders & in rapes delight,
And 'gainst my dearest Friend for madness fight.
Thou far from me the greatest Woes wou'dst dare,
Rather than live with me in safety here:
O Cruel! Still let not thy haughty Scorn
Bring on thy pitiless Soul a like Return:
Now, now, of Lover's fatal Woes I sing,
And Charms, of Sorrows like my own, the Spring.
Yes—in the Woods midst Bears & Wolves I'll roam,[2]
And think no more of Flavia & of Home:
There shall the Trees my fatal Passion wear,
The Marks of my fond Love their Barks shall bear.

Meanwhile, *Scotch-Irish*[3] shall my socials be,
Wild as they are, quite good enough for me.
Or 'gainst the grizley Bear my Rage I'll vent,
To trace his Haunts in Freezing Cold content.
Now over Rocks & ecchoing Woods I fly,
The friendly *Indians* all my arms supply,
As if by this my Soul a Cure cou'd gain,
And Heav'n had taught me thus to ease my Pain.
Now neither Nymphs nor Songs can yield me Peace,
And all the Charms the woodland's gave me, cease;
Not all my Cares can change the Tirant-Boy;
My Summer's Thirst *Patuxent*[4] may alloy;
Winter's most piercing Cold I might endure;
But Love still governs all, & will not know a Cure.

Enough has *Worthy* mourn'd—enough I've sung,
Due Thanks, ye Planters, to my Lays belong;
No more my Pipe with spritely Strains shall swell;
Go mind your Hogs & Crops,—& so farewel.[5]

Author's Notations

1. Crabs very plentiful in the seaside, tho no Lobsters.

2. The Author here has the advantage of the Bardling at Home, for here are both Bears & Wolves in great Plenty.

3. Great numbers of these Gentry [live] in the back Parts of the Provinces & tis hard to say whether the Indians or they are <the wilder> greater Savages.

4. A River on the Western Shore, on which the suppos'd false one lived.

5. My friend here has finish'd, but has left out not imitated the seventh Eclogue of Virgil; What can be Reason; I'm at a Loss; But tis most likely that he died before he had finish'd his Design, for certainly had he liv'd longer, he would have imitated that & left these Poems, he has done, more perfect than they are.

9
The Death of Socrates

[<u>Cast of Characters</u>

Socrates	Philosopher of Athens
Xantippe	His wife
Plato	
Crito	His students
Phedon	
Melitus	
Lycon	His accusers
Anitus (Anytus)	
Apame	Melitus's sister
First Areopagus	Judges of Athens
Second Areopagus	
Crier	Bailiff
Gaoler	Jailer
Citizens of Athens]	

[Act the 1st]

[Scene 2d]

[Melitus, Anitus]

[Melitus]

The heavenly powers no doubt entrust their secre[t]
With that vain wretch, who dared defy their godhead,
And slight their altars.

Anitus

Thus the bold *Lysistratus*[1]
Won on the people by a like pretence;
He too had his *Minerva*[2] to protect him,
To aid his counsels, and support his cause.
High on the shining car with him she rode;
And the gull'd commons, struck with stupid wonder,
Gaz'd on the feign'd divinity, till they
Lost their dear liberty, and hug[g]'d the chain
Of a foul tirant—Doubt not, *Socrates*
Hath the same view; and if the worthy *Melitus*,
With others that are wakeful for the state,
Use not the noble talents heaven has given them,
Their pow'rs of speech, their energy of sense,
In firm defiance 'gainst his guileful schemes,
And timely ward the fatal blow he aims,
What can ensue but slavery and ruin?

Melitus

Such slavery and such ruin as slate
Gall'd [illegible] that villain traitor, *Critias*.[3]
He lorded nobly o'er his fellow-citizens,
To death devoted ev'ry man of virtue,
And was indeed a tirant—such the ruin
The haughty son of *Clinias*[4] had essay'd,
(Whose vile contemptuous usage of the god
That guards, benign, our doors still strikes our
souls
With chilling terrors) had not *Athens* fear'd

Th'impending peril—These thy pupils, Socrates!
These are the youths that fondly listen'd to thee;
These had'st thou taught in all the secret arts
Of thy philosophy; conspicuous proofs
Of thy attachment to the publick weal!

Anitus

What wait we then? Why waste we still the hours
In vain complaint? And since our patriot hearts
Burn for the injuries our state hath suffer'd,
Why don't we rather haste to execute
What nobly we've resolv'd—th'applauded deeds
Of all the heroes that our Athens boasts,
However great, are poor, compar'd with this.
T'assert the dread divinities that guard us,
To shield their shrines, to vindicate their
    temples;
To free our youth from impious fallacies,
From vain illusions and destructive tenets;
Our freedom to establish on a base
That will be solid, these are godlike toils,
And, if we fall, our fate will yet be glorious,
Worthy the sons of Athens!

Melitus

And I'll dare it,
Whatever perils face me in the conflict.
But there's no peril—be we staunch and honest,
And all his subtleties and nice evasions
Can's stem the torrent that comes pouring on him.
My sister! hah!—I know her simple businesses—
Retire we for the present—Well-inform'd
Of our design, and stupidly enthral'd
In love's fond bondage, her romantick head
Thinks high of Socrates, and much she labours
To thawart my soul in her confirm'd resolves.
In vain! The cause is heav'n's, and I'll be steady.
I dearly love her, and she cou'd not ask
A second favor that I shou'd deny her.

Notes

1. Lysistratus was a Greek sculptor of the late fourth century B.C. noted for his realistic portraiture. All notations to this drama are those of the editor.

2. Minerva was the Italian goddess of handicrafts usually identified with the Greek goddes Athena.

3. Critias (c. 460-403 B.C.) was an aristocratic Athenian politican and poet exiled from the city in 406 B.C. for his support of Alcibiades. See note 4 below.

4. Clinias was an Athenian commander killed at Coronea in 447 B.C. and the father of Alcibiades (c. 450-404 B.C.), an Athenian general and politician noted for his insolence, haughtiness, and extravagance. He was a friend of Socrates. He was accused of multilating the Hermae (square figures surmounted by the head of the god Hermes) that stood at the entrance of private homes in the city. For this impiety Alcibiades was tried and convicted. He fled to Sparta to avoid punishment.

Scene 3rd

Apame

Thou fly'st me; ah! infatuated brother!
Thy sly insinuating *Anitus*
And the fool *Lycon* lead thee on to ruin.
Big with high notions of thy own desert,
Thy boasted eloquence, thy cry'd-up wisdom,[1]
And proudly swol[le]n with their pernicious praise,
Fondly thou think'st to bear down all before thee,
To manage *Athens*, as thy own vain will
Suggests, and trample e'en beneath thy feet
All that oppose thee in thy windy schemes.

'Cause thou art angry, and yet know'st not why.
The venerable *Socrates* must bleed;
That *first* of men, who mates a god in wisdom,
Sent surely as a blessing from above,
To teach sublimest truths, to rear the soul
'Bove earthly views, and form her, to embrace
Joys more than mortal, bright, etherial, pure
And yet this excellent, this peerless sage
Must fall the sacrifice of villain malice,
Of wicked men who hate him for his virtues.

Meanwhile, what sorrows swell my anguish'd bosome,
Rent 'twixt distressful passion and the tie
That binds me to my brother. Love for *Phedon*,
For *Phedon*, worthiest of the youths of *Athens*,
Whose truth wou'd shame the constancy of swains;
Phedon, adorned with ev'ry mainly grace,
That cou'd engage a virgin's tender heart,
Fills all my soul, and makes it his entire.
Alass! Dear, gen'rous youth! What boots the love,
The faithful fondness of thy charm'd *Apame*,
While still her brother with relentless hate,
Thwarts all the schemes thou form'st to save thy friend,
And aims the ruin of thy dear instructor,
The reverend sage thou lov'st to call thy father?
The dire result of this I well forebode,
And e'en anticipate that weight of woe,
That follows close his obstinate pursuit.

Note

1. Line 5 is Cradock's line number 200.

Scene 4th

Apame, Phedon

Phedon

That pensive posture, and that tearful eye

Betray fair excellence, the ill success
Of my Apame's pleadings with her brother.

Apame

O Phedon, Melitus, I fear, is doom'd
By the just gods to force his own destruction,
His strong inveteracy 'gainst Socrates
To them is painful; and for righteous ends
Tho' that great man may suffer, still my brother
Must feel the utmost fury of their vengeance:
For well I know, their justice yet will punish
The wretch, a foe to virtues like their own,

Phedon

Then he's resolv'd?

Apame

Resolv'd? he shuns his sister;
Soon as he saw me, from my sight he fled,
Like a base murderer, conscious of his guilt,
Who dreads each whisper'd nothing that he hears,
And flies the phantom that himself hath form'd.

Phedon

Then thou must fall, my Socrates: thy soul,
Great as hath yet e'er animated man,
I know, will bear this stroke of fate undaunted:
Will smile at all the malice of her foes,
And look with calm indifference on death.
Hence spring our fears: Were he like other men,
Had he the same weak frailties to lament,
Life wou'd appear to some importance to him,
And he'd be more sollicitous about her.
For, far from this, he thinks not of his danger,
As danger; but pursues his wonted course,
Directing others in the paths of truth,
As if no foes endeavour'd his destruction,
And all without was, like his own pure soul,
Sweet harmony and peace.

Apame

This binds me to him,
Weak as I am, and of that thoughtless sex,
Who seek no further for their rule in life
Than the dull road their mothers trod before them;
Yet ever hath my heart leap'd at the name
Of Socrates; and scarce had reason dacon'd[1]
In my young mind; but I grew fond to hear
The lessons that he taught; to learn from him
Truths, hid before in sophistry's dark guise,
And close to follow, where he led the way.
The more I knew, more was my joy athirst
For higher knowledge; and he still encreas'd,
Still as he hed me on, my love of wisdom.
But, more than all his wondrous eloquence,
His choice expression, and his flow of reason,
His practice pleads; unerring in his life,
He walks conspicuous in each godlike virtue,
And lives himself in the great good man he teaches.

Phedon

He is indeed the man thy justice speaks him,
Nor did he want a herald to his virtues,
Cou'd he employ a nobler tongue than thine;
For thou art even wanton in his praise,
And then shin'st loveliest, when his worth's thy subject.
Oh! my Apame! how unlike thy brother.
But I'll evade the contrast—he's thy brother,
And therefore to a softer theme I'll turn,
Such as demands the eloquence of gods,
Thy heav'nly beauties, thy divine perfections.

Apame

Forbear, presuming Phedon—

Phedon

Listen to me,
Nor with that frown indignant kill your Phedon.
Say rather; dearest object of my vows;

Thou first and only mistress of my heart;
Say, wilt thou now with kind relenting eye
Hear me pour forth the truest noblest passion
That ever swell'd a fond and faithful soul;
A soul that lives not but upon the hope,
The distant hope that goodness, nigh divine,
Will look with pity on the pangs she suffers.[2]
Oh! thou art all that fancy's self can paint—
All harmony, all excellence, all beauty!
Thy form so exquisite, that wou'd the maid,
Last of the gods that left our earth reluctant,
Once more forsake her natal plains above,
And with her presence gladden thankless man;
She'd sure shine forth in all the bright
    effulgence,
In the divine attractions of *Apame*,
O stay that killing look—forgive my rapture—
Indulge my wanton tongue while she essays
A task more arduous, to display the charms,
The heavenly beauties of thy matchless mind.

Apame

Say, is this *Phedon*, this the strenuous friend
Of *Socrates*, of *Socrates* the sage,
Form'd by his rules, and won by his example,
Who can thus poorly waste the precious hours
In wordy compliment and vain encomiums
On the mean trifle of a woman's beauty?
Now when thy friend, thy father, thy instructor
Walks on the verge of fate, can thy low soul
Sink in the soothings of an idle passion?

Phedon

Chide not, *Apame*, chide not; deep I feel
The pressing dangers of that virtuous man;
And oh! if I had twice ten thousand lives,
I'd part will all, nay, almost part with thee,
To save him from the direful fate that threats him;
For much I fear the pow'r of those that hate him.
For what inures my heart amid it's sorrows,
What firms my soul, but love of thee, my charmer,
Of thee the lover and the friend of *Socrates*?

This ardent passion arms me 'gainst my grief,
With manly fortitude, with intrepidity.
Forgive me then, nor blame thy faithful Phedon,
If in the fullness of his love he speaks
The glorious charms of that transcendant maid,
Which thus inspires him to sustain each shock,
To dare all danger for the friend he loves.

Apame

No more; but that I know thy honest heart,
This flattery wou'd be grating to my ear,
Harsh and discordant as an ill-tun'd instrument.
'Tis not by sounds like these I can be won.
Yet still forgive me, virgin—modesty—
I own thy worth, thy virtues, and thy truth
Have made my soul a sharer in thy griefs.
But oh! I leave it to thy thought to form
The various evils that will thwart our bliss.
Still be thyself, still be the friend of Socrates;
And if the gods join with thee in thy cares,
And crown thy filial friendship with success,
Apame then with honour—spare my blushes—
What have I said?—my maiden heart condemns me—
I dare not stay to tell thee, how I'd thank thee.

Notes

1. Daconed could be a variant of docent, from the Latin docere, "to teach". It means "teaches or instructs; teaching."

2. Line 68 is Cradock's 300th line of this act.

Scene 5th

Phedon

Transporting sounds! O my enraptur'd soul!
Yes; I will be the friend of Socrates,
Will be myself, and will deserve Apame.
Thou shalt be mine; for sure the righteous powers

Must crown my truth, and thy consummate virtue
With ev'ry happiness this earth can yield—
But talk'd she not of evils that might bar,
Might thwart our bliss? forbid it, heav'n!—the thought,
Shou'd I dwell longer on it, wou'd distract me.
I'll strive then to forget it, and away
To my expecting friends.

Scene 6th

Plato, Crito, Phedon

Plato

Tis now the hour
That *Phedon* said he'd meet us.

Crito

He appears.

Phedon

Alass! My tiddings bear but slender hope:
The foes of *Socrates* resolve his Death:
Apame's not allow'd to see her brother;
Sullen he flies her presence, and in vain
She strives to turn him from his fatal purpose.

Plato

What frenzy hath possest the men of *Athens*?
Think they the gods will thank them for their hate
To that great man, whom only they allow
Sincerely wise? Have they so soon forgot
What dread *Apollo* from the sacred tripod
Divinely answer'd to th'enquiring *Cherephon*,[1]
That *Socrates* was wise, and only *Socrates*?
And well the sage responds to the great character
The oracle bestows; for sure if wisdom
E'er dwell on earth, within his virtuous breast

The heav'n-born goddess lives, and sways the man
Sways ev'ry action, dictates all his words.
Well ye repay the pow'rs divine, *Athenians*,
To work his death, who forms your greatest glory,
And makes you foremost in the states of *Greece*
For true philosophy, for solid knowledge!
Lo! this is ample gratitude to heaven!

Crito

Such gratitude hath *Athens* ever shew'd
Where worth illustrious shone. In arts or arms
Whoe'er excell'd, but met the like return?
Thus *Homer*, thus *Tirtous*[2] bore their despite;
Thus *Anexagoras* was once condemn'd;[3]
Miltiades[4] thus languish'd in a prison,
And great *Themistocles*[5] was forc'd to fly
For refuge to the monarch, 'gainst whose tiranny
His prudent counsels had preserv'd his country.

Phedon

Th'unruly populace, who're ever won
By the loud rhetorick of a noisy demagogue,
Forget the noble actions of their heroes.
Their city sav'd, their pow'r maintain'd, enlarg'd,
Their wives, their daughters snatch'd from direful rape,[6]
And peace and affluence to their streets restor'd;
Their youth instructed in each patriot-duty,
And form'd to virtue from their infant-years;
All these plead vainly with a boistrous rout,
Who're giddy with th'authority they bear;
And call it glorious freedom to devote
Their worthiest citizens to death or exile.

Plato

Else *Socrates* who bends beneath the weight
Of seventy years, years spent in noblest toils
For his dear country's safety or her glory;
Might hope to wear away the few poor minutes
That yet remain of life, amid his friends,
In honourable ease, exempt from danger.

Phedon

And might he not, did not the 'unworthy *Anitus*,
Whose flagrant guilt can't bear the kind rebuke
Of one who but endeavors to reclaim
His soul from ruin, urge the prosecution?
For *Melitus* and *Lycon* are but tools[7]
To his iniquities and mean revenge.
Base, he gives up to an unmanly passion,
Beneath the soul that is not worse than brutal,
Revenge for good intended, such a man,
As *Athens*, if she yields to his delusions,
Will ne'er remember but with tears of repentant
penitence.

Plato

Then be't our care to save her from her shame.
O friends, O youths, that have with me imbib'd
The sacred truths, which, like *Hyblean* sweets,[8]
Flow'd on your souls from his mellifluous tongue;
Who've often with unutterable transport
Felt the glad influence of his blest instructions;
O let us know, unanimous, resolve
To thwart the machinations of his foes;
To stay the low'ring mischiefs that impend
Over our great preceptor. Much we owe
To his directing hand. If we are virtuous,
If for our country or our friend we feel,
If our hearts glow with love of ev'ry grace,
That can exalt us 'bove the groveling crowd,
Twas he that form'd us; he the sacred spring,
From whence our souls drank deep the cordial draught
Of heaven-born truth, of knowledge that aspires
'Bove sense, bove appetites, and penetrates
Yon empyrean[9] heights; of rapturous wisdom,
That teaches us to scorn this lower scene
Of mean delights, beneth th'enlightened mind,
T'emerge from out the prison of the body.
And seek for our inheritance, amid
Etherial beings in the realms above.

Crito

Doubt not, my *Plato*, but our inmost souls

And seek for our inheritance, amid
Etherial beings in the realms above.

Crito

Doubt not, my *Plato*, but our inmost souls
Are link'd with his; and, if he falls, we feel
Griefs that wou'd dumb expression.—Name thou then
The means to save him, and we joy to dare them
E'en at the utmost peril of our lives.

Plato

Alass! that's only in the will of heav'n,
At least, what project can we form at present?
If he won't fly, he must submit to trial;
All therefore we can do, is to be active,
Strenuous, and resolute in his defence;
To plead with all the eloquence of tears,
To battle 'gainst his enemies, and rather
To die—

Phedon

Imortal gods! wou'd that preserve him,
I'd dare a tirant's tortures.

Crito

So wou'd I,
And bless the hand that took my life for his.

Plato

Bravely resolv'd, my friends! Methinks we are
Like a poor people, who beneath the rule
Of a just prince have long been blest and happy;
When the stern-fates the cruel mandate give
To close his precious life: the direful news
Link them in wild astonishment, they look
Aghast, and, struck with terror, deep they mourn,
Fly to their altars, with incessant prayer
Plead for his life, recount his gracious deeds,
Run o'er his gen'rous cares, his gentle reign;

Suppliant, the mercy of high heaven implore,
And, to retrieve their prince, will be themselves no more.[10]

End of the 1st Act

Notes

1. Chaerephon, a youthful friend of Socrates and a member of the democratic party in Athens that was now persecuring the philosopher, once asked the oracle of Apollo at Delphi if there was anyone wiser than Socrates, to which the oracle replied that there was none wiser. Plato, *Apology*, 20e–21a.

2. The reference to Homer is unexplained in this context. Tirtous or Tyrataeus was a seventh-century B.C. Spartan general and patriotic poet. Some claimed he was an Athenian schoolmaster before going to Sparta. Cradock's allusion seems to be to the Athenian belief than no Spartan could be a poet, so he had to be a former Athenian.

3. Anaxagoras (c. 500–c. 428 B.C.) was probably the first philosopher to reside in Athens. He was exiled for alleged impiety during an attack on his friend Pericles, c. 450 B.C.

4. Miltiades (c. 554–489 B.C.) was the Athenian general who directed the victory over the Persians at Marathon in 490 B.C. He was imprisoned by political rivals and died shortly thereafter.

5. Themistocles (c. 524–c. 460 B.C.) was the Athenian admiral who saved Greece from Persian domination as the result of the destruction of Xerxes' fleet off Salamis in 480 B.C. Exiled from Athens, he eventually served Xerxes' son as governor of some Greek cities in Asia Minor that were under Persian control.

6. Line 38 was Cradock's line 400 for Act 1.

7. Anytus is considered to have instigated the proceedings against Socrates for worthy motives. His objective was not to execute Socrates but rather to exile him as a threat to political stability. Anytus chose an obscure, young religious fanatic named Melitus to prosecute the case. About Lycon very little is known. See A. B. Taylor, Socrates: The Man and His Thought (Garden City, N.Y.: Doubleday, 1953), pp. 102-4.

8. Hyblean refers to the town of Hybla in Sicily that was celebrated for the honey produced in nearby hills. The bees of Hybla are mentioned in Vergil, Eclogues, 1.54.

9. Empyrean pertains to the highest heaven in the cosmology of the ancients.

10. Line 115 is Cradock's line 486. In the subsequent acts there were no numbered lines in the manuscript.

Act 2nd

Scene 1st

Socrates

How beauteous springs the morn! yon golden beams,
That burst all glorious from the rising sun,
To glad approaching day, and cheer mankind
In their repeated toils, but late were hid
Beneath night's dreary mantle, and black darkness
Shaded a sleepy world: and yet that sun
Rose yesterday as bright, and will tomorrow.
—Say, is not this to die and rise again
Each even and morn? for death itself's no more
Than the dark instant that removes the soul
From *this* world to a *better*, when she rises
More free, more active, to etherial life;
In this superiour to yon blazing orb,
That, when she once hath risen, she sets no more.

This to a listless, an ungrateful world
I long have taught aloud, and pointed forth
The way to solid wisdom. By that pow'r
Inspir'd, who long with unremitted goodness
Hath on my anxious, my enquiring mind
Beam'd heavenly knowledge,—such as ancient sages
In vain essay'd to learn,—have I to man
Laid ope the hidden stores of true philosophy,
And shew'd her plain and naked to the eye.
For this what worthy recompence is mine?
E'en taunt and despite: Man that will not know.
—His real good, insulting, thus repays
For him my gen'rous cares; nay more; grown tir'd
With being freely told ungrateful truths,
They scheme against me; 'gainst a weak old man,
Emaciated with toil, with pain, with indigence,
They level all th'artillery of their malice.
They work my ruin, merely 'cause I love them,
And labour for their welfare in *Hereafter*.
But be it so; be this their kind return;
Persist, my soul, in thy benevolence;
Be firm in doing good—Beneath thy thought

Are life's vain scenes, and death to thee but opens
A brighter prospect, rich with endless life,
With rich happiness! Not to be told,
Not to be thought, while thou art confin'd below!

Scene 2nd

Socrates, Plato, Crito, Phedon

Socrates

What gloom is this, my worthy youths, that sits
So heavy on the visage? You're no more
Lightsome and gay, as when you us'd to crowd
Around your old philosopher, to hear
The smooth and easy dictates he unfolded.
You seem distrest, as if some sudden evil,
Some unexpected blow, had stunn'd your souls,
And wretchedness and you were grown familiar.

Plato

Alass! we're now no strangers to each other.
Ah! Socrates, canst thou demand the cause
Why all thy friends have lost their wonted glee,
Why they look sunk in thought, in deep anxiety,
When thou, who long hast been their heart's best solace
Their dear-lov'd object of esteem and reverence,
Stands't tott'ring on the precipice of fate,
The horrid precipice, nor seem'st to hear
The gulph that roars beneath thee?

Socrates

Pho! my friends;
This all your cause? I am not worth your sorrows.
Too long already have I toil'd, depress
By this dull clayey covering, this incumbrance,
That keeps me downward; while my soul aspires
To something higher, something that she whispers
As far exceeds what we call bliss below,
As man himself excells the vilest worm,

That groveling crawls the earth. Then why for me
This needless anguish? Wou'd you please your Socrates,
Be cheerful still, be gay, as you were wont,
And listen, blithe, to those important truths,
I'll never cease to speak, while life informs
This old and tottering fabrick.

Crito

Chearful, say'st thou?
O Socrates, in vain wou'st thou instruct us
To bear serene the perils, that we fear.
While thus our big-swol[le]n hearts bleed inly for thee,
Too piercing is the anguish that we feel,
E'en to be sooth'd by thee.

Phedon

We mourn, we mourn
For thee our dear-lov'd friend, our blest instructor,
And therefore are we come once more to move thee,
To yield awhile to this thy pressing danger.
Well do we know the firmness of thy soul;
Dauntless she views the rancour of her foes,
And smiles at all the efforts of their fury.
But oh! forgive us, if we urge thy flight;
Evade at present what will else destroy thee:
The citizens will yet return to reason,
Soon will they wonder at their own mad folly,
And blush to think they e'er could hurt their Socrates.

Plato

Then to thy wishing friends mayst thou return,
With glory soon; again from thee they'll hear
The words of wisdom, nay, the words of life;
For what is life without that heavenly guide,
To lead us onward to eternal day?
Consider; Oh! reflect, if thou art lost,
We lose the hand that guides us, and again
Sink in that rayless state, wherein the world
Long time had grop'd in vain, till heaven sent thee
To drive the darkness, and illume our hearts.

Socrates

What means my <u>Plato</u>? how! must <u>Socrates</u>
Fly from his country like some villain—traytor,
Who bears within him all the guilt, for which
He fears the just resentment of his citizens?
Is life so very valuable, that he
Must give the lie to what himself had taught,
Poorly resign his yet-unsullied fame,
And bid farewel to all his peace of mind,
Meanly to save it? Never, friends, o never,
Shall your Preceptor thus condemn his Doctrines.

Plato

Sure when a desperate enemy resolves
To ruin worth, any by fallacious arts
Betray that virtue which he hates to death;
The guiltless sufferer can fear, no stain
Will soil his honest praise, if he awhile
Leaves his ungrateful country, and retires,
Till she at length recovers from her madness,
With tears calls back her dear, her injur'd patriot,
With open arms receives him to her bosome,
Owns her offence, and begs him to forgive her.

Socrates

The man, that flies the justice of his country,
Must have some inward reason for his conduct;
He wou'd not fly but that his conscious mind
Urges his flight;—he knows too well he's guilty,
And therefore he escapes; I know my innocence,
And therefore am resolv'd to stand my trial.
O friends, conceive the transport I must feel
To hear my foes with all their busy malice
Rack their poor thought to find one single circumstance,
Whereon to ground their cruel accusation.
How shall I smile, to hear the twist and torture
Each harmless word, and each indifferent action,
To mould them to their purpose, but in vain.

Plato

Alass! Thou wilt not see the fearful danger:

The people, when a noisy Orator
Pleads 'gainst exalted merit, quick enflam'd
By his insidious, his bewitching eloquence,
Lose all destinction soon 'twixt right and wrong,
And madly vote to death the man they love,
The man by whom they live, by whom they're free.

Phedon

Hast thou forgot, how those unhappy chiefs,
Who fought victorious at the Arginuse,[1]
And dyed the azure main with Spartan blood,
The blood of enemies that struck at Athens,
Fell victims to an inflam'd populace?
What was their crime? fatal necessity.
The winds, the waves, the very gods oppos'd them;
Yet still they suffer'd; nor their own high merit,
Nor even thou, tho' nobly didst thou plead
In their defense, cou'dst save them from their fate,[2]

Crito

They perish'd—so wilt thou—remember yet;
Thy Alcibiades[3] cou'd boast a soul
Equal to ev'ry danger; yet he thought
It well befitted his high fortitude
To avoid his partial trial, when he knew
His judges were his foes, and stood determin'd
To satiate their resentment with his blood.

Socrates

In vain are these examples urg'd—I still
Will front the danger, be it e'er so dreadful.
But why do I say, danger? Life to me
Long time hath worn indifference. Even now
Death hath not one poor terror to appall me:
And, if such base injustice sways my country,
Meanly to yield to my causeless foes,
Tho' well ascertain'd of my innocence;
I'll meet this death, this bug-bear to mankind
E'en as a courteous friend that kindly takes me
From a base world, which knows not how to value
A patriot-citizen, devoid of guile,

Who only sought the welfare of his country.

Plato

Yet let *Xantippe*, let your children plead;
Yet *live* for them—your little innocents
Deserve your life, as long as heaven will grant it.
Tis sure not like a father, thus to waste it,
When their young tender years demand support
From thy directing hand—O think, think of them,
Think, what they lose, when they're bereav'd of thee.

Socrates

Xantippe and my children share my heart:
Forbid it, heaven, that shou'd want for them,
That strong affection, which our common mother
Enforces to the meanest of her offspring!
Yet still there is a more coercive law,
Which the mind will obey; and, when that tells me
To stay and face the malice of my foes;
I think, I'm well absolv'd, if to that pow'r,
Who ever guards the orphan and the widow
I leave them, with a firm and holy confidence,
That he will be to them a friend, a father.

Notes

1. At the naval battle of Arginusae off Lesbos (406 B.C.), the Athenian fleet decisively defeated the Spartans, but the victors were unable to rescue the crews of some of their sinking ships. For this the Athenians arrested, tried, and executed six of their admirals.

2. Socrates' defense of the six accused admirals may be found in Plato, *Apology* 32b-32c, and Xenophon, *Hellenica* 1.7.

3. Rather than face trial for impiety due to the multilation of the Hermae, Alcibiades fled in 415 B.C. to Sparta. See Act 1, Scene 2, note 4. His advice to the Spartans in the Peloponnesian War contributed significantly to their eventual victory

over Athens. Alcibiades, an open traitor condemned to death by Athens and cursed for sacrilege, was a supposed pupil of Socrates. This association was a critical factor in public opinion relative to Socrates' alleged corruption of the youth of the city.

Scene 3d

Socrates, Xantippe, Plato, Phedon, Crito

Socrates

Thy looks are wild, Xantippe, and thou tremblest—

Xantippe

Ah! Socrates, have I not cause to tremble,
When thy inveterate enemies combine
To take thee from me, and will sure succeed,
Merely 'cause thou art wanting to thyself;
When thou goest on in thy old beaten track,
Like one forsaken by the gods he scorns,
To teach those doctrines whence they form thy ruin,
And art indifferent to what ill betides
Thy little ones or me.

Socrates

You wrong me much,
To think youself or them to me indifferent.
I bear about me all the tender passions,
That throb the husband's and the parent's breast;
And wou'd be all an honest man can be
For your support. But tell me, wou'dst thou have me,
Now, that I'm tott'ring on the on the verge of fate,
And death by natural means must very soon
Divorce me from thee, meanly save a life;
That can't be long of much emoulment
To them or thee? I never can, Xantippe—
Haply my enemies may not succeed,

And Athens have that great regard to justice,
Not to condemn an innocent old man,
Only because the wicked rage against him.
But if it is resolv'd that I must fall,
For thy dear sake, and for my children's sake,
I will not, must not finish with dishonour
A life, as yet unstain'd with guilt or baseness;
I must not meanly fly, but dare the danger,
And bravely suffer, as a good man ought.

Xantippe

Ridiculous! But such hath ever been
Thy life's wild conduct. Vainly dost thou boast
Thy wise philosophy, if this th'event,
Thou'lt suffer, how?—like a delirious fool,
Who in a fever's rage eludes his keepers
And plunges in the flood—the same thy madness;
Drunk with thy idle sistems, wild with notions
Of what thou can'st not know, thou hast brav'd
our gods,
Derided our religion; warp'd our youth,
And made thyself obnoxious to the state;
And yet thou calmly talk'st of innocence!
They'll not condemn an innocent old man;
I'll bravely suffer, as a good man ought.
Stuff! stuff! mere stuff!—ah! Socrates, thou say'st
Thou art old; thou art so; for thou doatest Socrates;
And all thou say'st, is folly, mere, rank folly.

Socrates

Have patience, my Xantippe

Xantippe

Patience? preach it
To thy kind friends, to Melitus and Lycon;
They'll listen most attentive; yes; they'll hear thee
With most observant reverence—preach to them—
They'll be thy Platos, Phedons, Critos—all
Their passions will be sooth'd no doubt to peace,
When thou preach patience to them; they'll no more
Plot 'gainst a poor and innocent old man;

They will admire thy virtue and thy wisdom;
Thy wondrous virtue, that can leave thy wife—
Thy children—in the most severe distress—
Thy wisdom, that can bid thee not t'evade
The ills that threat thee—Heavens! can this be wisdom!
Can this be virtue?—Curse such hair-brain'd
maxims—
And yet I wou'd preserve thee—I shall rave—
Say, wilt thou save thyself?

Socrates

As how?

Xantippe

Why fly,
Fly till the storm is over.

Socrates

No, Xantippe,
I cannot fly—

Xantippe

Thou can'st not? Driveling wretch!
The gods are even with thee for thy madness;
They will repay thee for thy wild contempt;
They now laugh at thee; for their high abodes
They dart their vengeance, and thou diest their victim;
Infatuated fool! thou diest their victim.
O I cou'd tear myself to atoms—Thus
To see thee—Heavens? my brain—Curse on—O Socrates!
—Dull stupid wretch! Thou art not worth my tears.

Scene 4th

Socrates, Plato, Phedon, Crito

Socrates

Strong is the virulence of female passion;

Poor woman! how her boistrous temper sways her!
And yet she loves me with sincere affection
'Mid all this tirant-madness that deforms her—
But tis beneath philosophy, to heed
A woman's idle rage.

Plato

O Socrates
Greatly she's worthy of your kind regard;
Her soul's bewilder'd in the killing fears
Of your approaching danger; and she knows not,
By nature violent, in her distress
To moderate her anguish.

Socrates

Therefore be she
No more the subject of our thoughts at present:
For you, for her, and for the tender pledges
Of our most holy loves, I will do all,
I will bear all the humane heart can bear.
But there's one rule I must constant follow;
The rule my soul imposes on herself:
I have already said, I can't transgress it.
Great are the transport of an honest conscience,
E'en in the severest trials! he that knows
That he means well; and by that inward law
Hath modell'd all his actions, stands secure,
Tho' all around is waste and desolation.
Tis this compels me to my present conduct:
Think not, tis vanity directs my heart;
I know too well our nature, to be vain.
I will be Socrates, will be the man
I've ever taught mankind; and if my foes
Prevail, and I'm unjustly doom'd to suffer,
I'll die as I have liv'd,—I will die Socrates.

Scene 5th

Apame, Melitus

Apame

At length I've found you, Brother; long you've shunn'd
me,
As if _Apame's_ presence were unwelcome;
The cause yourself best knows; but sure you need not
Fear the reproaches of a simple sister.

Melitus

I own, I fled your presence for a while,
'Cause well I know your high attachment to
The man your brother hates—I blame you not—
Phedon's pathetick eloquence hath power—
But therefore I declin'd a conversation,
Guessing the mighty purport of your errand.

Apame

An errand, _Melitus_, that much concerns you:
For know, your malice 'gainst the godlike _Socrates_,
Rebounds upon yourself—You may succeed;
But sure, unhappy youth, you only work
Your own perdition; your insidious wiles
Will in the end ensnare you in a ruin
I dread to think of.

Melitus

Then e'en spare thy terrors
For me, dear sister, I despise that ruin,
But say, what ruin? Brave, don't I defend
Our country-gods, whom this vain man insults?
Will they desert me, when in their own honour
I firmly dare? When I assert their godhead,
And strive to save their temples from contempt?
No sister; they're themselves too much concern'd
T'expose the man, who fights their cause, to ruin.

Apame

Ah! brother; vainly dost thou urge a plea;
Which can't convince one single soul that knows thee.
The worship of the gods affect thee little.

Long might they mourn their want of votaries,
Their shrines neglected, their forsaken altars,
Did not thy own resentment trail thee in
To their assistance.—*Socrate's* friendship
His gen'rous candour, and his honest zeal
To wean thee from thy idle, fond amusements
The stupid figments of a poet's brain,
Words without meaning; and to lure thee thence
To solid studies, such as wou'd inform thee
In life's importance, and advance thy soul
To real pleasures—this his love for thee
Hath rais'd thy spleen, and drives thee to repay
him
With such ingratitude as wants a name.
Therefore thou join'st the villain *Anytus*,
And ideot *Lycon*; one, a half-learn'd fool
Fraught with his empty *self*; the other, Heavens!
A wretch the meanest, guiltiest, most abandon'd
Of all that plagues our *Athens*—worthy fellowship!

Melitus

Well sister, hast thou learn'd thy sexes talent;
Thou bandiest purely; but pray I stope[1] no more;
My friends will laugh at all thy woman's railing;
Nor think thy modest appellations worth
A wise man's notice—still, if thou art prudent,
Thou wilt forbear, and not provoke me farther—
I may perhaps forget I am thy brother.

Apame

These threats to me, dear *Melitus*, are idle;
I have, as well becomes me, all the love,
Nay, all the reverence, you can claim as brother.
Yet sure there's something due unto a sister,
The rather, when her tenderness alarms her,
And she forbodes some very sad event
From her dear brother's conduct. If he's angry
Merely because she fears he may regret
The steps he's blindly following, she will pity him,
But smiles—contemptuous at his empty threats.

Melitus

Well; my pert sister, I'll for once be calm,
And hear the wondrous lesson thou wou'dst teach me,
Tho' much compliance sits but awkward on me.

Apame

Away with this derision! More important
Is the sad subject of our present converse.
You're tempting your own fate; and, like the bestial,
That heedless roves the flow'ry plain along,
That feeds securely on the verdant herbage,
Nor views the dreadful precipice before him,
Till suddenly he tumbles down it's height;
Gaily you rush into your own destruction.
The cruel prosecution you intend
'Gainst *Socrates*, whatever flattering dream
Deludes you on, will have most woeful issue.
Say, you succeed—oft-times the gods permit
A good man's fall, for wise and secret ends,
Which puzzle man with all his boasted wisdom.
But be assur'd the wretched instruments
Of these their sacred counsels are by them
Devoted to inevitable ruin.

Melitus

Full learnedly, *Apame*, hast thou pleaded;
I fancy *Phedon* understands his business;
He tutors well; and, I will do thee justice,—
His charming pupil hath a coming genius.

Apame

Twice you've unkindly mention'd *Phedon* to me;
O *Melitus*, wou'd you but act like him,
Your sister's aching heart wou'd be at peace;
The horrid image that now strikes her soul
With fearful horrors, strait wou'd disappear,
And leave her calm and easy.

Melitus

What Enigma
Is this that thou wou'dst fain unravel to me?

Apame

It is my brother's pale and haggard carcase,
Drag'd by a ruthless mob along the street,
Spurn'd and insulted by each scoundrel citizen,
That now applauds thee; nay, while yet thou liv'st,
Me thinks e'en now I see thee scorn'd and loath'd;
Not one will speak to thee; they shun thee, like
The most abhor'd production of wild nature;
And thou at length will thank the executioner
For the kind blow that rids thee of thy being.
Say, can thy sister think this without horror?
And yet her fancy paints it to her view
In colours still more hideous.

Melitus

Well sayst thou
Thy fancy forms this to thee.—Pray, *Apame*,
No more of these imaginary terrors.
I stand resolv'd; and, were th'event to prove
As thy sick mind hath imag'd, such strong hate
My soul[2] resentful bears thy idol, *Socrates*,
That I wou'd dare the horrors thou hast painted.
Away!—I'll hear no more thy wild surmises—
Why, thou hast rais'd such phantoms, as e'en shock
My firmest powers—Be gone, or I shall something
That—prithee, leave me.

Apame

Yes, I will be gone;
Unhappy *Melitus*, thou bidst me leave thee;
And oh! forgive a sister's pious prayer,
May the tumultuous passion, which now writches thee,
End in a fair resolve to quit thy purpose,
And free *Apame* from her killing fears.

Notes

1. Apparently Cradock refers to the fable that Melitus was put to death by remorseful Athenians who erected a statue in Socrates's honor. Taylor, *Socrates*, p. 118.

2. Note how Melitus has adopted the Socratic notion of a soul. See also Anytus's comments, scene 7, line 9.

Scene the 6th

Melitus

Gods! how she hath unman'd me! She has drawn
A shocking pourtrait—say, shou'd it prove real?
Why, be it so;—the man, that dares a guilt,
Must have a soul like *mine*, which braves the gods
To thwart it's purpose.—*Socrates*, I hate thee;
And thou shalt pay me ample retribution.
My friends?—I thank them; they are come in time,
To firm me 'gainst the horrors she hath rais'd.

Scene the 7th

Melitus, Anytus, Lycon

Melitus

I've had a glorious lecture from my sister,
Why; the girl's grown a mere philosopher;
And mouths her maxims, out as well as *Socrates*;
Had not my soul been iron-proof against her,
I shou'd have faulter'd—

Anytus

Sure the noble *Melitus*

Will laugh at a weak woman's idle reasonings.
The sex will oft assume a fancied power,
And rate it shrewdly; but they're tinsel arguers;
The man, whose soul is constant to herself,
Carries with ease the pretty things they say.

Melitus

Nay; had she spoke with sevenfold eloquence,
With all the energy of Hermes,[1] still
Her eloquence were fruitless—I am determin'd,
Nor all the powers of heav'n or hell can move me.
Can shake my soul, or alter her resolve.[2]

Lycon

Spoke like my friend, and now we soon shall see
How this sage reasoner, this intrepid Socrates,
This mighty man of wisdom will behave,
Aw'd by the solemn presence of a court,
And all his baleful schemes produc'd against him.
Tis well, if his philosophy supports him:
He'll then appear like other common mortals,
Sunk in his fears, and cover'd with confusion.

Anytus

No; Lycon, no; his philosophick pride
Will bear him up against us; we shall see him
E'en smile contempt upon us: 'Twere unworthy
Of the wise Socrates to hint a fear.
Therefore he'll summon all his hoard of maxims,
All he hath gather'd from a long experience,
To arm his haughty stubborn soul against us:
For tis the boast of madmen, like himself,
Not to confess their frenzy, but stand out
E'en Against the strongest Evidence.

Melitus

We'll prove him;
We'll work up all his patience; I'm deceiv'd,
Or we shall make him totter on the basis
Of his assum'd Integrity—Be it

Firm and immoveable, as he pretends,
We'll undermine, till like a tumbling tower
It falls at length in hideous ruins on him,
And crushes him to atoms.

Anytus

Twill be so;
He ne'er can stand th'assault—he falls—he dies.
And then, my friends, our souls will be at ease;
Our virtues too our own without a monitor;
Our youth will tread the good old path
Of their forefathers; Heaven will have it's votaries;
Our sacred fanes,[2] as usual, will be throng'd
With hallow'd victims; *Athens* rise anew
In wonted glory; horrid war forbear
To fright her matrons and her tender maids;
O'er distant realms supreme once more she'll reign,
And hold her envied empire o'er the main.

End of the second Act

Notes

1. Hermes or Mercury was the Greek messenger god and the patron of eloquence.

2. A *fane* is a temple.

Act 3d

Scene 1st

Phedon, Apame

Phedon

This day, this solemn day, my dear *Apame*,
Will stand recorded in *Athenian* Annals,
As the most black and dismal: Not the period,
When Heav'n sent forth the raging pestilence,
When the dank air we breath'd was big with death,
And *Athens* shew'd a heap of carcases,
Will wear a gloomier aspect to posterity.
Our after-race must blush to read, their fathers
Brought to an infamous, a cruel trial
The man, whose virtues made their state renown'd
Bove all the *Grecian* Cities; heav'n, they'll cry,
Had let the Furies loose, and given them leave
To dart their venom in each *Attick*[1] breast.
O *Athens*! O my country! how my soul
Indignant glows, that she within thy walls
First view'd yon glorious sun!

Apame

Thou art happy, *Phedon*,
Thou hast been a steady friend to *Socrates*:
Hast shewn a soul well worthy his instructions,
Nor will desert him in the day of evil;
Thou hast no brother, whose prepost'rous hate,
Whose perverse enmity, to worth, to virtue,
Can give thy heart a pang.—Too wretched I!
Long as I've lov'd that venerable sage,
And almost reverenc'd him as a divinity,
When I reflect, the man that calls me sister,
That drew his first, his infant-nourishment
From the same honour'd breast, resolves his ruin,
And joins with impious men against his life;
How I am struck with horror at the thought?
How I am lost in my excess of misery?

Phedon

Strange! that a man who in the spring of life
Promis'd a glorious harvest of brave actions,
Shou'd thus run counter to his fair beginnings,
And hate that virtue, which he once rever'd!
We then were friends; at least I call'd him mine,
And with delight I saw him close attend
The virtuous *Socrates*, and catch each sentiment—
As it came from him—How alass! he's chang'd!
Sure some malignant Planet sways his conduct,
And drives him head long on the guilty course,
He now with such determin'd will pursues.

Apame

Oh! he is lost, my *Phedon*, he is lost;
The gods have destin'd him to be the dupe
Of his remorseless folly;—Late I saw him,
And strove to win him from his dread design;
In vain—his fury rose—his form look'd madness—
Wild were his eyes—his voice grew loud and rageful,
And he in heighth of passion drove me from him.

Phedon

How I am mov'd at thy too just complainings?
O my *Apame*, Life is fraught with misery;
Few are our joys and many are our woes.
For me, had they denied me thy dear love,
If thou hadst not with kind compassion heard me,
Heard my fond suit, and bad me hope, that time
Might ballance all my miseries with thee,
Sure I shou'd sink beneath the pondrous load.

Apame

Ah! *Phedon*, cease t'indulge this weakness farther;
T'will but delude thee—Heaven forbids our loves—
Far from each other we must fly for ever;
Must bid adieu to ev'ry fond desire,
Each tender thought that knit our souls together;
I can't be thine—I must not—Nature, virtue,
The ties of blood, the rigid laws of honour,
Severly bar me from thee.

Phedon

Aweful powers!
What do I hear? *Apame* now forbid me
T'indulge my faithful love!—It must not be!
O thou art all to me the Gods can grant,
And, if I lose thee, Heaven hath not beneath it
A wretch more lost in misery than *Phedon*.

Apame

Phedon, be calm; to thy impartial reason
Will I appeal, and she'll I'm sure, acquit me.
My brother is the foe of *Socrates*,
Th'inveterate foe, and e'en to death pursues him.
However guilty, he is still my brother,
A Brother too, for all his wayward conduct
Something within commands me still to reverence.
Say, can I marry then the youth, whose friendship
For that illustrious, that much injur'd sage,
Must make him look on *Melitus* with hatred,
As on the base destroyer of his friend?
How wou'd it suit with thy *Apame's* virtue,
With that chaste fame she values far above
All that mistaken man calls great and splendid,
To lose herself in softnesses of love,
So to be led away by her fond folly,
As to forget that great, that innate law
Nature makes indispensable, forget
My brother is my brother, thou his enemy?
No *Phedon*, n'ever can *Apame's* soul
Bear the reflection of so wild a conduct.

Phedon

Good heavens! Where am I? Are they all a dream,
These golden hopes, that have thus long entranc'd me?
To all the dreaded woes, that now alarm me,
Must this be added yet?—*Apame* lost!
Apame never mine!—Assist me, fair one,
Say something to relieve thy sinking *Phedon*,
Or, like the bark, that on the stormy surge
Hath long been tost, the sport of raging winds,

And sinks at length deep down to the opening gulph.
I fall victim to my love and thee.

Apame

Alass! what can I say to ease thy anguish?
That I have lov'd thee—witness, ye chaste Stars,
Witness, ye holy powers, that know our hearts,
And search the inmost passions lurking there;
Long have I lov'd thee, and to death will bear
The virtuous flame—but oh! *Apame* can
No more—

Phedon

How I am lost in many sorrows?
Thou lov'st me, my Apame! What avails
This fond confession, if I still must live
Unblest without thee, and must languish out
A tedious, hated life in dread despair?

Apame

Learn, *Phedon*, to support the awards of Heaven
With noble fortitude, with true philosophy;
And copy with more firmness thy great master.
He sets a glorious pattern—act like him.
This is unmanly whining—if he falls,
All I can promise, since I can't be thine,
Is, ne'er to be another's—if he lives,
(But oh! my heart forebodes, the god's decree,
That he must fall, and by my brother's means)
Yet, if he lives, and *Melitus* at length
Sees and laments his present wayward conduct,
I'll only say, that life without my *Phedon*
Will be a burden heavier to my soul,
Than to the chained slave, that tugs the oar,
And hourly dies beneath a tirant-lord.

Phedon

Too slender solace for my bleeding heart!
And yet I thank thee—yes; thy *Phedon* thanks thee.
O may high Heaven with piteous eye look down

On our transcendant loves!—But I'm all fear—
My trembling heart—forgive me, my Apame—
But when I think what I shall lose in thee,
Oh!—I will copy my great Master's firmness,
I'll copy thee—Do thou, my virtuous maid,
Support me—O I wou'd, wou'd hope, and yet
Some envious demon glooms upon my soul,
And e'en forbids my hope—O help me, Socrates,
Help me, Apame; help me all that virtue,
That I've imbib'd from Socrates and thee.

Note

1. Attica was the region in Greece where Athens was located.

Scene 2d

Socrates, Plato, Phedon, Crito, and others

his friends attending him to his trial

Socrates

No, Plato; no, my youths; it must not be.
Dear is the offer of your friendly hearts,
And Socrates will to his dying hour
Retain a kind remembrance of your love.
For me you shan't expose your precious lives
To needless dangers, to the rude resentment
Of a licentious people—I'm prepar'd
Gainst the worst fury of my mad accusers;
And can myself support my character.
Good Heaven hath not so left me; I can plead
With firmest resolution all my services,
My constant, faithful services to Athens,
And, if they will condemn me, they shall own,
Spite of their malice, that I die unjustly.

Plato

That the kind powers have blest thy sapient tongue
With all the energy of soft persuasion;
That virtues like thy own might well reject
The feeble aid of our imperfect eloquence;
That the severest trials of ill fortune
Cannot unnerve thy firm and manly soul,
We're well assur'd—But yet forgive thy friends,
If they still hope, their faithful cares may prove
Of solid service to thee 'gainst their slanders.
Mean tho' our powers of speech, we yet may urge
Something, that in the hurry of thy thoughts,
May slip thy memory, of great import—

Socrates

Alass! of what emolument to me
All you can say? my judges, if they're just,
From my own mouth will be convinc'd—However,
I'll be my own defender, and assert
My innocence of soul with honest freedom:
Firm and serene I'll meet the pouring tempest,
And smile at all the horrors they wou'd raise.

Plato

And can thy pupils, they, who've learn'd from thee
The road to wisdom, and the paths of peace
Whose tender minds thou hast form'd with pious care,
And, kind, instructed in each godlike virtue,
Silent, can they behold thee stand alone
Gainst the united malice of thy enemies,
And not reach out their helping hand? Must tears
And patient suffering only be their share,
And not one word drop from them to defend thee?
Much twill alleviate our heart-piercing sorrows,
If we're allow'd to plead thy righteous cause,
To shew Mankind that not in barren soil
Thou hast planted thy own virtues; that we know
Our heavy loss in being bereav'd of thee,
And will dare all that honour bids, to save thee.

Socrates

Enough, dear youths; I do believe, you love me,
And tis no moderate solace to my soul,
That I've not toil'd in vain'; that you deserve
My cares and labours.—Greatly it rejoices me,
To know, if Heaven determines I shall die,
That I shall leave in Athens worthy men,
Firm patriots like myself, sincere to friendship,
True to their country's interest and to virtue;
For such, I'm sure, are you—pursue the track
With steady resolution—but you will.
For me, you have my thanks; but know, 'twill pain me
More than my trial, to involve my friends
In the same ruin—Leave me to myself;
I shall not be dismay'd; my steady soul
Suffices 'gainst the assaults of all their fury,
And will repel their slanders—let us on;
The venerable court is set, and I
Wou'd not delay their more important business
For an old man, not worth the mighty pother,
Some wild and busy heads have made about him.

Scene the 3d

The Court of the Areopagus[1] in the open air

The orator's desk

Melitus, Anitus, Lycon, as accusers of Socrates, with the Athenian populace attending them: After some time enter Socrates, Plato, Crito, Phedon and numbers of the Athenian youth; he gay and cheerful, they under the greatest dejection.

Areopagus

Give out the business of the day.

Crier reads

Melitus, son of Melitus of the people of Pythos[2]

accuses *Socrates*, son of *Sophroniscus* of the people of *Alopece*.

Areopagus

Read the accusation.

Crier

Socrates is criminal, because he acknowledges not the gods, that the republick acknowledges; and because he introduces new deities; he is farther criminal, because he corrupts the youth.

Areopagus

Bid *Melitus* stand forth.

Crier

Melitus son of *Melitus* of the people of *Pythos*, appear and prove your accusation against *Socrates* son of *Sophroniscus* of the people of *Alopece*.

Melitus ascends the Orator's desk and speaks.

Much I'm abash'd, most grave and reverend Senators,
Thus to appear, unequal as I am,
To this important cause, but 'tis the cause
Of Heaven and *Athens*—and the fervent zeal
That warms my heart for our immortal gods;
That dear regard my native soil demands,
Compel me to accuse the great delinquent.
I say then, *Socrates* abjures our gods;
He laughs with high contempt as all the honours
We pay to their divinity, and stiles them
Mere empty *nothings*, creatures of the brain,
The idle dreams of ancient superstition,
Grown sacred from the ignorance of our fathers,
Grown venerable from a length of years.
When was it, *Socrates* wou'd condescend
T'attend their fanes, and pay that holy reverence
Which their divine protection of our city
Claims from the sons of *Athens*? He, more wise,

More deeply read in nature and her powers,
Inspir'd, no doubt, with wisdom from above,
Forms to himself a deity unknown,
A *being* sole, and independent of
All other beings, o'er the world supreme.
To him this God benign communicates
The secrets of his will, to him alone
Unfolds his counsels; and, to guide his steps
To guard him from the frailities of our nature;
T'inform his reason, and inspire his soul,
Directs a special demon to attend him.
This his assertion; vain, presuming man!
Thus he divests those ever-gracious deities,
By whose propitious aid our *Athens* long
Hath been the pride and wonder of the World,
Of all their virtues, attributes and powers.

Nor yet content with his own blasphemies,
He lures our youth to listen to his doctrines,
T'imbibe his vile pernicious fatal errors;
He trains them up to sins of horrid kind,
To guilt that wants a name, to monstrous mischiefs.
Him do they follow wildly 'long the streets,
Nor hearken to a parent's kind rebuke,
Nor hearken to their country's solemn voice;
Nay, e'en religion pleads with them in vain;
For *Socrates* to them is parent, country,
Their god, their *all*; and madly they're prepar'd
To act all his commands, however wicked,
However fatal to our weal and peace.
These, dear *Athenians*, these ye rev'rend Judges,
These are the crimes of this all dearing man.
To you, as well becomes me, I shall leave
The Award of his demerits; but if ever
Pernicious citizen deserv'd to die,
If every *Athens* bore a son ingrate,
Who sought clandestine to undo his country,
To rob her of her liberties and laws,
To innovate her ancient sacred rites,
And level all the objects of her worship,
The son of *Sophroniscus* is that traitor.

Socrates to his friends

Heavens! what a stranger am I to myself?

Say, friends, am I this wretch, this impious parricide?
If Melitus hath search'd my heart so deeply,
And found these dreadful mischiefs lurking there,
Sure never man was more unknown to man
Than Socrates to Socrates.

Melitus

To strengthen
What I've asserted 'gainst this vile deluder,
The worthy Anitus and gen'rous Lycon
Men of sincere affection to the state,
Faithful and active in their country's interest,
Are both prepar'd and willing to support me.

Areopagus

Let them attend, and speak their thoughts with freedom.

Anitus

Small is the trouble I shall give the senate;
I have not learn'd the niceties of speech,
And can but bluntly say what I've to offer.
Nay, tis with great reluctance I appear
Against the man that once I call'd my friend.
But when I see to what irreverent use
His talents are applied; when I observe,
Against those very gods that gave him all
The wondrous faculties he justly boasts,
He lavishes their blessings, and does outrage
To all that we hold sacred and divine,
When the wild listless youth of this great city
Run after him, and catch with eager gape
Each impious tenet he profanely utters;
When Heaven must soon lament it's want of votaries;
And the avenging gods,justly incens'd
At our neglect of their most holy worship,
Will curse this city with severest evils,
Will sink us deep in most deserv'd distress,
In woes more fatal than we've felt already,
Unless we timely hinder the result
Of their tremendous anger, I no more
Look on the ties of friendship to be binding:

And therefore I conjure you, rev'rend Senators,
As you are men of *Athens*, as you're citizens,
That have the welfare of the state at heart,
To rouse yourselves against these threatening perils,
To clear your city of these novel doctrines,
T'assert your gods, and most severely punish
The man who dares to speak against their power,
That dares deny their providence and being,

Phedon aside

Poor tender *Anitus*! his righteous conscience
Can't bear the least infringement on the rites
Of his dear country. Sure his virtuous heart
Is clear from ev'ry stain of base injustice.

Lycon

It is no mean offender, ye *Athenians*
Today demands your cognisance; if ever
Presumptious man hath dar'd beyond forgiveness
Or of the gods or you, this vain declaimer
Against our hallow'd rites, this mighty reasoner
In speculative knowledge, this arraigner
Of our dread gods is he.—I wou'd be calm,
I wou'd be master of myself, my faculties,
While I lay forth the insolent attempts
Of his insidious heart. But when already
We feel the fatal issue of his conduct,
When even now our gods dart down their vengeance
In fearful bolts of wrath; and *Athens* mourns
Almost in Ashes their severe displeasure,
Say, can a citizen, can one that Loves
His dear maternal land, command his utterance,
And speak with temper?—O reflect, *Athenians*,
Consider coolly the successive evils
That long have ravag'd this devoted city;
Then say, if all the gods have not conspir'd
To pour destruction on us.—Why, my countrymen,
Why are we thus the objects of their wrath?
Why? 'Cause an old irreverend dotard lures you
To horrid guilt—grown desperate in impiety,
He charges you with folly in your worship,
Deprives high Heav'n of it's undoubted powers,

And quite annihilates it's blest inhabitants.
Are ye asleep, *Athenians*? Lo! Your youth,
Mad with his baneful dogmas, slight the temples,
No more the consecrated victim bleeds;
No more the solemn vows are paid;—nay further,
He draws them from the duties of relation;
In vain with his ungracious son the father,
In vain the mother, pleads parental cares.
Their children fly their precepts, and return
Unnatural ingratitude—Can this,
Can this be pleasing to the powers divine?
Will *Athens* flourish, when the holy bond
That shou'd subsist between a child and parent,
Is thus dissolv'd?—Let our experience teach us.
What an abandon'd wretch was *Alcibiades*?
What a remorseless savage tirant, *Critias*?
These left their friends to listen to his lore;
These were his pupils; these had long imbib'd
His boasted maxims; these were once his favourites,
And bore the appellation of his *sons*.
Awake, ye rev'rend Senators; no more
Sleep in the dangers that alarm the state;
Call forth your courage, let your country rouse
you;
Be just, be earnest—Heaven and earth conjoin,
And claim your verdict 'gainst this dangerous man.
He will, I know, endeavour to amuse you;
He'll soothe you to forgive him; he'll smooth over
His base detested conduct—but beware—
He hath a winning, a bewitching eloquence;
His words are oil, but oh! there lurks within
Poison of killing force; and, if you hear him,
If to the magick of his tongue you yield,
I can but mourn the ruin of my country,
Shall weep, religion, thy deserted altars,
Shall wail, dear liberty, thy fall in *Athens*.

Plato aside

O eloquence, what a pernicious bane
Thy beauties are, when basely they're adapted
To screen a villain, or defame the good.

Areopagus

Who speaks for the defendant?

Socrates

Even he
That best knows how to answer his accurers

(*Plato* attempts to mount the desk)

Plato, forbear; thou dost me great injustice
To think I want assistance 'gainst a heap
Of falsehood so absurd; if *Athens* boasts
An honest senate, I've no cause to fear.
E'en their own hearts will plead with them for *Socrates*,
And safely guard him 'gainst such frontless malice.

1 Areopagus

Gods! he e'en braves the senate.

2 Areopagus

Let him on
He'll say enough to make him guilty.

Socrates

Whence comes it, ye *Athenians*, that I am charg'd
With a denial of our country-Gods?
Have I not always worship'd in their temples?
Have I not always bow'd before their altars?
What festal days hath *Athens* e'er ordain'd
That I have not kept holy? Many are there
Can prove my presence, there, and *Melitus*,
Had he so will'd, might have observ'd me too.
They say, I introduce new deities:
What are they, Senators? inform me, do.
I own I'm ignorant, unless to say,
The voice of God directs me, is, to assert
Some novel deity you have not known.
They who divine by thunder, they that mark
The notes of birds, the priestess on her tripod,

Are they not guided by the voice divine?
What difference, tell me? only this, that I,
Pious as well as wise, ascribe to Heav'n,
What only they ascribe to second causes,
to mediate powers, whence they derive their Omens.
Alass! no base design, no wicked purpose
Hath ever swayed my heart: if heav'n declares
That I am wise, I sent not *Cherephon*[3]
To *Delphos* to enquire; and yet the God
Pronounc'd me more than wise,—both just and free.
But why am I not so? No slave to sense,
Above temptation, faithful to my poverty,
Still searching after knowledge, teaching others
What have I learn'd myself; Is this not wisdom,
Is this not justice, freedom, all that's right,
All that is grateful in the eyes of men,
Nay, I'll go farther, in the eye of Heaven?
Thus many of our citizens have thought,
Thus all the virtuous in the states of *Greece*
To me they've travell'd; and from me, well-pleas'd,
Imbib'd the maxims of philosophy.
But I corrupt your youth;—What youth corrupted?
Name even one, who with a mind sincere
Ador'd the gods, that I have made an infidel;
Name one remark'd for chaste and modest bearing,
That I have render'd impudent and leud;
Name any sober, frugal, hardy, brave,
That have become debauch'd, or profligate,
Or coward, or effeminate, from pursuing
The rigid path I've pointed to their steps.

Melitus

Many there are, unthinking, heedless youth,
Who, tho' regardless of a parent's will,
Bear most submissive reverence to thee,
And pay thee the submission that they owe
To them alone or Heaven.

Socrates

They have obey'd me
In following virtue; I was their preceptor;
Their parents knew not how to teach them wisdom,

And therefore they applied themselves to me.
Who heeds relation in a dangerous fever?
Is it their parent's counsel that they take
Or the Physician's? In the trade of war,
The general's skill, and not his friends are weigh'd.
Instruction is my province; therefore justly
Submissive reverence from them is my due.
Is this a cause, why I shou'd suffer death?
Is this so dread an evil to the state,
That nothing but my life can recompence
The mischiefs I have done?—Speak, *Anitus*;
Speak, *Lycon*, *Melitus*—but, O my judges,
Let them succeed; they hurt not *Socrates*
Death bears to me no terrors.—who can say,
Whether he is an happiness or evil?
But he that dreads him, for that very reason
Can not be wise—however he may palliate
His servile fears—his soul's estrang'd from wisdom.

The Areopagus consult for some time,
and by their Suffrages bring him in guilty.

Areopagus

The justice of the senate, *Socrates*.
Hath found thee guilty; and thy punishment
By law is death—However, if thou'lt
Pay the fine awarded, thou'rt allow'd to live.

Socrates

A fine? for what *Athenians*? I a fine?
Yours is uncommon justice—Innocence
Hath ever sway'd my conduct; and no guilt
Cleaves to my soul; and she shall ne'er upbraid me,
That, dastard-like, I'd meanly save a life
I ever held indifferent at the forfeit
Of what I hold most dear, my fame and virtue.

Plato

O *Socrates*, have pity on your friends,
Your relatives, your country—curb a little
This grandeur of thy soul; impartial men

Will ne'er conceive thee guilty, and thy life
May yet be long a blessing to the world.

Socrates

No, *Plato*; were the wealth of *Athens* mine,
I wou'd not buy my life so basely from them.
But since they're in suspence, myself will rate
My services—be this my punishment.
As I've been ever faithful to my country:
Have frelly shed my blood in her defence,
And sav'd her noblest citizens from death,
Have taught her yout the road to solid glory,
To real virtue, and immortal happiness,
The publick shall maintain me, while I live,
A cheap reward for what I've done for them.

The Areopagus shew marks of high resentment, and after some consultation give the final sentence.

Areopagus

Thy haughty soul, thou son of *Sophroniscus*,
Compels us to condemn thee; therefore be it
As thy high crimes deserve—the poison'd bowl
Thy portion;—when arrives the sacred ship
From *Delos*' hallow'd Isle, that day's they last.
Be on thyself thy blood—dismiss the court.

Notes

1. The Areopagus was the high judicial tribunal of Athens. Cradock also uses the term to mean a member of the court rather than the more normal *Areopagite*; for example, see the first speaker of this scene.

2. By *people* is meant deme or administrative district of Attica. Melitus was from the deme of Pitthus and Socrates from the deme of Alopece.

3. See above, act 1, scene 6, line 13.

Scene 4th

Socrates and his friends returning from the trial. Guards attending.

Socrates

Tis then determin'd, and I die, Athenians;
Why then I leave a base ungrateful world,
And hie me to those calm, those blessed regions
Where misery is no more, and all is peace.
Forbear, my friends; these unavailing tears
Betray unmanly weakness; tis beneath
Philosophy, to weep and grieve like women.
Compose your hearts; and bear my loss with firmness,
Like men that have not learn'd in vain my lessons.

Crito

O Socrates, th'injustice of thy country!
That thou so wise, so good, so innocent,
Shou'dst thus be sacrific'd?

Socrates

What means my Crito?
Tis better thus, than die an abject wretch,
Condemn'd by by own heart, my friend's disgrace.
My foes may take my life, but can't deprive me
Of what is more than life and all it's joys,
Unsullied innocence and firm integrity;
They are above their reach, above their malice;
Therefore they hurt not me—Cheer up, my youths—
Come, lead me to the prison—I can die.
The man who walks the path of life sincere,
Nor deviates from the truth, disdains to fear:
Tho' Death each horrid, ghastly form assume,
My hopes are fixed on better world to come:
Long, long ago the arduous task I learn'd
And view his fancied terrors unconcern'd.

End of the third act

Act 4th

Scene 1st

Xantippe, Plato

Xantippe

Ye gods! what hath Xantippe done, to feel
This deep excess of misery?—Life! What art thou?
—A Curse—at least I've found thee so—the brute,
That knows no care but happily enjoys
The present hour, boasts nobler bliss than man.
He roves along the fields in joyous plight,
Selects his food, drinks free the christal stream,
And to the moment of his fate is happy.
But we, that vaunt ourselves superior beings,
That proudly talk of reason and her powers,
What bliss have we? incessant fears alarm us;
Incessant ills o'ertake us; and our joys
So thinly scatter'd, that they fleet unfelt,
Like empty bubbles on a watry mirror.

Plato

This springs from Heaven's peculiar love to man;
Too well he knows, how fond our hearts wou'd grow
Of mundane bliss; and therefore wisely mixes
The cup of life with gall. Sublimer joys,
Than what this life can furnish, he intends
In future, brighter Worlds; but, if our souls
Met here the full completion of their wishes,
They'd grow unfit for more exalted pleasures,
And cling to earth as to their only stay.

Xantippe

These are the idle rants of Socrates,
And he hath madden'd thee with his delusions.
Whence springs this knowledge or to him or thee?
Or why to you alone is given to know
The after-state of men? Tis all mere Rhapsody,
And he, inebriated with his whimsies,

Hath quite cast off all thought of what I feel,
Of what his harmless, helpless children feel,
Knows not the anguish of parental tenderness,
Forgets the love he owes to his Xantippe,
And wraps himself in his ideal prospects
Of something, but of what he does not know:
While I, distracted with my sore distress,
Rave to the Gods in fruitless exclamation,
And have no glympse of hope t'allay my sorrows.

Plato

Yet may'st thou hope,that that Omniscient Power,
Whose will he hath ever sought, and taught to others,
Tho' in his boundless wisdom he ordain,
That Socrates must fall, may yet to you
And to your little ones extend his mercy.
He may have glorious reasons for his sufferings,
Beyond our ken; and wou'd exhibit forth
His chosen favourite, as a blest example
To shew to others, how the man of virtue,
The man of wisdom, like to his shou'd act.
You therefore he'll forsake not in affliction,
But still will raise you friends, to heal your griefs,
To aid your wants, and drive away despair.

Xantippe

Alass! thou talkest wildly, Plato; How!
Must Socrates, who boasts that he hath serv'd
This unknown Deity with strict sincerity,
Be given a victim up unto his foes,
And feel the vengeance of their villain-malice;
Yet I, who never had a thought about him,
But worshipped merely as our father worshipp'd,
Regardless how, or whom, I must forsooth!
Be the peculiar object of his favour?
Gods! this is worse that womanish reasoning,
And shews us, how absurdly man will argue,
When he pretends to fathom what he knows not.

Plato

'Twere vain, Xantippe, now to plead submission

To Heaven's high will, to bid thee arm with patience,
Thy soul, too much opprest with sore calamity.
But sure afflictions are not always evils,
And *Socrates*, me thinks, in future times
Will shine the brighter from his noble conduct
Under the pressure of his present woes.
Like yon gay sun that glads the world with day;
Sometimes a black invidious cloud conceals him,
When he emerging with redoubled vigour,
Darts all his beams with more resplendent glory.

Xantippe

No more of this—to me he's ever lost—
By *Socrates*, thou'rt gone—thou diest, my *Socrates*;
But a few hours, and death's unpitying hand
Gives the dread final stroke—O hear me, Heaven!
Hear a lorn widow's prayer—shower down, shower down
Thy deadliest curses on those villain-wretches,
That have bereav'd me of my *Socrates*:
O let them feel the pangs I suffer now;
Heap all thy vengeance on them, till they groan
In deepest anguish, till they're curs'd like me.

Plato

Restrain, thou consort of my god-like friend,
This mad disorder; yet, if thou'lt be calm,
And bear submissive what the Gods ordain,
Yet may some unexpected change disperse
Thy present woes, and thou again be happy.

Xantippe

Happy? I happy? No; I've long shook hands
With happiness; tis writ in heaven, that I
Must be the most unhappy of my kind.
O I am all affliction—Socrates!
Thou hast brought this misery on me—I forgive thee,
Yet hadst thou listen'd to me, hadst thou yielded
To my persuasions—but tis vain t'upbraid thee
Thou art lost, and I am—O support me, Heav'n!

Scene 2d

Plato

Her killing griefs have so possest her soul,
That 'twere a needless task to speak to her.
I wou'd have told her of our friendly scheme—
To free her Socrates; but, shou'd it fail,
Shou'd he himself (as much I fear) obstruct
The honest mean we've taken to preserve him,
And, obstinate, resolve to die, her grief
Wou'd have return'd with double weight upon her,
And sunk her soul to utter desolation.
But why delay my friends? tis now the hour
They promis'd here to meet me with the gaoler.
If he is firm, and Socrates will hear us,
He'll yet escape, and triumph o'er the malice
Of his invet'rate foes—grant Heaven, he may!

Scene 3d

Plato, Phedon, Crito, Apame, Gaoler

Plato

Welcome, my mournful friends; tis then resolv'd
And you're unanimous t'attempt his rescue?

Phedon

Unanimous? Who wou'd not dare their fate,
To save the man who e'en the gods behold,
With rapturous wonder, from so base a death?

Crito

Yes, Plato, we're resolv'd; and Heaven in pity
To Athens, to relieve her from her shame,
Inspires this generous man to aid our purpose.
He blushes for his country, and determines
To share with us, the brave attempt, or die.

Gaoler

Who, that beholds his great, his god like patience,
His nobleness of suffering, but wou'd join
With earnest resolution, to preserve him?
I am a stranger to _philosophy_,
Nor know her influence on the sons of men;
But this man's more than humane; his demeanour
Hath in it something of divinity.
Calm and serene he smiles at my compassion,
And bids me not to be concern'd for him;
That life and death he hath weigh'd in equal
    ballance,
And finds himself indifferent to either.
Oft, when I speak th'inveteracy of those
That work'd his cruel sufferings, strait he pities them,
And begs of Heaven that they may be forgiven.
I heard him with amaze; he won my soul;
And O, were I the humble mean to save him,
Methinks I cou'd forgive the gods, shou'd they
Ordain my death the moment he escap'd.

Plato

Thy honest heart! But doubt not but the gods
Will shower their blessings on thee. Thy regard
For virtue in affliction, claims their goodness,
And they will pay thee worthy recompence.
Why, my good friends, this looks as if the Powers
Above took care of him—let's seize th'occasion,
Spite of himself preserve him, and become
Th'asserters of exalted worth in _Athens_.

Apame

Yes, ye _Athenians_, dare the utmost perils,
Bid brave defiance to severest tortures,
Rather than he shou'd fall; the world hath not
In it's extended regions one that mates
With him in virtue. Hapless that I am,
To have my nearest relative his foe,
I'd dare for him above my feeble sex.

Plato

O sweet *Apame*, worthiest, matchless maid!
How shall I praise thee, as thy worth deserves?
Thy dear esteem for *Socrates* demands
Our highest gratitude, and makes us almost
Forget, thy cruel brother sought his death.
O thou transcendant excellence! had he
But half thy virtue—O forgive the thought!
I see how it transports thy gentle soul.

Phedon

Gods! how she's mov'd! O *Plato*, thou hast rais'd
Tumultuous war within her—heavenly fair One,
Summon thy own great virtues to thy aid,
Calm thy afflicted soul—thy *Phedon* asks thee
Speak solace to thyself—support the conflict—
What can I say to ease thy strugling heart?

Apame

O the severe distress that hangs upon me!
You're all the friends of *Socrates*—be mine.
Ye know, how I revere him, how I love him;
And oh! if ye succeed (and grant, ye Gods,
They may succeed) have pity on *Apame*,
And give her back, if possible, her brother.

Scene 4th

Plato, Phedon, Crito, Gaoler

Plato

Her soul is deeply wounded—may the gods
Prosper our righteous scheme, and give her peace.

Crito

We must succeed; he cannot long withstand
Our earnest prayers and tears; do you, my friends

Be ready to admit us; when escap'd
From out the loathsome prison, I'll convey him,
Ere dawn beams forth, beyond the reach of malice.
A gen'rous band of youths, who mourn his fate,
Await our coming at the gate, that leads
To Thebes; They'll there receive the sage with
    transport,
And safe conduct him to the destin'd place
Of his concealment.

Gaoler

Hence an hour exact,
The prison-doors are open—you be there,
And I'll attend you to him.

Plato

You've our thanks
But that's but poor; you'll have the thanks of *Athens*.
Believe me, when their present madness leaves them,
And they reflect th'injustice of their conduct
To you illustrious prisoner, much 'twill please them
He hath escap'd their sentence; they will then
Heap with caresses, with assur'd applause,
All that have bravely ventur'd for his safety.

Gaoler

That as they list; the goodness of the deed
Weighs more than me, than e'en a world's applause.

Scene 5th

Anitus, Melitus, Lycon

Lycon

The sacred ship is then return'd from *Crete*?

Melitus

She is; and now yon cool philosopher

Must yield to fate; few are the hours he numbers,
Ere he is reckon'd with the dead.

Lycon

My soul
Longs for th'important moment, much I fear'd,
His friends wou'd try their utmost power to save him.

Anitus

No doubt they have, and will; but won't succeed;
Their greatest obstacle will be himself;
The senate wou'd have wink'd at his escape;
And had been glad he had evaded punishment.
But here my anchor held; I knew his temper;
I knew he wou'd not fly; he laughs at dying,
And calls the apprehensions mortals form
Of death, the brain's delirium—how? he fly?
What inconsistence? No; that king of terrors
Affrights not him, he'll brave him to the last,
Or rather meet him as a friend.

Melitus

Absurd!
To spurn our gods, and so insult their powers,
And yet presume that, when he goes from hence,
Eternal wretchedness is not his lot!
Fine reasoning this! but so are fools deluded.
Had he, content with what his fathers knew
Liv'd as we liv'd, and, when his country call'd,
Fought, like ourselves, her battles, and been silent,
Nor sought presumptuous things above his sphere,
Of woful issue to the publick weal,
He might have liv'd for Melitus

Lycon

Or me.

Anitus

O say not, had he fought his country's battles;

For righteous cause tho' I've pursued his death,
Yet still I'll do his virtues ample justice.
Myself have seen him—on that fatal day,
When fierce *Beotia's* sons in *Delium's* plain
Pour'd their victorious thousands on our troops,
And we, like timerous flocks, when wolves pursue,
Fled from them daunted; *Socrates* alone
Bravely maintain'd his post, or, if receded,
Twas as a lion, that disdains his hunters;
He turn'd and fac'd them, and repell'd their fury;
Till by his bold resistance he gave time
To the disheartend'd soldier to retreat,
And hide their shame in safety. Brave he stood;
Not *Ajax* nor *Achilles* match'd his force;
He dar'd them to the battle—they beheld him,
As a divinity that fought for *Athens*,
And, struck with reverence, check'd their full pursuit.

Melitus

Well; be his virtues what they will; no matter,
Fate has him now, and, thank the gracious powers,
Athens and we shall fear our foe no longer.
But I will curb my joy—my worthy *Lycon*,
My noble *Anitus*, good night to both,
And let our hearts be blithe—he dies tomorrow.

Note

1. Socrates is credited with exceptional bravery in covering the retreat of the Athenian forces after the disaster at Delium (424 B.C.), where the Attic forces were routed by the Boetians. See Plato, *Apology*, 28e, *Symposium*, 219e, *Laches*, 181b. Cradock misspelled Boetia.

Scene 6th

The Prison

Socrates discovered asleep; to him enter Plato, Phedon, Crito, and Gaoler

Gaoler

See, there he sleeps; thus ever hath he slept
When nature call'd; his troubles seem not his;
He feels them not; thus calm and thus resign'd,
He lays him down and takes his sweet repose,
As fate fear'd him, and he, her sovereign Lord,
Cou'd stay her progress, and controul her power.

Phedon

Who, that views him, wou'd envy Persia's monarch?
Surrounded by his guard, yet still embitter'd
Are all his hours, some sudden plot he fears,
And starts amid his slumbers, well aware
Of might mischiefs, brooding o'er his head,
And breaking quick upon him.

Plato

Tis not thus
With virtuous men; our great preceptor shews us,
E'en by that smile that now englads his face,
That in his sleep he's happy—O ye Gods!
Who wou'd not be that glorious man of virtue?
Tomorrow comes, and he is then a corse,
And yet—but see, he wakes—ye guardian powers,
Inspire us with your own blest energy,
To win him to our purpose, and to save him.

Socrates awaking

Thanks to that gracious Being, that now supports me:
O this is heavenly rapture! Have I then
E'en now a foretaste, what I soon shall be?
Dear Melitus, I thank thee; thou wilt send me
Strait to the region of immortal Spirts
There to enjoy—my friends, what calls you forth

In this inclement season of the night,
To visit this dank dungeon? tis your love;—
But sure tomorrow is our own—the laws
Of Athens are not chang'd, that I must die,
Ere I cou'd take or give a last farewel.

Plato

No, Socrates, tomorrow yet is yours;
Spite of your cruel foes;—a noble cause
Now calls us hither; fate's a length propitious
And ere tomorrow dawns, are you secure
From all the villain-efforts of your foes.

Socrates

What means my friend?

Crito

Oh! he hath glorious meaning;
And wou'd the man, on whom our all depends,
The dearest solace of our lives on earth,
The nobler prospect of our joys hereafter,
But listen to his pleadings, Athens yet
May boast the blessing of her Socrates,
For years to come; and he may long continue
The pattern of all virtues of his Country.

Socrates

Unfold yourselves.

Phedon

The vessel is arriv'd

Socrates

I know it, and that I'm to die tomorrow.

Crito aside

O how I fear that steadiness of look,
That firm demeanour—all our hopes are vain.

Plato

That you must die tomorrow? No, my father,
Good Heaven reserves you still for nobler purpose;
To make you yet his substitute below.
This earth is still too rank to lose her <u>Socrates</u>;
His lessons are too needful to her peace;
She must not want you; and in kind compassion
To erring mortals, he that wakes o'er all,
That gracious providence you've long ador'd,
Inspires this honest man to aid our counsels,
To free you from your fate, and ope the way
To your deliv'rance.—Some selected youths,
The pupils long of your divine instructions,
Are ready to convey you far from <u>Athens</u>,
From the ungrateful citizens, to life
To peace, to safety. O regard your friends,
Your family, mankind—fly hence, and give
Your future lessons to th'applauding world.

Socrates

How, <u>Plato</u>; this from you; from you, to whom
I've long unfolded all my inmost soul?
Is <u>Socrates</u> so little known by those,
Who from their infant-years have learn'd his lore,
That they shou'd think him meanly fond of life;
Shou'd think he'd fly the death his country dooms him?
My Country hath condemn'd me, her's the blame,
If causeless she condemn'd—for me, I glory,
That, innocent, I quit a thankless world,
And spring to regions of immortal joy;
To regions—cou'd my tongue express the rapture,
My soul conceives at her desir'd release,
My friends no more wou'd strive to stop her progress,
But kindly aid her in her flight to Heaven.

Plato

Full well we know that life hath lost it's relish,
That all it's glitter, all it's tinsel joys,
Have not one charm, to win you from that Heaven.
And yet—forgive the yearning of our souls—
We still wou'd keep you, still wou'd we be blest

With that divine, that more than heavenly sapience
That flows so strongly from you, and leads on
By inpersceptible degrees, our hearts
To love of ev'ry virtue. Without thee
Darkling bewilder'd we shall madly wander
In life's vain errors, like the simple traveller,
Lost in the mazes of a devious wood,
Who knows no path to lead him on his way.

Socrates

Have then my precepts had so poor effect?
What say'st thou, Plato? have I toil'd so long
To guide you to your bliss, and toil'd in vain?
O no, my friends; you're rich in ev'ry virtue;
Form'd by my hand, you know each step is wisdom;
Charm'd with her beauty, you will ne'er desert her.
Tho' the world frowns, tho' wicked men exclaim,
Tho' tirants threaten, you will ne'er desert her.
And my glad soul presages, future times
Will learn the lessons you have heard from me,
Will copy from your page the fair example.
There's no occasion I shou'd violate
My country's laws by which I stand condemn'd,
Nor stain my soul by acting 'gainst their verdict.
Believe me, this would give me greater pangs,
Than e'en a thousand deaths, such as I'm doom'd to.

Phedon

Yet wou'd we save thee—

Crito

O forgive our love,
And yield thee to our prayers.

Plato, pointing to the gaoler

View this good man;
Behold his honest eyes suffus'd with tears;
He speaks not, for his heart's too full to speak,
And yet his ev'ry gesture pleads thy pity,
On him, on us, on all. Apame too,

Her heart now bleeding for her brothers cruelty,
Is wearying heaven—in vain? Must she in vain
Plead to heaven for thee?—And need I say
How thy Xantippe, how thy children—Oh!
Will nothing move thee? bend thy soul a little,
Be still a man, or soar above thy nature;
Struggle with thy perfection for a while,
And want thy happiness a little longer,
To sooth the sorrowing hearts of those that love thee.

Socrates

Indeed, my friends, you love grows painful to me;
The more, 'cause all your pleadings will be fruitless.
I stand resolv'd—tis sure the will divine
Which thus resolves me—I must die, my Plato,
Tomorrow I must die; and oh! might life
Be mine for yet a long, long round of years,
And spritely youth and vigour wou'd return,
New—string my nerves, and make me as I have been;
I wou'd not quit the hopes of what my soul
Assures herself that she shall be tomorrow.
Leave me—I thank you for your pious friendship,
But leave me—nature still demands repose,
She will claim her debt out—When the morn
Wakes to fresh life the tenants of the worlds,
Again I'll see you, give one kind embrace,
The last on earth—indeed I wou'd not grieve you,
But part we now—I find, whilst I am mortal,
I've all the weakness of a man about me—
I must submit—farewel—my eyes grow heavy.

Goes to his couch, and composes himself to rest; they continue fix'd for some time in amaze & sorrow, when at length

Plato

Tis vain to urge him farther—he's a determin'd:
His righteous soul won't in her own defence
Act 'gainst the hallow'd statutes of his country.
Good heavens! The godlike virtue of this man!
O let us have him ever in our eye;
Make him our precedent, like him support

The World's despite, in conscious worth secure:
And the like peace to our last hour ensure.

End of the fourth act

Act 5th

Scene 1st

Melitus

What means this dreadful vision of the night?
Ha! Sure it was not fancy? fancy breeds
A thousand megrims in the brain, and loves
To tease her e'en to madness.—No; twas real;
I saw it plain, and horrid was it's figure;
It glar'd upon me with the eye of death;
And spoke too—sure it spoke—it mention'd *Socrates*,
And told me, heav'n was pouring down it's vengeance
On my accursed head—It was no dream;
My slumbers left me soon, and long I lay,
Stretch'd on the rack of conscience, when it came.
It came—I saw it stalk into my chamber.
How I'm distracted? Gods, was it for this,
That I maintain'd your godhead 'gainst the wretch
That wou'd have rob'd your temples of their
worship?
O for that peace I once enjoy'd—tis gone,
And now I feel such tortures—I will feel them—
My sister, ha! I wou'd not see her now.

Scene 2d

Melitus, Apame

Apame

Alass! my brother, what uncommon terror
Speaks in your countenance? you look so wild,
So sternly sad; that you alarm your sister.

Melitus

Apame, you've succeeded in your wishes;
Your brother's lost; you pray'd the foes of *Socrates*
Might feel the pangs of fell remorse—I feel them,
And fall the victim of my own resentment.

Apame

Does Melitus relent? O heavely powers!
The venerable sage will yet find mercy;
My brother will retract the wrongs he did him,
And haste to save him from the fatal potion.

Melitus

No; by the gods, I'll have my dear revenge;
Save him? I save him? Were it possible
To have my tortures doubled, (and I feel
All that the most distracted mind can form)
So strong the hate I hear him, he shou'd suffer,
Shou'd die the death my vengeance draws upon him.

Apame

What horrid resolution? Are there gods?
You say, there are, and have yourself asserted
Their dread divinity. Say, will not they
(They must be just) inflict severest torture
On guilt like yours? O hear me, dearest brother;
Give to your soul her peace, implore their mercy,
To aid you in the justice you shou'd act;
To make you gentle, humble, mild, forgiving,
That you may yet—

Melitus

Ha! sayst thou? I implore
The gods?—they'll hear not me, or, if they wou'd,
I'll not implore them, for I'll not retract
All that my injur'd soul hath urg'd against him.
He merited my vengeance—I implore them?
No; I'll not ask the mercy they'll not grant me.
—Avaunt, foul spectre! What is Socrates
To thee? art thou his wife, his child, his friend,
That thus thou haunt'st me?—Well, I will be wretched;
Away! I tell thee, that I will be wretched—
O my pain'd heart!—Ha! hath he suffer'd, say you?
Thank heaven for that the dotard then is gone
To his reward—to what reward? Ay; there,
There lies the question—If he shou'd be right—

What's that to me? I'm sure, I must be wrong—
Apame—sister! how dar'st thou intrude
Upon thy brother's privacies? Phedon sent thee;
I know him—he's the friend of Socrates,
And he has sent thee to behold thy brother
Curst e'en beyond redemption—hold, my brain!
—Gods?—what Gods?—there are none—or if there are,
They are the gods of Socrates, not mine—
I'll have no Gods—Yes, roar, ye changeling crowd,
Drag, tear me e'en to atoms, if you will;
You're true Athenians, and I'm—horror, horror!

Scene the 3d

Apame

Unhappy Melitus! I mourn thy crimes,
I mourn thy punishment—alass! thou'st rack'd
With the most cruel torture, conscious guilt.
How wondrous sad thy fate? thou feel'st the pangs,
Without the blest result, of dear repentance.
Thou wou'dst be sorry for thy fault, but can'st not,
So harden'd is thy heart! In what strong chain,
The sinner's soul is bound? he wou'd be free;
Vain is his wish; stern fate's inexorable,
And holds him fast enfetter'd in his wretchedness.
Oh! poor ill fated brother! I will pray for thee;
Spite of my reverent love for Socrates,
—Tis nature's dictate—I will pray for thee—
With thee compar'd, he's happy, whilst thy soul
Feels even now the measure of it's woes.

Scene 4th

Apame, Phedon

Apame

Alass! I've heard your kind attempt was fruitless;
That all your eloquence, your prayers, your tears

Mov'd not the god-like sage. He'll not escape;
And _Athens_ must receive a stain, which all
The tears of her repenting citizens
(For sure I am they will regret his death[)]
Will ne'er wash out.

Phedon

No, my _Apame_, no;
He will not hear us; he hath weigh'd it well,
And on the ballance finds it best for virtue
To quit at once a base and sordid world,
A world unworthy of the Good she offers.
We sued, as pious children to a parent,
On whose dear life hung all their future welfare;
In vain; he answer'd all our pleaded reasons,
Said, he must die; that it was Heaven's high will;
And he'd obey it: then with that authority
That firm, commanding, yet endearing aspect,
He wonted to instruct us, bad us leave him;
His seem'd the voice of Heaven; in wonder lost,
Sunk in our grief's distraction, we submitted.

Apame

O _Phedon_, what a day is this to _Athens_!
How will she rue—yet she deserves it all—
The dire result of her inhumane cruelty?
Indeed I pity her—she demands my pity—
Yes, O my country, I will pity thee.
But for the virtuous man she hath condemn'd,
Condemn'd unjustly; by his godlike firmness,
He shews he has made his peace with those above,
And only waits the destin'd hour for happiness;
Therefore, an object only now of wonder,
Rather, of envy, he's above our pity.

Phedon

I joy, my dear _Apame's_ soul regains
Her wonted calm; you look resign'd, my charmer,
And quit your _Socrates_ with that tranquillity,
As suits his great philosophy.

Apame

Ah, Phedon!
My soul is stunn'd;—it is indeed a calm—
But what th' event?—that we must leave to Heaven.
The death of Socrates, my brother's madness,
For oh! he hath lost—

Phedon

Your brother? say, Apame
What of your brother?

Apame

Now he left me, frantick,
Mad with his guilt, and sunk in desolation

Phedon

Good Heaven! how you surprise me!—but, no wonder—
When guilt like his recoils upon the soul
Tis then a dreary waste, a dreadful gloom,
And not one ray of comfort darts upon her
But I forbear—O pardon me, Apame.

Apame

Yes; I will pardon thee; thou say's no more,
Than what becomes the friend of Socrates;
Myself condemns him, tho' I am his sister;
A sister, that much loves and pities him.
O Heavens! What means my heart?—it seems too easy;
These two great evils, that shou'd sink her down
To deepest woe—

Phedon

Oh! add a third, my charmer,
A third, that, spite of all I feel for Socrates
Gives me more cruel pangs, our hapless loves.

Apame

Yes; Phedon: I must own, I once indulg'd

A fruitless hope, that thou and I were form'd
By Heaven's blest power, to give each other happiness,
But tis determin'd, tis *above* determin'd
That we must meet.

Phedon

Thus mortals oft
Plan to themselves their flattering schemes of bliss,
And, spite of all their vaunted art and forsight,
Drop from their airy hopes to dire despair.
What must I say? at this tremendous moment
What can I say? And yet I wou'd say something.
Alass! O can't—My soul distrest, desponding,
Wants e'en conception to describe the pangs,
That rack her now, and makes her more than wretched.

Apame

Say this; that thou art still *Apame's* friend
That thou wilt ever bear within thy breast
Her dear Idea[1], as she will do thine;
That thou wilt still pursue the glorious track
Thy great Preceptor led thee; and endeavour
T'improve in ev'ry grace, in ev'ry virtue;
Say this; and thy *Apame* yet will promise
To love thee still, t'indulge the holy friendship
That flames her soul for thee, to weary Heaven
With prayers for *Phedon*, and to her last hour
Think on thee with affection and with rapture.

Phedon

Say this! O Heavens! My feeble tongue wants
utterance
To tell thee—this is more than I durst hope;
To be subject of *Apame's* prayers,
The constant object of her tender thought,
The sole delight of her remaining hours!
What can't I promise thee? divinest maid!
Oh! I'll be all that thou wou'dst have me be;
And, if not here, yet sure in future worlds,
Transporting thought! our gentle souls shall meet,
Where no impetuous storms of fate shall part us.

Apame

Be that our hope; tis time we now retire,
You to the prison, to perform the last
Kind, filial service to your dying master.
Tell him, *Apame* never will forget
Th'important lessons that she learn'd from him;
Tell him she deeply mourns her loss, not his,
Much will she want him—but she hopes to see him
In better worlds, where she and thou and all
That lov'd him here, and listen'd to his lore,
Will yet attend him in an endless state
Of peace, of happiness.—farewel—my soul
Sinks to her heaviness—farewel, my *Phedon*.

Phedon

One kind embarce—Sure modesty forbids not
This last—forgive me; but my soul hangs on thee,
As o'er the body it's departing spirit,
Unwilling to forsake her long-lov'd mansion.
Do not refuse me—tis the last sad favour
Thy *Phedon* asks—
She inclines to him
O Heavens! and I must lose thee?
Farewel;—sure, sure, it will not be—for ever.

Note

1. In Platonic philosophy, an *idea* is an archetype of which all real things are but imperfect imitations.

Scene 5th

The Prison

Socrates

Today I am to die—What art thou, death?
Some say, a dread, a formidable tirant,

That mak'st mankind thy quarry, and devourst them,
Till they're no more than what they were, ere first
The great Eternal call'd them into *being*.
Thou art not so; and such I shall not find thee.
I've noblest prospects far; and to my soul
So mild thy aspect, that I'll call thee friend.
Thou'lt lead me, where at least my better part
Will meet with perfect virtue, certain knowledge,
With all th'improvements that she sought in vain
In this low scene.—Her state is sure progressive,
She still went on each day acquiring something,
Yet still dissatisfied, met not completion,
And wanted something farther still to *be*.
Nay more; her innocence, her constant bent
To sweet philanthropy, to doing good,
Was given by that dread power for noblest ends.
Are those ends answer'd? No. I feel, I am not
Contented with the little I have done,
And wou'd do farther—but I must not here;
My judges have forbad me—Therefore, therefore,
I go from hence to where no vile incumbrance,
No base abuse of power, no impious malice
Will hinder me from doing all I can:
Where I shall still be virtuous; nay be all
What wisdom tells me, I have not been yet;
And feel each ardent faculty within me
Fully employ'd, and blest in it's attainments.

Scene 6th

Socrates, Plato, Phedon, Crito and others

Socrates

Socrates

Welcome, my faithful pupils; you are come
To bid your *Socrates* a last farewel.
A last? No sure; we yet shall meet again.
I've been debating with myself, my friends,
And find upon the upshot, I have gain'd.
Tis true, I might have liv'd a little longer;
But oh! that little longer I had liv'd
Had rob'd me just so much of happiness.

Plato

Thou peerless man! how I adore thy virtues!
Now on the confines of eternity,
Thy looks, thy words, thy gestures are so calm,
So full of inward peace, my soul admires thee.

Socrates

For what, my *Plato*? He that acts aright,
At such a time as this is ever easy.
It may be hard to know we act aright;
Yet, if no conscious thought within disturb us,
No nauseous *bitter* mingles with our *sweet*,
But all is peace and pleasantness, sure then
Death's a mere phantom, and must lose his terrors.

Phedon

Alass! so wretched is the state of man,
We know not what we must be; thou art right;
My soul assures me, *Socrates* is right;
And yet—forgive me—still my darken'd mind
[Is] lost in her surmises, and she knows not
How to unriddle these thy causeless sufferings.

Socrates

Phedon, I can't inform thee more than what
I know myself; I've yet no full conception
Of *how* it will be; but my soul forebodes
Joy 'bove expression: Heaven for noblest ends
May yet delay to great enquiring man
The knowledge of his future fate above.

Crito

That's our distress; we've view'd the constant tenor
Of thy applauded life; and to reflect
The vile indignities thou hast endur'd
The base, insidious villain schemes against thee,
The woful death that thou must die today,
Fills us with vain incertitude; we wonder—

What mean the powers above, that they shou'd yield thee
Thus to thy impious foes.

Socrates

You quite surprise me,
How, *Crito*, don't I tell thee I'm ascertain'd
Of being something nobler than I am
While I am here—but what—that lies beyond
The ken of present knowledge—God is good,
Is gracious ever—In some future time,
When man's prepar'd to hear the happy tidings,
Some blessed sage will rise t'instruct him, whither
He goes from hence, to teach the certain road
He must pursue to reach his destin'd goal.
Meanwhile tis but our duty to await
That glorious period; we not know it yet;
[But] if I bode aright, our after-race
Won't be bewilder'd in a fruitless search
Of this important question.

Plato

Be it so!
Be heaven thus gracious to his creature, man;
And let all those, who've learnt from thee the rule,
I had almost said, th'unerring rule to live,
Await that welcome instant—Ah! my *Socrates*,
Xantippe comes; she comes to bid forever
Adieu to her dear *Socrates*; look on her
With eyes of tenderness; she's deeply wounded,
And merits all the pity thou canst shew her.

Socrates

She is my best-belov'd; heaven only knows
The true esteem that warms my heart for her.

Scene 7th

Socrates, Xantippe, Plato, Phedon, Crito & c.

Xantippe runs to him and embraces him

O *Socrates*!

Socrates

My dear, my best *Xantippe*.

Xantippe

And art thou going? have thy foes prevail'd
And must I lose thee? On this fatal day
Fore'er lose thee? O my bleeding heart!
My *Socrates*, do we now part for ever?

Socrates

So heaven ordains; and tho my soul reflects
[...]fondness all the happy hours
And yet—

[end of manuscript]

10
Trifles, Part 2d

By the Author of the first.

I, fuge; sed poteras tutior esse domi.

Martial[1]

Martial to his Book. B[ook] 1, E[pigram] 4.[2]

Thou o'er the various shops delight's too rove,
When with thy Lord shou'dst greater safety prove,
The Scoffs of haughty Rome thou dost not know,
All the whole I own have taste—thou'lt find it so—
Unluckier drolls not o'er the globe appear,
And old and young are playing fond of sneer.
While their applause thou madly hop'st to share,
Swift will they toss their dancing in the air.
But, that thy masters blots thou may'st not feel,
Nor fear thy pleasant jokes his anxious guile;
Abroad, gay, wanton thing, thou ask'st to roam;
Go, fly—but thou had'st better stay at home.

Mart[ial] to Attalus. B[ook] 2, E[pigram] 7.[3]

Your smartly declaim, & as smartly you plead,
Smart histories write, & smart poems indeed.
Your farces & epigrams are all of them smart,
And the smartest by far of stargazers thou art.
Full, smartly you dance, & as smartly you sing
Strike smartly the ball, & as smartly the string
Yet you do nothing well, tho' in ev'rything smart.
—In troth! thou no more than a smatterer art.

Mar[tial] to Sextus. B[ook] 3, E[pigram] 38.

What woundrous confidence brought you to Rome;
What do ye expect or hope for, now you're come?

'Causes, as well as Tully,[4] I can plead;
'Not one can equal me—much less exceed.'
Yes, Caius[5] plead & Lucius;[6] both you know;
To live, was more than they e'er yet could do.
'If that shou'd fail, Heroicks I'll compose;
'Hear them; you'll say, that Mine is Maro's[7] muse.'
Mere madness! these you see so poorly clad—
You'll find them Ovids,[8] Virgils all, egad!
'Turn courtier then'—but few e'en so succeed,
The rest scarce gain enought to find them bread.
'What must I do? I'm here resolv'd to stay.'
If on mere honour you can live, you may.

Mar[tial] to Posthumus.[9] Book 4, Epigram 40.

Where flourish'd Piso[10] with his num'rous race,
And Seneca[11] in highest honour was;
Thee, Posthumus, did I to them prefer;
Tho' a poor knight, to me you Consul were.
With you full thirty winters I have liv'd;
One couch in common both of us receiv'd.
Now you can give—now lose—with wealth replete;
With honour too—your favours I expect.
Nought will you do? Alass: 'tis now too late,
For me to hope another king[12] to get.
Say, fortune, is't agreable to thee.
That Posthumus shou'd thus impose on me?

Mar[tial] on his stay in the Country.
B[ook] 4, E[pigram] 90.[13]

You ask, while in my Country-farm I stay,
My Business there—first, to the Gods I pray;
My servants next, & next to look o'er my land.
And there to all their diff'rent tasks command;
Next; I some gay diverting Author read,
Then dare the muse, & ask Apollo's aid.
Then oil my body, for the ring prepare,
Strain at the sport, my mind quite free from care,
'Cause free from debt—then dine, drink, sing & play,
Then walk, then sup, then end in rest the day,

Till the small oyly lamp exerts her light,
My studies alway take from me the night.

Mutual love, On the friendship between Mary Queen of *Scotland* and Elizabeth Queen of England.

By Buchanan[14]

With steel darts his right hand arm'd,
His left with poysons fill'd;
Rage *Death* around the universe,
While all things to him yield;
Let time now down with ruthless scythe
What does on earth appear;
Or dire old age with hasty steps
To atoms all things wear:
Yet there's a chaine defies their pow'r
Two faithful hearts which binds;
Nor *Death's* approach nor length of time
Dissolve the love of *minds*.
Great *Scipio* with his *Lalius*[15] true
Both age and *Death* o'ercame;
But now with all their force destroy'd
Their friendship's noble flame.
So now between two *British* Queens,
The *Heroines* of their time,
Their friendship firm fore'er will reign
In one unfolding prime.
E'en when the final lot of things
With Heaven Earth shall join,
Still in it's purity shall last
A Friendship so divine.
Maria, *Scotia's* peerless queen,
Her *English* friend shall love;
Eliza, *England's* noblest boast,
For her as faithful prove.

On the death of *Adonis*[16] From Theocritus[17] Idyll: 30.

When *Cytherea*,[18] mournful, sad,
Beheld her dear *Adonis* dead,

His shining tresses stain'd with gore,
His cheecks, late blooming, pale all o'er
Haste, seize, she to her Cupids cried,
The bestial, by whose tusks he died.
Swift as the tenants of the sky
To ev'ry wood around they fly,
The murdrous boar full soon they found,
With joy their hapless prey they bound.
With mighty triumph led him strait
To Love's fair queeen to know his fate.
The boar but sullenly did move,
For much he fear'd the queen of Love.

'Art thou, the Goddess fiercely said
'The wretch that struck Adonis dead?
'Didst thou his beauteous body tear,
'To my lovesick heart so dear?

The beastial trembling thus replied,
'The cruel fact can't be denied;
'But, Goddess, by thyself I swear,
'These Loves, this chain that binds me here,
'Far from my aim it was to've harm'd
'A youth, whose ev'ry feature charm'd.
'I saw and lov'd—was that amiss?
'And sought his snowy thigh to kiss.
'But I, alass! to madness lov'd;
'The kiss I gave, too fatal prov'd.
'Take then these tusks, Goddess fair,
'For they the great offenders are;
'Tear, root them out for what they've done;
'Glad shall I be, when once they're gone.
'And if my tusks won't suffice,
'E'en punish all—my lips—my eyes.

The gentle Goddess griev'd his fate,
And bad the Loves unbind him strait.
And now no more in woods he roves,
But follows Venus and her doves:
And, since so cruel their embrace,
His Love-teeth to the flames conveys.

Epigram from Theocritus

With thou, now the eve is fair,
Breathe, my boy, some pleasing air
On thy softly-worbling flute?
I myself will take the lute;
Meanwhile Daphnis's[19] to his lip
Shall apply his reedy pipe;
Thus all three will sweetly play,
And beguile the night away;
And, while nigh yon mossy cave
We the sprightly concert have,
From his nap we Pan[20] shall take,
And keep the God all night awake.

Epigram from Moschus[21]
Love at plough

His torch and quiver laid aside,
Pernicious Cupid takes the whip,
To drive the plough was now his pride,
And down his shoulders hangs his scrip.[22]

He to the yoke the steers submits;
The toilsome burthen long they'ad born;
And briskly, as for business fit,
Along the furrow strews the corn.

Then leering up at amorous Jove,
Cries, parch the fields, dear Daddy, do.
Else soon Europa's bull[23] may prove
My power, oblig'd to drag the plough.[24]

Anacreon's[25] Dove. Ode. 9.

Pretty dove, that wing'st along;
Whence dost come? to whom belong?
Breathing sweets around you fly;
All the air perfum'd anigh:
Heav'ns! what fragrance! prithee shew
Whose thou art—I want to know.

Anacreon has sent me here
To his sweetly-charming fair.
Dost thou know her? great her pow'r
Ev'ry heart she triumphs o'er
Venus, for a spritely ode
Me upon the Bard bestow'd;
And, in such like things as those,
I my master learn to please.
Now these letters—what they are
I know not—he bad me bear;
And he tells one, I shall be
Instant from his service free.
But tho' he shou'd bid me go,
My good hap I better know:
I with him will still remain:
O'er the hill or o'er the plain.
What need I to rove, or be
Nestling idly on a tree?
Eating what wild fruits I find,
And leave his dainty cates behind?
Now from his own hand I'm fed
With the choicest wheaten bread.
From the cup, whence he'as his tip;
I the richest nectar sip;
Then I dance, and while he sings,
Hover o'er him with my wings,
Neer him constantly I keep,
And upon his musick sleep.

Thou hast all that I can tell;
Gentle stranger now farewell;
Thou hast made me prattle more
Than e'er Corornis[26] did before.

The Poet's Petition to Apollo
Horace[27] B[ook] 1st, Ode 31st.

1

From bright Apollo, God of wit;
What does his humble bard require;
What while he pours the new made wine,
Is the full height of his desire.

2

Not the rich fields, replete with grain,
That crown _Sardinia's_ fruitful ilse;
Not the fine flocks that jocund graze
In hot _Calabria's_[28] sunburnt soil.

3

Not golden treasures of the great;
Not ivory brought from distant _Ind_;
Not the gay plains round which the still,
The silent streams of _Liris_[29] wind.

4

Prune they, to whom indulgent fate
Allots, the fam'd _Calenian_[30] vines;
Drink merchants in their cups of gold;
Full dearly bought, their choicest wines;

5

(By Heav'n beloved: else scarce so oft
They'd pass secure th'Atlantick sea;)
Sweet olives and the mallows light,
And endive are the food for me.

6

Give me, O great _Latona's_[31] son,
T'enjoy what I my pittance find;
With strength of body, and yet more,
With superior strength of mind.

7

Give me to live a length of age;
From turpitude, from folly free;
Give me still to indulge the muse:
'Tis all thy _poet_ asks of thee.

A Poem from Boethius[32]

1

Yes all the various sons of Earth
Draw from one general Origin their birth;
One Father is the source of all,
And universal _being_ hears his call.

2

They feel his influence; he the sun
Supplies with beams; with milder light the moon;
Man, to inhabit earth, he has giv'n;
And all yon spangling host, to people heaven.

3

A spirit of the etherial flame
Hath he infus'd into the human frame;
Hence mortals all can boast a line
Of high descent, of origin divine.

4

Then why, vain fool, that pride of heart,
'Cause of peculiar ancestry thou art?
Reflect that God's the source of all,
And all of humane race thy brethren call.

5

None e'er degenerates from his birth,
Unless his soul lies groveling on the earth;
Unless, forgetful of her native skies,
She clings to dust, and does not aim to rise.

Celadon and Amelia, from Thompson's[33] Summer.

1

Young *Celadon*, a matchless swain,
Of all *Arcadia's* youth the pride,
Amelia lov'd, nor lov'd in vain;
She gently listen'd, when he sigh'd.
Guileless his flame, as was his mind;
His honest heart the charmer knew;
Pleas'd with a passion so refin'd,
The joy'd to prove the shepherd true:

2

The rural day in converse sweet
And blithesome sport the lovers spent;
The bow'ry grove their blest retreat,
Whose bows a grateful covert lent:
There while the welcome cool they prove,

Nor Sol's fierce scorching beams offend;
Oft talk'd they o'er their faithful love,
The joys that innocent attend.

3

Thus their fond hours they whil'd away;
In raptures but to lovers known;
When on a day (ah! luckless day!
O Sun why hast thou on it shone?)
By the fair face of heaven betray'd
(Their wayward fate, ye shepherds, mourn)
They joyous sought their wonted shade,
They sought it, never to return!

4

For oh! while in each other's arms,
They feel the sympathy of souls;
Sudden th'impetuous storm alarms;
The lightning glares, the thunder rolls:
Close to her swain the charmer clings;
Alass! he shelters her in vain:
The bolt with death fate, direful, wings,
And she falls breathless 'fore her swain.

5

See, see her blooming beauties fade;
Beauties, that now must charm no more;
Th'insulting Tirant, see, invade
That form, that conquer'd all before!
So the gay Blossom's vernal bloom
The blast's devouring pow'r destroys;
And, thus devoted to the tomb,
Ambition's early fav'rite lies.

6

But where's her sad dejected swain?
Aghast with murdring grief he stands;
Adown his cheeks tears fall amain,
He rends his hair, he rings his hands:
'And art thou gone? won't heav'n secure
'Such spotless innocence; he cries;
His big-swoln heart, can bear no more;
He falls, he grasps her corse, he dies.

Mars; Mercury a dialogue from Lucian[34]

Mars

<u>Hermes</u>, you heard the idle rants of <u>Jove</u>,
His empty menaces my laughter move.
Shou'd I from Heav'n be bluster'd, hang a chain;
Ye Gods, you'd strive to drag me down in vain.
But shou'd I chuse to Heav'n to draw you up,
Tho' earth and sea were fasten'd to the rope,
Soon wou'd you kick the stars—you heard the rest.
'Tis true, 'tis e'en by <u>Mars</u> own self confest,
That if one single mortal 'gainst him strove,
His Godship's strength wou'd far superior prove;
But that so great his force, that he cou'd bear
Both earth and sea and Gods aloft in air,
[. . .]nts[35] & brags, his <u>Juno's</u> son,
[. . .]e the feat, will never own.

Mercury

Good words, friend <u>Mars</u>, your raillery is unsafe;
Knew <u>Jove</u>—you'd pay, Sir, dearly for your laugh.

Mars

Psha! fool—I only mention this to thee.
I know too prudent thou to injure me.
Some babling Gods I wou'd not trust so far;
But safe with thee all my reflections are.
Well then, arn't all his vaunting threats absurd,
When <u>Neptune</u>, <u>Pallas</u>,[36] & my mother[37] dar'd,
Against his galling Tyranny to rise,
And made that dreadful hubbub in the skies,
How many shapes this monarch of us all,
Thro' fear, took on him, to prevent his fall.
And had not <u>Thetis</u>,[38] silverfooted maid;
Brought fierce <u>Briareus</u>[39] to his Godship's aid
For all his noisy thunder he has found
Himself a prisoner, & in shackles bound.
Remembring this, who cou'd a[. . .]
My own dear Daddy's empty [. . .]

Mercury

Prithee, good Mars, this idle chat forbear,
Not fit for thee to use, not me to hear.

The Dog and the Wolf from Phadrus.[40] B. 3. Fa:7.

My aim is now to let you see,
How sweet the charms of liberty.
A Wolf as lean as wolf e'er was,
Once met a dog in jolly ease.
They stopp'd and chatted—whence, quoth Grim,
Are you, my friend, so sleek and trim?
I that am stronger far than thou art,
No flincher for my guts, no coward
Am nought, you see, but skin & bone.
The fault, cries Jowler, is you own:
You need but do the same as I do,
You'd live as well, and look as spry to.
[. . .] why watch at night the door;
[. . .]ard the house from thieves secure.
[. . .]do't for faith! my life at present,
Is very far from being pleasant;
Rambling in woods whate'er the weather.
I scarce keep life and soul together.
'Tis easier to live under roof,
And at one's leisure have enough.
They soon agreed, and now they walk,
And of each other's matters talk;
When on dog's neck, with some suprise,
The marks of collar, wolf espies.
What's this? Pho! nothing. Tell me tho'.
I'm something sharp & fierce, you know,
For this they tie me up all day,
Which commonly I doze away,
But then at eve they let me loose,
And I can then my freedom use.
Besides, I eat while I am able.
My master e'en from his own t[able,]
Sends crusts and scraps & soups to fee[d me,]
And not a servant too but heeds me:
So free, so liberal they give,
I live as well as dog can live.

But tell me, have you with all this
Freedom to go where'er you please?
Quoth Jowier: No. The wolf replies,
Enjoy the servitude you prize,
For me, without my liberty,
A sov'reign prince I d scorn to be.

On The two Miss *****'* as they Sat before
me, hearing of Mr. Whitefield——[41]
An Extempore Epigram.

Plac'd as I was, such charms within my view,
Say, Whitefield, what could all thy Rhet'ric do?
In vain the nonsense trickl'd from thy tongue,
In vain with canting harmony you Sung;
Their blooming beauties more perswasive prov'd,
My heart with greater energy they mov'd,
Their Swan-like necks my ravish'd eyes did bliss,
Courted the touch, and tempted me to kiss.—

Notes

1. Marcus Valerius Martialis (c. 40-c. 104 A.D.) was a Roman poet best known for his fourteen books of empigrams that attacked the degenerate lifestyle of his age. The Latin phrase is translated in the last line of the first epigram below.

2. Cradock is mistaken; this is a translation of Book 1, Empigram 3.

3. Martial's original epigram is to Atticus.

4. Tully is Marcus Tullius Cicero (106 B.C.-43 B.C.) Cicero was one of the great stylist of the Latin language.

5. Caius Sallustius Crispus or Sallust (c. 86 B.C.-c. 34 B.C.) was a Roman historian best known for his account of Rome from 78 to 67 B.C., which he modeled after Thucydides.

6. Possibly Lucius Licinius Lucculus (first century B.C.), Roman soldier and ally of Caesar. In Martial's version the two eloquent men mentioned are called Atestinus and Civis. See Martial, Epigrams, trans. Walter C. A. Kerr, 2 vols. (Cambridge, Mass.: Harvard University Press, 1947), 1:184-85.

7. Maro is the cognomen for the poet Publius Vergilius Maro, better known as Vergil (70 B.C.-19 B.C.).

8. Publius Ovidius Naso (43 B.C.-c. 18 B.C.) was a Roman poet best known for his Metamorphoses.

9. Martial's original epigram is to Postumus.

10. The Piso family was prominent in Roman politics in the first century B.C. and A.D. Its members usually met with violent death. The reference is probably to Gaius Calpurnius Piso, who killed himself after being betrayed while leading an anti-Nero conspiracy in 65 A.D.

11. Lucius Annaeus Seneca (c. 4B.C.-65 A.D.), philosopher and tutor of Nero, was a close friend of Martial. Seneca committed suicide after being implicated in the Pisonian conspiracy against Nero.

12. "The name given under the Emperor by flatt'rers & dependents to their Patrons" (Cradock's notation).

13. There is no epigram 90 in Book 4. The one being translated has not been found.

14. "This is translated to shew that Poets are not always prophets" (Cradock's notation). George Buchanan (1506-82) was a Scots historian and Latin scholar frequently caught in the religious controversies of his age. He taught in Scotland, France, and Portugal and was tutor to Queen Mary of Scotland and her son James. He was not only a professor but also a political figure of major consequence in Scotland from 1562 until 1578. He

is generally considered the best Latin poet of modern Europe.

15. The friendship of two Roman generals of the Second Punic War, Publius Cornelius Scipio Africanus and Gaius Laelius, was a famous one in the ancient world.

16. The myth of Adonis outlined in this poem was a favorite of antiquity.

17. Theocritus was third-century B.C. Greek idyllic poet born at Syracuse. He is credited as the founder of pastoral poetry and his Idylls became models for Roman poets like Vergil. There is some doubt as whether Theocritus wrote this particular idyll, known as "The Dead Adonis." See J. M. Edmonds, trans., The Greek Bucolic Poets (Cambridge, Mass.: Harvard University Press, 1912), pp. 479-83.

18. Another name for Venus or Aphrodite, who was said to be born on the island of Cythera.

19. Daphnis was a mythical Sicilian shepherd said to have invented postoral music. He appears frequently in Theocritus's poetry.

20. Pan was the divine patron of pastoral poets.

21. Moschus was a poet from Syracuse flourishing in the second century B.C.

22. A scrip is a bag or wallet carried by wayfarers.

23. Europa's bull refers to the creature sent by Zeus to bring the daughter of the King of Tyre to Zeus's home on Crete. Hence a very powerful oxen is meant by this passage. Moschus wrote a poem about the rape of Europa, but there is doubt that this particular epigram may be ascribed to him. See Edmonds, Greek Bucolic Poets, pp. 427-41, 457, 461.

24. After this point in the manuscript "The Maryland Divine. A Parody on the 4th Eclogue of Virgil" is crossed out.

25. Anacreon (c. 582 B.C.-c. 485 B.C.) was a lyric poet from Teos noted for his poems of love and wine. However, there is no proof he wrote this particular poem. See J. M. Edmonds, ed., Elegy and Iambus . . . with the Anacreontea, 2 vols. (Cambridge, Mass.: Harvard University Press, 1931), "The Anacreontea," p. iv.

26. Coronis was a nymph of Naxos to whom Zeus entrusted the care of the infant Dionysus who eventually became the Greek god of wine. Presumably Coronis's fondness for that beverage made her talkative. Coronis is not mentioned in the original. Cradock has not made a literal translation but modified the last line while maintaining the original intent The Greek literally reads "you have all; go your way, you have made me more talkative, sir, than a very crow." Edmonds, ed., Elegy, "The Anacreontea," p. 41n.

27. Horace, actually Quintus Horatius Flaccus (65 B.C.-8 B.C.), was a Latin poet most famous for his Odes.

28. Calabria was the southernmost division of Italy.

29. Liris is a river in central Italy.

30. Calenum, modern Calvi, is a town north of Capus noted for its good wine.

31. Latona was the mother of Apollo and Diana. Her Latin name was Leto.

32. Boethius was a sixth century Christian philosopher, humanist, and active Roman official who eventually was executed in 525 for treason. He is most famous for "The Consolation of Philosophy," written while he was imprisoned. "The Consolation" is a Ciceronian dialogue interrupted

by brief poems. This poem comes from Book 3 of "The Consolation" in a discussion of "The Vanity of Noble Birth." See Boethius, The Consolation of Philosophy, introduced by Irwin Edman (New York, 1943), p. 53.

33. James Thomson (1700-1748) first published the poem "Summer" in 1727 and it became one of four pieces collected into The Seasons, first printed in 1730. In the 1746 edition, this tale, which Cradock modified slightly, is found in lines 1170-1268.

34. Lucian of Samosata (c. 120-c. 180 A.D.) was a Greek-language poet known for his essays in dialogue.

35. The brackets and ellipses here and elsewhere in this and the next poem indicate a tear in the manuscript.

36. Another name for Athena, the goddess of handicrafts and peace, who is identified with the Roman goddess Minerva.

37. Mars was the son of Jupiter and Juno. See line 13 above.

38. Thetis was a sea nymph and the mother of Achilles.

39. Briareus was a Greek mythological sea monster with 100 arms who freed Jupiter from imprisonment by Juno, Neptune, and Athena.

40. Phaedrus (c. 15 B.C.-c. 50 A.D.) was the first Latin writer of books of fables. He is best known for "The Fox and the Grapes." In the early eighteenth century, thirty new fables were discovered, giving him added popularity.

41. Not part of the "Trifles" booklet, this extempore epigram on "some young Ladies in Church, while the Reverend Mr. [George] Whitefield was holding forth from the pulpit" is credited to Cradock. "The two

Miss *****'*" are probably the daughters of Sheriff John Risteau of Baltimore County, one of whom would shortly become Cradock's wife. The epigram is from the Alexander Hamilton, "Record Book of the Tuesday Club," book one, chapter 7, folio 185, John Work Garrett Library, Johns Hopkins University, Baltimore, Maryland.

11
Textual Notations

Authorial modifications in the manuscript are noted below. Citation is by line number unless otherwise noted.

A Fragment

7 whose <shade> Oaks.

16 that is inserted above <tis>.

Crurulia

This manuscript is not in Cradock's handwriting, although the cancellations and interlineations appear to be his.

The Check

21 genuine inserted above <gen'rous>.

44 And bravely <act> inserted above <Then sure thou'lt> act.

Afflictions mercies

2 severest evils interlined above <acutest sorrows>, which had been inserted above the original <afflictions real>.

7 must inserted above <shall>.

9 word inserted above <thought>; action's inserted above <word is>.

10 thought inserted above <deed>.

12 yet present inserted above <offer up>.

24 whiten thro' inserted above <brighten from>.

33 vain fantastick <aims> pursue inserted above <for a diadem contend>; hopes inserted above <aims>.

35 view inserted above <end>.

The Resolve

2 noisome inserted above <the oile>.

7 Duely originally written Daily with the ai canceled and ue inserted above them; temple<s>.

15 <The ways of righteousness to understand,>.

16 <And> with the flame of <Love devine> to glow? is the first version; <all> inserted between With the <capitalized W written over the lower case w>; heavenly zeal inserted above <Love devine>.

18 direful inserted above <dreadful>.

19 in <all> my; sad inserted after my.

26 heart inserted above <soul>.

29 I stand inserted above <Yes, I'm>; thou, written over Oh.

30 se added to the to form these.

The Release

1 Vain inserted above <Poor>, empty efforts, which was interlined above <Oh! efforts vain> of <frail>.

2 . . . I keep the vow <I've made?> is original version; 've added to I; kept written over keep; solemn inserted after the; ? placed after vow.

4 <My poor weak heart so easily betray'd> is original version, above so was inserted thus, which was not canceled; The wretch . . . now written below the earlier line with the same inserted below <that wretched>.

8 where . . . obey inserted above to the God I shou'd obey.

14 her inserted above <me>.

15 <Yet sure> the resolutions <I> was original version; T capitalized on the; noble inserted after The; she inserted above I .

16 arm'd her sure inserted above <taught me all>.

17 sacred inserted above <solemn>.

22 enormous inserted after The; deserts his post inserted above <enormously offends>.

24 <And but obedience to his God pretends.> is original version; In the <first onset of temtations lost.> inserted above the original line; wild whirl of <furious madness> lost inserted below the

original line; impious anger inserted above furious madness.

28 contest inserted above <struggles>.

30 in . . . career inserted above <and their force restrain>.

31 poor weak inserted after Our; too . . . way inserted above <full oft they so resistless sway>.

32 <That our attempts to humble them are vain;> original version; And lose <all> their fortitude <the> danger near. inserted original; when inserted below <the> in revision; possibly 's on danger added at this time.

The Recovery

4 Again . . . celestial inserted above <And with the fire of Heav'nly>.

5 Wild inserted above <Base>.

6 base inserted above <vile>.

15 E'en inserted before Pleasure's; gaudy inserted above <gay>; and gilded inserted above <temptations gaudy>.

16 Firmly inserted before I scorn, <I hate>; can inserted above <e'en>.

17 prove, inserted after <be,>.

19 God and his inserted above <dear>; love inserted above <God, on me>.

20 On me inserted above <All>; flatt'ring, fatal inserted above alluring ; <wholly> lost.

23 song<s>.

27 rule inserted above <guide>.

32 mark inserted above <aim>.

The Prospect

6 prelude inserted above <foretaste>.

8 Who <make their lives one grateful sacrafice> was original version; strive replaced <seeks>; win replaced <gain>; eternal replaced <immortal> in a revision inserted above the original.

9 weary inserted above <much-tired>, which had been inserted above an original <weary>. Who <has> travel<led> with an s added to the last word.

11 *breezy* inserted above *bloom*<*ing*> to which a *y* was added, then the whole word canceled.
12 *harast* inserted above <*weary*>.
19 *joyous* originally <*happy*> which was replaced by <*blissful*>, and then by <*glorious*>.
25 *mistrelsy* inserted above <*melody*>.
32 *'re* written over last letters in *whose*; *t* written over *s* in *wish*.
36 *in* inserted after *count*; *extended ocean's scatter'd* inserted above <*azure sea's extended*>; *glitt'ring* inserted below original line, apparently replacing *scatter'd*, which is not canceled.
41 *Saviour-God* inserted below *gracious-Being*; *to* inserted before *provide*<*s*>.
42 *his . . . give* inserted above *to Him thou only live*,>.
43 <*And scorn to fix thy views on ought besides*>.

First Eclogue

English Text

24 *length* inserted above *last*, which was not canceled.
34 <*Than holy Pope at Rome does Scarlet Whore*.>
69 The <*liquid*> liquid Plain
75–76 '*Ere* <*I forget e'en to my dying Day*,>
<*For the kind Donor of my Bliss to pray*>
91 *juicy* inserted above *good*, which was not canceled.

Latin Text

17–18 *Saepe . . . cornix* does not appear in the standard editions of Vergil's first eclogue. It may be translated: "Often from a hollow tree the crow made unfavorable predictions." T. E. Page, in *P. Vergili Moronis Bucolica et Georgica* (London: Macmillan, 1910), p. 95, notes that *Saepe . . . cornix* is sometimes inserted after line 17 in "bad MSS." It is also possible that Vergil used *sinistra* to mean *favorable* rather than *unfavorable*, as it had such a connotation in early Roman literature. Vergil used a somewhat similar phraseology in the ninth eclogue, line 15.

45 boves boves should read ut ante boves; submittite should read summittite.

52 sacros <capta> frigus

60 pisces should read piscis.

74 felix quondam should read quondam felix.

79 poteres should read poteras.

Second Eclogue

English Text

7 hills wou'd inserted above Mountains, which is not canceled.

37 Piggies replaces <Hogs>

51 fairest inserted above sweetest, which is not canceled.

60-61 <Madly thou shun'st our Huts—when first they came>.
The <very> Whites themselves were glad to use the Same [not canceled].

61 To use the like, our Masters thought no Shame [not canceled]. Shame inserted below Blame, which was not canceled. Master's self inserted above <Lord's>. Sequence of lines 60-61 in MS. Probable sequence of composition, 1-5.
4—Surely our Hut . . . [interlined above]
1—Madly thou Shun'st . . .
5—Our Master's self . . . [interlined above]
2—The very Whites . . .
3—To use the like . . . [interlined below previous line, at bottom of page.]

62 Lamb pursues replaces Lamb<kin views>.

63 the <flow'ry> Glade; with rapture views replaces <pursues>.

64 My Daphne; the alone replaces <make thee my sole Delight;>.

65 Each follows that most lovely in its sight [not canceled]. follows inserted above and between Each that; that replaces <pursues>; charming inserted

above *lovely*, which is not canceled. Sequence of lines 62-65 in MS.

The Wolf . . .
The gentle Lamb . . .
I follow thee . . .
Each follows that . . .
All follow . . . [interlined between the above and line 66.]

66 *Toil is done* replaces *Toil*<*s quite*> *done*.
69 *Flames* replaces <wounds>.
70 *Frenzy* inserted above *Madness*, which is not canceled.
73 <*Thy Quarters & Tobacco most require*>*?* is original line; *Which both for Wants* <*Use most needful are*> inserted above original; *thy use & ease more needful are* inserted below original line.
74 *since* replaces <*if*>.
75 *Rant* inserted above *noise*, which is not canceled.

Latin Text

1 *Alexin* should read *Alexim*.
4 *Assidue* should read *Adsidue*.
9-10 Lines are in reverse order.
21 *meis* should read *meae*.
22 *desit* should read *defit*.
32 *plures* should read *pluris*.
41 *ambo* should read *albo*.
53 *&* should be deleted; *malo* should read *pomo*.
67 *crescentes* should read *crescentis*.

Third Ecologue

Argument *make* replaces <*charge*>.
1 *Kine* inserted above *Hogs*; which is not canceled.
2 *They . . . Trees* inserted above *I feed them as I please*, which is not canceled; *brousing on* inserted above *cropping of*, which is not canceled.

6 And <all> the; few inserted with caret after the; Cows inserted above Hogs, which is not canceled.

24 thy shrill Roar's inserted below <Noise like thine>.

25 us inserted with caret between of best.

26 prize 'bove any earthly inserted above value most of any, which is not canceled.

49 Knave inserted above Puppy, which is not canceled; does trudge inserted above <comes>.

50 who sings the better song inserted below <which best deserves the Lay>.

51 thy very inserted above & sing thy, which is not canceled.

56 Cows inserted above Hogs, which is not canceled.

59 first; inserted with caret after Cutpurse.

68 Cows inserted above Hogs, which is not canceled.

74 catch inserted above <hear>.

78 glut inserted below fill, which is not canceled.

101 L-as the first letter changed from another, which is illegible.

103 Yearlings inserted above <Young + illegible>.

105 reason inserted above Cause; at inserted above go, neither of which are canceled.

Fourth Ecologue

Booklet Text

62 we've have hardly is correct in manuscript, see "Trifles" text below where have is omitted.

63 to my <equ> Will.

67 L<ew>-s in MS.

74 Doctrines inserted above Systems, which is not canceled.

Trifles Text

A second version of this bucolic exists in the

"Trifles" booklet between the "Epigram from Moschus: Love at plough" and "Anacreon's Dove. Ode 9." Entitled "The Maryland Divine a Paradoy on the 4th Ecologue of Virgil," this rendering is remarkable in that all the personages left blank in the other version are spelled out here—particularly the name of the poet Richard Lewis. It is probable that this is a second text since such obvious errors as *we've have* in line 62 have been corrected to *we've hardly*. Only significant alterations are noted here; thus changes in capitalization, italicization, and punctuation between the two ecologues are ignored, as are minor spelling variants such as *tryed* for *try'd*. The "Trifles" version is crossed out in the manuscript.

Argument *gentile* replaced by *genteel*.
4 *Numbers* replaced by *mumbers*.
14 *'em* replaced by *them*.
22 *Hibernio's* replaced by *Hilario's*.
23 *Bombalio's* inserted below *Thomaso's*, which is not canceled. The new interlineation appears to be by a shakier hand than that of the original MS.
26 *Hilario* replaces *Hybernio*.
27 *Hilario* replaces *Hybernio*.
31 *To you in clusters shall resort the fair*,
32 *preach* replaces *teach*.
36 *Woolstan* replaces *Whoolstan*.
37 *Shaftesbury* spelled *Shaftburg*.
41–42 Lines reversed.
42 *will still endure* replaced by *will yet endure*.
43 *art* replaced by *are*
44 *transports* replaces by *transport*.
46 *Godly* replaced by *Christians*.
51 *wont* replaced by *us'd*.
55 <*self*> *self-sufficient*.
58 *Let's* replaced by *Now*.
61 *starves, too well* replaced by *starves us, well*.
65–66 Lines 71–72 inserted here.
67 *Favours* replaced by *Favour*.
69 *Shall* replaced by *Shou'd*.

"Trifles" Notations

by footnote number

2 They are Gentleman, which sometimes replaced by some Gentlemen. are meant, who at one time; in the Author's company replaced by in the cause of freedom, which terminates the note.

3 Changed to read: This must not be understood were of the greater part of the Clergy; who many of them have done honour to their profession; and 'tis observ'd those Gentlemen who have come over of late have more learning and Piety too, than their Predecessors.

6 of the omitted.

7 has . . . for it replaced by if he offers himself.

8 A Gentleman replaced by Lewis a Gentleman.

Fifth Ecologue

English Text

Argument Ever-Drunk <meeting> two planters . . .

6 bid inserted above ask, which is not canceled.

21 Weevil's inserted above Mite was, which is not canceled.

26 She . . . her, inserted above, <we thought she had lost her> Tongue.

27 Ham & Cheese inserted above Greens & Bacon, which is not canceled.

50 Value inserted over Love for him, which is not canceled; our great Regard inserted above we <neer> can [with an 't inserted after can] shew enough. [Obviously the notation to this line is a final version.]

54 when I awake inserted above & all that, which is not canceled.

66 continual inserted below, external inserted above Constant, none of which is canceled; care inserted above joy, which is not canceled.

73 Hardships quite forgot inserted above Slavery forgot, which is not canceled.

75 Indolence inserted above <Idleness>.

76 *all* inserted above <*illegible*>.
80 *the* inserted above *our Punch* and over *our Flasks*, which are not canceled.
81 *Honours* inserted over <*off'rings*>.
82 *very souls* inserted over *ev'ry Sense*, which is not canceled.
87 *rove* inserted over <*love*>.
101 *being* inserted above and between *Tho' an*; *he's* changed to *his*; *wound is* inserted above <*wondrous*>.

Latin Text

2 *leves* should read *levis*.
10 *ignes* should read *ignis*.
19 *Sed* . . . *antro* credited to Manaclas in Vergil.
27 *in gemuisse* should read *gemuisse*.
30 *Baccho* should read *Bacchi*.
50 *quocunque* should read *quocumque*.
51 *Daphninque* should read *Daphnimque*.
55 *Stimicon* should read *Stimichon*.
84 *valles* should read *vallis*.

Sixth Eclogue

2 An illegible word is inserted above *speak*, which is not canceled.
10 *blither* inserted above *happier*, which is not canceled.
23-24 *Thus* . . . *condemns* interlined below line 22. There was no subsequent renumbering of lines except for line *109* below.
24 *Thoughtless* inserted above <*Fabian*>.
45 First *God* has ink blurred in MS, but *G* is apparent; a dash exists where second use of the word appears.

Eighth Ecologue

9 *Jemima* inserted above <*Maria*>.

16 Jemima written over another word; which is illegible.
24 O'er Ghosts . . . Pow'r inserted above More Wondrous Feats she 'ad done, than e'er done before, which is not canceled.
51 raging inserted over tickling, which is not canceled.
115 vain <m>.

Ninth Eclogue

English Text

1 Hoa inserted above Say, which is not canceled.
3 Tachanoontia written over Gachradidow.
6 which once inserted between Sounds we; to replaces <we once sh[oul]d>.
62 explore inserted below adore, which is not canceled. No room existed to interline above adore.
64 golden inserted above <plenteous>.
66 when a boy inserted above <to our youth>.

Latin Text

3 nunq[ua]m should read numq[ua]m.

Tenth Ecologue

71 ecchoing correct MS spelling.

The Death of Socrates

Act 1, Scene 2

46 dare inserted above <meet>.
47 Conflict inserted after <way>.

48 and honest inserted above <sincere>.
51 simple inserted above <foolish>.

Act 1, Scene 4

28 Directing inserted above <Instructing>; paths inserted above <ways>.
34 trod appears written over another word, possibly took.
114 bliss inserted above happiness, which is not canceled.
117 filial inserted above thy; <deserv'd> success.

Act 1, Scene 5

3 <thee,> Apame.

Act 1, Scene 6

48 her inserted above <its>.
61 repentant inserted between of penitence.

Act 2, Scene 1

5 dreary inserted above <dismal>.
28 <fre> being.
39 rich inserted after With; <indeed>! not.

Act 2, Scene 2

11 wonted inserted above former, which is not canceled.
24 vilest inserted above meanest, which is not canceled.
33 hearts inserted after big-swol[le]n.
34 piercing is inserted above <great &>; <piercing> anguish.
36 dear lov'd inserted before friend; <our father> our; blest inserted before instructor.

53 lo<o>se

65 Meanly inserted above Merely, which is not canceled; never, <never,> friends; the final O never may have been a latter addition.

66 <Never shall Socrates condemn himself.>

93 quick inserted above strait, which is not canceled.

95 lo<o>se; soon inserted above <strait>.

111 <th> his.

133 thy inserted above <his>.

134 <you> thee.

Act 2, Scene 3

13 That <thwart> throb.

16 verge inserted above <brink>.

60 hair-brain'd inserted above stupid, which is not canceled.

Act 2, Scene 4

1 Strong inserted above Strange, which is not canceled.

Act 2, Scene 5

26 a inserted above <that>.

31 trail inserted above <draw>.

34 fond inserted above <vain>.

48 bandiest <well> purely.

89 like <Phedon,> him,

113 thy <mad> wild.

119 the inserted above <that>; which inserted above <that>

Act 2, Scene 6

6 retribution inserted above <for thy insult>.

Act 2, Scene 7

3 out inserted above <e'en>.
13 Her . . . fruitless inserted above <She wou'd have spoken in vain>.
16 my friend inserted above <thyself>.
17 wisdom inserted above <virtue>.
33 E'en inserted before Against.
40 T inserted between <It> will.
42 will inserted between souls be.
43 too inserted above <will be>; own inserted between our<s> without.
45 votaries; inserted above <worshippers;>.

Act 3, Scene 1

39 came inserted above <dropt>.
136 O I wou'd, <I> wou'd.

Act 3, Scene 3

38 our nature inserted above <his kind>.
39 inspire inserted above illume, which is not canceled; soul inserted above mind, which is not canceled.
50 monstrous inserted above <horrid>.
84 bluntly <spee> say.
131 Loves inserted after <mourns>.
267 no guilt <cleaves>

Act 3, Scene 4

20 Come, <to> lead.

Act 4, Scene 1

73 all inserted above forth, which is not canceled.

Act 4, Scene 3

26 the inserted between I humble.

Act 4, Scene 4

10 Thebes inserted above Corinth, which is not canceled; there inserted after They'll; the sage inserted above him there, which is not canceled.

24 they list is blurred in the manuscript.

Act 4, Scene 6

58 from <th> your.

70 him inserted after think.

89 ling added to dark; <and> bewilder'd.

92 Who written over previous words; s added to know.

93 Have written over How; <Plato> then.

147 support inserted over endure, which is not canceled.

Act 5, Scene 2

49 Drag, <thro>

Act 5, Scene 4

27 firmness inserted above steadiness, which is not canceled.

43 soul inserted after <heart>.

45 <thereon> inserted above upon <it>; her placed after it .

103 on inserted above <o'er>.

Act 5, Scene 7

3 lose inserted above <leave>.

Trifles

Marital, Book 1, Epigram 4

4 *I* *own* inserted above <*mob*>.

Martial to Sextus. Book 3, Epigram 38

10 *them* <*all*> *Ovids*.
13 *here* inserted after *I'm*.

On the Death of Adonis

33 *won't* written over what appears to have been *wil'st*.

Celadon and Amelia

10 *some* inserted above the last syllable in *blithe*<*less*>.

Mars, Mercury, a dialogue

20 <*my*> *my*.
28 *Godships* <*he*> *aid*

The Dog and the Wolf

30 <*Besides*> *And*.

Index to Part I

Addison, Joseph: Augustan style, 46, 48; "Ode," 48; lay sermons, 49; *Cato*, 49–50, 72, 75
Allen, Rev. Ethan, 54
American Magazine, 53
Anglican Church. *See* Church of England
Annapolis, 19, 28, 50, 60, 90

Bacon, Thomas, 20, 51, 88, 89; *Laws of Maryland*, 25, 89
Bailyn, Bernard, 51
Baltimore, Lords, 19, 26, 27, 34, 65. *See also* Calvert, Charles
"Baltimore Bards," 52, 62
Baltimore County, 27, 28, 53
Baltimore Town, 19, 28, 52
Barton, Thomas, 91
Bedford, Duke of. *See* Russell, John
Bentley, Richard, 46
Berkeley, George, 27, 33, 51, 89
Boorstin, Daniel, 84
Bowers, Fredson, 97
Boyd, Julian P., 96–97, 98
Bray, Thomas, 33, 89
Breslaw, Elaine, 86
Bridenbaugh, Carl, 84
Brinton, Crane, 31
Buchanan, George, 57, 58, 59
Butler, Samuel, *Hudibras*, 59
Byrd, William, 52, 71, 72, 84, 85
Byron, Lord, 59

Calvert, Charles (Baron Baltimore), 33, 67
Carroll, Charles (of Carrollton), 51
Carroll, Charles (of Doughoregan), 57
Carter, Robert (of Nomini Hall), 57
Cato, Marcus Porcius, 49–50, 55, 72
Chandler, Edward, 36, 37
Chase, Thomas, 19, 52, 62
Church of England: in America, 27, 33; clerical authors, 49, 51, 89; clerical misconduct, 19–21, 34, 65–66, 67; evangelicalism, 32, 36, 40–41; High Churchmanship, 35, 49; history of, 31–35; latitudinarianism, 32, 35; Low Churchmanship, 35, 49; in Maryland, 26–27, 33–34, 65–66; rationalism, 34–35, 37
Clarke, Samuel, 36, 37
Clive, John, 51
Cole, Charles, 60, 61
Collegiate Church, Wolverhampton, Staffordshire, 23
Cook (Cooke), Ebenezer, 51, 70–71
Cooper, John Gilbert, Jr., *Socrates*, 73, 74
Cradock Papers, 20, 38, 63, 72, 95–96
Cradock, Ann (Marson) (mother of TC), 23, 24, 57
Cradock, Anne (wife of Rev. Wm. C), 23, 24, 25
Cradock, Anne (daughter of TC), 24, 28, 96
Cradock, Arthur (father of TC), 22, 23, 24, 25, 55
Cradock, Arthur (son of TC), 24, 28, 54, 96
Cradock, Arthur (1869–1960), 24, 95
Cradock, Catherine (Risteau), 24, 27, 63
Cradock, Elizabeth (Taylor), 22, 23, 24
Cradock, John (d. 1687), 22
Cradock, John (archbishop), 23, 24, 26, 32
Cradock, John (son of TC), 24, 28
Cradock, Sir Matthew (1468?–1531), 22
Cradock, Matthew (1520–92), 22
Cradock, Matthew (mayor of Stafford), 22
Cradock, Matthew (of London), 22
Cradock, Richard, 22
Cradock, Thomas (1718–70), 32, 57; cultural values, 51, 52, 64–65, 70, 77–79, 88, 89–91; deferential social order, 43; emigration to Maryland, 26–27; evangelicalism, 40–41; and Dr. A. Hamilton, 60–63; marriage, 27; Methodist Society, 41–42; ordination, 25; orthodoxy, 43; reputation, 25, 59, 70–71, 90–91; at Tuesday Club, 60–61; youth, 25
—Poetry, 52–79; classic poetry transla-

tions, 54–55, 60; "Crurulia," 55–57, 95; 8th Eclogue, 64, 68–69; 5th Eclogue, 64, 65, 68, 69; 1st Eclogue, 64–66; 4th Eclogue, 64, 67–68; "A Fragment," 55, 95; hymns, 55; "Maryland Eclogues," 28, 32, 63–71, 72, 95, 96, 97, 98; "Mutual Love," 59; 9th Eclogue, 64, 69–80; *Psalms,* 28, 57–58; 2nd Eclogue, 64, 66; 6th Eclogue, 64, 68; *Socrates,* 28, 72–79, 95, 98; 10th Eclogue, 64, 65, 68, 70; 3rd Eclogue, 64, 66–67; "To Thyrsis," 53–54, 68; "Trifles," 58, 63, 95
—Sermons, 28, 57, 91, 95; on Catholicism, 39–40; on church governance, 19–21, 34, 65, 95; on education, 38; fast sermon, 40–41; "Merry Sermon, The," 40; on patriotism, 38–39
Cradock, Thomas (son of TC), 24, 28
Cradock, Thomas (son of Rev. Wm. C.), 25
Cradock, William (of Trentham), 22
Cradock, Rev. William, 22, 23, 24, 25
Cumberland County, Pennsylvania, 38

Davies, Samuel, 59, 72
Davis, Richard Beale, 40, 51, 52; British values in America, 51; *Intellectual Life,* 86–88; Southern mind, 86–87, 88
Deism, 32, 34–36, 67, 68
Donnington, Salop, England, 23
Drama, English, 49–50; American theater, 50, 71–72; Cradock's *Socrates,* 72–79

Fitzhugh, William, 63
Franklin, Benjamin, 37–38, 51, 57

Garrison Forest, Baltimore County. *See* St. Thomas' Parish
Gay, John, 47
Gay, Peter, 34
Gentleman's Magazine, 25
Gibson, Edmund, 26
Godfrey, Thomas, 78
Gower, Lord. *See* Leveson-Gower, John
Great Chain of Being, 42, 90
Green, Jonas, 20, 63
Greene, Jack P., 51–52

Hamilton, Dr. Alexander, 51, 52, 60–63, 68–69, 85
Hamilton, James (governor), 57
Hargreaves, John, 25, 26, 57
Hooker, Richard, 31
Hulse, Dr. Randall, 55, 90–91, 96

Indians, Iroquois, 27, 63, 65, 69–70; at Lancaster Treaty, 63, 69

Jensen, Thomas Cradock, 95
Jesus College, Cambridge, 23, 25

Lancaster, Pennsylvania, 63, 90
Lawson sisters, elegy to, 54, 79
Lemay, J. A. Leo, 52, 88; *Men of Letters,* 85
Leveson, Katherine, 23, 25, 26
Leveson, Richard, 22, 23
Leveson-Gower, Evelyn (Pierrepont), 25
Leveson-Gower, Frances, 27, 53, 70
Leveson-Gower, John (first baron Gower), 23, 25
Leveson-Gower, John (first earl Gower), 26, 27
Lewis, Richard, 67, 68, 71, 85
Locke, John, 35
London, bishop of, 26, 34
London, England, 25, 26, 28, 49, 57, 89
Lux, William, 60, 61

Magdalen College, Oxford, 36
Magdalen Hall, Oxford, 26, 52
Marambaud, Pierre, 85
Maryland Gazette, 20
Maryland Historical Society, 20, 72, 95
Menzies, Adam, 72
Methodism, 36, 49, 91
Montagu, Mary Wortley, *Town Eclogues,* 47
Morgan, Edmund S., 87

Negroes and slavery, 50, 65, 66, 90

Oglethorpe, James, 33

Philadelphia, 28, 51, 90
Poetry, Augustan style, 46–48; classical poets, 46–47, 58, 60–61. *See also* Addison, Joseph: "Baltimore Bards"; Buchanan, George; Cradock, Thomas; Montagu, Mary Wortley; Pope, Alexander; Sterling, James; Swift, Jonathan; Tuesday Club; Vergil; Watts, Isaac; and Wesley, John
Pope, Alexander, 89; *Pastorals,* 47
Presbyterian Church, 59, 91

Risteau, John, 27, 62
Rollin, Charles, *Ancient History,* 73–74
Roman Catholic Church, 31, 39
Russell, John (fourth duke of Bedford), 26, 27, 32

Sackville, Lord John, 27
St. Anne's Parish, Annapolis, 19
St. John's College, Cambridge, 23, 26

St. Paul's Parish, Baltimore Town, 19, 52
St. Thomas' Parish, Baltimore County, 19, 27, 38, 43, 52, 57, 63, 91, 96
Satire, English, 48–49, 59–60; Maryland, 60–71
Scotch-Irish, 70, 71
Seed, Jeremiah, 37
Servants, indentured, 65, 66–67, 70
Sharpe, Horatio (governor), 19, 57
Smalbroke, Richard, 26, 36, 37
Socrates, Augustan image, 72–73; Cooper biography, 73; Cradock's play about, 76–79; life, 74–76
Sterling, James, 51, 88, 89; drama by, 49; *Epistle,* 89
Sterne, Laurence, 49, 89
Swift, Jonathan, 35, 51, 52, 89; satire, 48, 59

Tanselle, G. Thomas, 96–97
Taylor, Arthur, 22
Theocritus, 64
Thomson, James, *Seasons*, 47, 72–73, 74
Tillotson, John, 36, 64, 85
Trentham, Baltimore County, Maryland, 28, 52, 90, 95, 96
Trentham, Staffordshire, 22, 23, 43
Trentham Free School, Staffordshire, 22, 23, 25–26, 57
Tuesday Club, 52, 60–63, 85–86

Vergil, Augustan imitations of, 46–48; *Eclogues,* 63, 64, 65, 68, 69

Watts, Isaac: hymns, 49; psalms, 58
Wesley, Charles, 58
Wesley, John, 58, 89
Woodforde, James, 32
Woodward, C. Vann, 87–88
Worcester, David, 59
Worrall, John, 25
Wright, Louis B., 85

York County, Pennsylvania, 38